Henry VIII and the Merchants

Henry VIII and the Merchants

The World of Stephen Vaughan

Susan Rose

BLOOMSBURY ACADEMIC
LONDON • NEW YORK • OXFORD • NEW DELHI • SYDNEY

BLOOMSBURY ACADEMIC
Bloomsbury Publishing Plc
50 Bedford Square, London, WC1B 3DP, UK
1385 Broadway, New York, NY 10018, USA
29 Earlsfort Terrace, Dublin 2, Ireland

BLOOMSBURY, BLOOMSBURY ACADEMIC and the Diana logo are trademarks of
Bloomsbury Publishing Plc

First published in Great Britain 2023
Paperback edition first published 2024

Copyright © Susan Rose, 2023

Susan Rose has asserted their right under the Copyright, Designs and Patents Act, 1988, to be identified as Author of this work.

Cover image: © Artokoloro / Alamy Stock Photo

All rights reserved. No part of this publication may be reproduced or transmitted in any form or by any means, electronic or mechanical, including photocopying, recording, or any information storage or retrieval system, without prior permission in writing from the publishers.

Bloomsbury Publishing Plc does not have any control over, or responsibility for, any third-party websites referred to or in this book. All internet addresses given in this book were correct at the time of going to press. The author and publisher regret any inconvenience caused if addresses have changed or sites have ceased to exist, but can accept no responsibility for any such changes.

A catalogue record for this book is available from the British Library.

A catalog record for this book is available from the Library of Congress.

ISBN: HB: 978-1-3501-2769-2
PB: 978-1-3503-4349-8
ePDF: 978-1-3501-3410-2
eBook: 978-1-3501-3411-9

Typeset by Deanta Global Publishing Services, Chennai, India

To find out more about our authors and books visit www.bloomsbury.com and sign up for our newsletters.

For S. With my love.

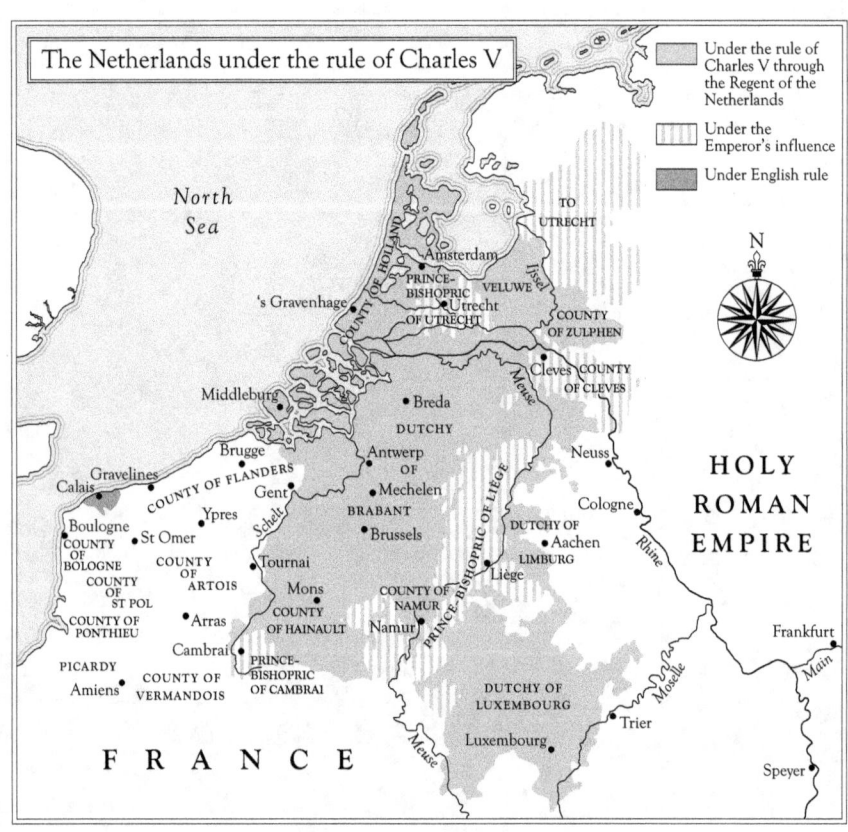

Map of the Low Countries.

Contents

List of illustrations	viii
Preface	ix
List of abbreviations	xi
Introduction	1
1 London at the start of a new century	7
2 Antwerp at the beginning of the golden age	21
3 A new century, new rulers and new ways on the money market	33
4 Stephen Vaughan: his family and youth	47
5 Vaughan as a diplomat	67
6 War with France	91
7 The final years in Antwerp	111
8 Stephen's legacy	137
Notes	155
Bibliography	174
Index	182

Illustrations

Figures

Cover   De Oude Beurs (the Old Bourse) *c.* 1515

1	Panorama of London *c.* 1543 by Anthon van den Wyngaerde central section engraved by Nathaniel Whitlock *c.* 1845	8
2	Map of Antwerp *c.* 1565	22
3	The new Bourse in Antwerp built 1530–31	34
4	Hof van Liere, the English House of the Merchant Adventurers, now part of the University of Antwerp	48
5	Hof van Savoy, at Mechelen the residence of the Regents of the Netherlands	68
6	Stephen Vaughan's coat of arms	69
7	William Paget first Baron Beaudesert	92
8	Mary of Hungary, sister of Charles V, Regent of the Netherlands	93
9	A holograph letter by Vaughan to Paget written at the time of the death of his first wife	112
10	A decoration in the dining room of the house built by Gaspar Ducci on the outskirts of Antwerp (undergoing restoration)	112
11	The Hearse Cloth of the Company of Merchant Taylors	138

Map

Map of the Low Countries   vi

Tables

1–4   Loans and repayments undertaken by Vaughan for the Crown in 1545   134

Preface

This book is an attempt to understand the world or the life and times of a Tudor official, one of the middling sort, and relate it to contemporary political and commercial affairs. As a direct result of his work for the Crown, he gained neither wealth nor greatly enhanced social standing. He did not follow the path to wealth and riches, particularly in land, taken by some of his colleagues at the court of Henry VIII, men such as Ralph Sadler or William Paget. He was not, however, of no account and, as we hope to show here, tells us via his career and personal life a great deal about contemporary society. His letters, even if written in the course of business as a royal agent or diplomatic envoy, reveal enough of his personality for us to appreciate him as a loyal, good-hearted friend and a devoted family man. He was at the same time a merchant to his fingertips and a competent and hardworking servant of both Thomas Cromwell and Henry VIII. His family to which he was devoted provides an individual and striking example of the way individual lives were moulded by public events here principally the Reformation and how different paths were taken even by those whose origins were very similar.

While working on this book I have been much in debt to the writers of earlier books and articles as will be evident in the pages which follow. I have also met with much help and kindness from archivists and librarians at a time when in-person visits to archives or libraries were impossible. This is particularly the case with the British Library and the Institute of Historical Research. I also received assistance in locating the digitized versions of theses which are not on the Ethos data base which was a great help. The amount of digitized material already available, principally in this case that to be found in British History online, is now very large and very valuable. It is what has made writing this book mainly in the Covid-19 years possible. Many other books and documents were to be found in odd corners of the internet by diligent use of search engines. There were very few key sources of information of which nothing could be found online. I am very grateful to all those who have made this possible. I must also thank my neighbour Hanne who translated very useful material for me from what she said was old-fashioned academic Dutch; I thought it was Flemish. Her help was invaluable.

I have also benefitted from all the help and loving support given by my family, including Tabitha the cat but principally of course by my husband. The book is dedicated to him as a small thank you.

Susan Rose
Highgate, 2021

Abbreviations

ODNB	Oxford Dictionary of National Biography
Ec. HR	Economic History Review
EHR	English Historical Review
H. of P.	History of Parliament
CPR	Calendar of Patent Rolls
T.N.A.	The National Archives, Kew
B.L.	British Library
L.& P	(References in footnotes are shown in the format L.& P. vol.no. item.no. As set out in British History online.) Letters and Papers of the Reign of Henry VIII
TRHS	Transactions of the Royal Historical Society
SP	State Papers

Introduction

At first sight Stephen Vaughan seems to be a typical royal official of the early sixteenth century, appearing more often in the footnotes of books dealing with the 'great and the good' (and the bad) of the first half of the sixteenth century than in the text itself. It seems that he can be safely dismissed in a few words as a useful functionary, a minor player in the dramas focussing on the king's marital affairs, court intrigues and the religious turmoil of the period.[1] This assessment ignores not only the intrinsic interest of his life and career but also the light this throws on an important but perhaps less dramatic aspect of sixteenth-century English society, the growing importance in both government and politics of trade and traders.

Stephen was closely involved both in the world of trade as a Merchant Adventurer and in the world of the court and the affairs of the king. He first entered public life as a close associate of Thomas Cromwell, one of the group of like-minded young men who were his assistants. At first he was involved only in Cromwell's personal business life but he later followed his master into public matters, in his case those largely concerned with the practical side of the process of dissolving religious houses. Vaughan's first direct commission from the king in 1531 gives an indication of the way the world of commerce and the world of high politics were often entangled. He was commissioned to seek out William Tyndale, the translator of the Bible into English, who was living somewhere in the lands of the empire. Tyndale's return was wanted as a possible tool in the king's policy with regard to the circulation of controversial religious texts in England. Stephen's contacts in Antwerp and with merchants, many of them inclined to Reformed religion, could be exploited to find Tyndale and convince him it was safe to return to England. Later when Vaughan became the king's agent and diplomatic envoy in Antwerp, he was at the centre of European finance and commerce at a time when the relationships between the English monarch, the king of France and Emperor Charles V were dominating public affairs amid the likelihood of the outbreak of war with France. Yet even in a time of tension and crisis, within a matter of days, he could be advising the king on the raising of loans on the Antwerp Bourse on the one hand and carrying out private commissions in the markets in the town for prominent courtiers on the other. His intimate knowledge of the conduct and financing of all kinds of deals both in England and abroad, however, became invaluable to the government, to the king and to his courtiers.

Much of this is revealed in his letters to and from the most prominent of Henry VIII's courtiers and advisers, and even the king himself, which survive among the State Papers. These letters allow us to follow his career in some detail and also make it possible for us to come to know his personality. Unlike the practice in more modern State Papers, important royal business of all kinds and his personal affairs were not kept separate but often discussed in the same letter. This makes up for the fact that there are no surviving purely personal letters although it is clear that Vaughan was evidently a frequent and eloquent correspondent with his friends and family beyond the court. For example, it is only by means of incidental comments in his correspondence on the king's financial affairs, largely with the king's secretary William Paget, that it becomes plain how deeply Vaughan cared for his family and the education of all his children both his daughters and his son.[2]

Two cities are particularly important in Vaughan's career: London where he was born, and Antwerp where he spent the most important part of his working life. Both were cities where both national and international trade was of great importance but which differed in other important respects. During Stephen's early years London was something of a backwater among the trading cities of Western Europe despite its size and dominance of commerce in England. There were few visible hints of its later rise to pre-eminence, especially if it was compared with centres like Venice (an independent city republic notable for its widespread overseas trade) and Lyon (notable for its active money market and enormous trade fair). There is some truth in the view that the English economy was 'not many leagues removed from that of the colonial economy dependent upon sales of primary products to more advanced regions and purchasing manufactures and services from them'.[3] London's trade relied heavily on wool whether in its raw state or made up into cloth. The export of these goods from its ports, pre-eminently London, was heavily concentrated on the nearest commercial centres in the Low Countries, with only a small amount going further afield by sea largely to Italy. Although London possessed an active and long-established system of local government with a degree of independence in the Corporation of London, ultimate control was in the hands of the Crown based nearby in Westminster. This political reality affected the careers of Vaughan and other important merchants. The wishes of the Crown would always take precedence over those of the city fathers. Antwerp, however, at the beginning of the sixteenth century was at the outset of its meteoric rise to become the most important trading centre of all in Western Europe. Its relative freedom from the interference of state authorities in its affairs was a factor in its success, since the court of the Regent of the Netherlands was in Brussels, while ultimate authority was in the hands of Emperor Charles V, who might be either in his German lands or in Spain. Its rise to pre-eminence entailed the decline of Bruges, the city with which English merchants had earlier had the strongest ties. Stephen was very active on the Bourse in Antwerp just at the time that the money market was growing rapidly.

This market was particularly successful in developing and increasing its ability to arrange loans for states and rulers throughout Western Europe as well as for traders. The increasing need of rulers in this period for loans to finance their plans for expansion or personal aggrandizement greatly affected the political situation in England and its nearest neighbours, France, the Low Countries and the empire. International politics also depended largely on the state of the relationship between the three rulers mainly concerned Henry VIII, Francis I and Charles V. This was the background against which Vaughan and merchants in general had to operate. Their deals and negotiations could be thrown into disarray by rumours of impending conflicts or the perils and difficulties caused by the war itself. They operated in a system in which hard news was difficult to come by and the personal credit of an individual or a monarch was of great importance. Financial systems were also rapidly developing at this time and any successful merchant, more particularly one who was also acting as the financial agent of a monarch, had to have a thorough understanding of the advantages and the pitfalls of the exchange system and the Bourse itself. Vaughan acquired some of the knowledge and the skills needed to act in this environment through his employment with Thomas Cromwell as a personal assistant and clerk. Equally important was his involvement in the Company of Merchant Adventurers and his first years abroad in Antwerp and elsewhere, sometimes fulfilling personal commissions largely from Cromwell as well as trading on his own behalf. In this way he became thoroughly conversant with the world of international trade and finance.

All this experience together with his evident desire at all times to serve his king to the best of his ability came together to mould the way Vaughan dealt with the most important period of his career; his years as the king's official agent in Antwerp. He was charged with raising the finance desperately needed to enable the king to pursue the war with France as the ally of the emperor. It can be argued that his successful fulfilment of this charge prevented this war from being a disaster both for Henry and ultimately England. The frequent exchanges of official letters and reports, between Antwerp and London, found in the *Letters and Papers*, allow this process to be followed almost on a day-to-day basis. By 1547, however, Vaughan was a sick man, worn out by the stresses of his work at Antwerp, but although facing the end of his career in royal service, this was not the end of his story.

It is true that within twenty years of his death the days of Antwerp as the centre of international finance and trade were drawing to a close. English merchants and English rulers were facing different problems on a larger world canvas. England's economic future would depend increasingly not on the old trade in cloth and raw wool with the Low Countries but on the exploitation of new markets in the East and in the Americas. There would be no successors to Vaughan or Gresham as individuals in their work to ensure the financial stability of the Crown in the seventeenth century. For Stephen Vaughan, along with his friends and colleagues, life as a merchant who was also in the service of the Crown exemplified many of the changes in economic and political life which began in the first half of the sixteenth century. As a merchant he was most concerned with trade between England and the Low Countries largely exporting woollen cloth and importing all manner of luxuries and manufactured goods. Apart from the primacy of cloth compared with raw wool in exports this was very little different from the bulk of English trade since the late twelfth century. He personally and many of the most prominent members of the Company of Merchant Adventurers had little involvement in the new avenues for trade opening up in the second half of the century. He was not one of the groups of traders largely centred on Bristol who moved on from trade with Spain to the beginning of trade with the Spanish Empire in the Americas.[4] Nor did he have either the inclination or the opportunity to explore possible new routes to the East or in the far North.[5] His world consisted largely of London and Antwerp and its environs. Where he did point the way ahead was in the development of money markets and their importance for rulers as well as traders. His work and that of those like him made clear to contemporaries that success in the competition for primacy among states and rulers depended as much on mastery of the contemporary financial world as much as mastery in warfare. The credit worthiness of a monarch was, in some ways, as important as their prowess on the battlefield. He himself ended his life quietly at home in Spitalfields with his family. The lessons to be learned from his career, however, became of increasing importance for future rulers in the succeeding years.

The fate of Vaughan's family also exemplifies the way in which in the later years of the sixteenth century more varied pathways in life opened up for those in his level of society. Vaughan's children, for whom he never ceased to care even when under the greatest pressure from events and from his ever-demanding master, the king made their own ways in the Elizabethan world. His son had an assured position as a gentleman with a not inconsiderable landed estate. One daughter, Anne, a close friend of John Knox, became a cultured and admired devotional poet and a much-valued member of the Puritan element in the Church of England. Her sister Jane was renowned by the end of the century as a heroine of the recusants with her children either in Holy Orders in the Catholic Church or in the case of one son fighting in support of the Catholics in wars in the Netherlands. The divisions between his children reveal how much life changed over the course of the sixteenth century from the secure if rather limited world of a London merchant family into which Stephen was born to the divided world full of new opportunities which faced his children.

1

London at the start of a new century

Stephen Vaughan was born around 1500–1 in the city of London, probably in a house near Cheapside in the parish of St Mary le Bow.[1] Stephen's precise date of birth is uncertain, but it can be narrowed down to the first year or two of the sixteenth century (Figure 1).[2] His father, Richard Vaughan, has been identified as, 'an undistinguished London mercer'.[3] It is true that he has the briefest of mentions in the Acts of Court of the Mercers' Company; once in 1527 as nominated by the Court of Assistants to serve at the feast of master William Hollys on his election as sheriff and in the same year in connection with a loan but listed as 'out of the livery'. He was clearly not one of the elite of the company fit to be mentioned with the like of the Gresham family and others who became aldermen and Lord Mayors. He was not, however, a person of no account, even if probably a fairly recent migrant to London.[4] The family came from the Welsh Marches, Radnorshire. Their property was at Harpton (the Welsh name being Tre'rdelyn) near Maesyfed or New Radnor in the Welsh Marches. His mother, Elen came from the nearby town of Presteigne, right on the border with England. The Harpton estate was quite considerable and by the mid-sixteenth century was in the ownership of Thomas Lewis, the sheriff of Radnorshire, whose descendants held the land until the mid-twentieth century.[5] He may have had an older brother, Watkyn, who was more likely inherit this property, giving Richard the need and the opportunity to seek his fortune in London like so many other young men from the countryside in this period. In making this move he probably followed the example of his own father Geoffrey Vaughan.

If Stephen's parents had speculated about what the future held for their newly born son, they might well have come to the conclusion that the prospects for England and its people looked more settled and secure at this time than they had done for many years. The arrest in 1497 and execution in 1499 of Perkin Warbeck, the Yorkist pretender to the throne in the assumed persona of Richard Duke of York, the long 'disappeared' younger brother of Edward V, had removed

Figure 1 Panorama of London c. 1543 by Anthon van den Wyngaerde central section engraved by Nathaniel Whitlock c. 1845. Public domain.

a long-standing threat to the security of the Crown and the establishment of the new Tudor dynasty. The machinations of Warbeck's supporters particularly Margaret of Burgundy in the Netherlands had dominated foreign policy throughout the 1490s even though Warbeck and his predecessor Lambert Simnel had found little support in England itself. The treaty with Spain was sealed with the marriage of Arthur, Prince of Wales, and Catherine of Aragon, in 1499 by proxy, in 1501 in person and had strengthened Henry's position as an influential player in European affairs. Relations with Scotland were also much improved as later signified by the marriage of the king's daughter, Princess Margaret, with James IV of Scotland in 1503. As far as commerce was concerned, the major concern of a family like the Vaughans where both Stephen's father and grandfather were merchants largely in the cloth trade, the improving relations between England and Low Countries were of great importance. The Archduke Philip of Hapsburg, the ruler of the Netherlands, and Henry VII signed a major treaty in 1496, known as the Magnus Intercursus. This had much to say about the conditions of trade between the two realms. Its major provision was to bring to an end the embargo imposed by Henry VII in 1493 on trade in cloth between England and Antwerp and the Low Countries, the prime outlets for this major export commodity. Traders like the Vaughans profited from this new agreement which guaranteed them almost complete freedom to trade and moreover exemption from the tolls on the seaway and reduced duties in this crucial market. The effect of the agreement is clear in figures for cloth exports through the port of London in 1496–7; those by denizen merchants rose from 12,000 p.a. to over 18,000 p.a. The exports of Hanseatic traders (exempt from the embargo) varied little falling slightly from 17,000 p.a. to 16,000 p.a. while the exports of other aliens also rose from c. 4,500 cloths to over 8,000 p.a. Exports of cloth from England, principally to both the Low Countries and Italy, had exceeded exports of raw wool from the beginning of the fifteenth century. Although the company of the Staple, the association of wool traders still enjoyed a special relationship with the Crown based on their close connection with Calais and its defence, cloth traders greatly exceeded them in numbers and wealth by this time.

English merchants and the Crown itself were also showing the first tentative signs of a willingness to grasp the new opportunities for trade with distant lands opened up by Portuguese mariners and traders. Interest in the intriguing New World of the Americas was growing. In 1496, followed up by further action in 1498 Henry VII set in motion the first effort by the Crown to exploit the potential offered by the newly discovered lands across the Atlantic. A royal patent to seek new lands was granted to John Cabot in 1496 and a second in

1498. Both patents were built on the earlier voyages of Bristol men to the fishing grounds off the coast of North America and, as the patents state, it was hoped that considerable 'profits, emoluments, commodities, gains and revenues' would result from their endeavours.[6] The success of the Portuguese in trade to the East was obvious to fellow merchants while the dawning realization of the potential for enormous profits of Spanish activity in the Caribbean and Central America could not be ignored. The city of Antwerp, which was displacing Bruges as the most profitable market for English goods in the Low Countries, was full of news of these new trading opportunities which doubtless reached the ear of the king and his advisers. This project, however, did not greatly disturb cloth merchants like the Vaughans; their attention remained focussed on the Low Countries.

This mindset, however, was not unusual in London. Though the capital and by far the largest town in England, it remained a medieval city, conservative in its social life and ways of thought. There was as yet little enthusiasm for the new ideas or modes of thought, conspicuous in Italian cities. There was little if any evidence of much dissatisfaction with the church as an institution or with its doctrines. Lollardry was no longer the important movement it had seemed in the early fifteenth century. What support it had came mainly from artisans and craftsmen outside London. The best-known group in this period, that in Coventry, only came under prolonged investigation by the bishop of Lichfield and Coventry in 1511 with a series of trials for heresy between 1515 and 1522.[7] Henry VII himself was conventionally pious and found little reason to quarrel with the papacy or other aspects of the church's authority. Looking at the printed books published in England between 1499 and 1503, of the fifty titles of which there are extant copies, half are concerned with orthodox Christianity, with some emphasis on personal religious experience and traditional practice. An extract from the writings of Margery Kempe, the early-fifteenth-century mystic *A shorte treatyse of contemplacyon taught by our lorde Jhesus Cryste taken out of the boke of Margerie Kempe of Lynn* is an example. Another called *The Hylle of Perfecyon* was an early work of John Fisher Bishop of Rochester, who was, at this date, Lady Margaret Professor of Divinity at Cambridge, a benefaction of Lady Margaret Beaufort, the king's mother. At this date his views and writings were accepted as mainstream. There was no hint of the disputes which led to his defiance of the king and his execution in 1535. The few printing houses in England at the beginning of the sixteenth century mainly produced 'devotional and didactic tracts designed to promote traditional piety and a better knowledge of the faith and practice of Catholicism'.[8] There was apparently only a small audience for advanced new ideas. The hold that the rituals and ceremonies of the church, as it had existed for many centuries, had on Londoners at large is well illustrated by the ceremonies that marked the funeral of Thomas Wyndout, a prominent mercer who was buried in a tomb in the chapel of St Anne in the parish church of St Antholin in Budge Row in 1500. His funeral, as befitted that of a former Lord Mayor, had all the expected accoutrements of burning tapers and torches with a congregation of city dignitaries in their official robes. Money was provided in his will for 400 masses for his soul and that of his parents with bequests to the London Charterhouse as well as the chapel of St Thomas of Acon the patron saint of the mercers.[9] As Caroline Barron has pointed out, there was 'little to suggest that London might become the stronghold of heretical opposition to the Church which developed in the 1530s and 1540s'.[10]

At the beginning of the sixteenth century there were twenty-three important religious foundations in the city apart from the parish churches. These convents, priories, hospitals and friaries, included the Charterhouse or Carthusian monastery and the grand priory of the Knights of St John. Their large and imposing buildings could be found all over the city and were an important element in the townscape. The spires of churches dominated views of London, as is evident from the Wyngaerde panorama of 1543.[11] The religious turmoil of later years was nowhere to be found. There was also no university in the city; English intellectual life, such as it was, was centred on the colleges of Oxford and Cambridge. The Inns of Court provided training for lawyers concentrating on the common law of England rather than the civil law favoured elsewhere in Western Europe. London was a centre of trade and business not of learning. It must not be forgotten, however, that London was a city of some 50,000 souls. It was by far the largest town in England even if smaller and less developed both economically and culturally than other European cities like Venice, Paris and Naples.[12] It gained much both in prestige and in wealth from its near neighbour, Westminster, the seat of the King's Court, the Law Courts and important aspects of the machinery of government like Parliament and the Exchequer. Westminster was not in any sense a rival to London as an urban centre. It was linked physically to the city by the great houses of the nobility established along the Strand but was outside the authority of the corporation and the Lord Mayor. Its governance was still in the hands of the Guild of the Virgin's Assumption based at St Margaret's, the parish church. Westminster only gained a modicum of self-government as late as 1587.[13]

A visitor to London in the early years of the sixteenth century would have found it still a medieval city, its shape defined by the line of the ancient walls first built by the Romans. As well as crowded alleys and a lack of amenities such as conduits providing water, there were many fine buildings and an exceptional number of churches of which St Paul's Cathedral was the most notable, dominating the skyline. The Guildhall, the centre of the government of the city, had been completed in 1411 and Leadenhall, the main produce market, in 1448, both were impressive civic buildings suitable for a city of more than national significance. Even so, there was still much greenery within the walls from the extensive gardens and orchards of great houses to the small yards behind more modest dwellings. The Scottish poet William Dunbar, writing at the end of the fifteenth century, extolled London as 'the flour of cities all'. In his eyes London was truly 'New Troy'.

> Strong be thy wallis that about thee standis
> Wise be the people that within thee dwellis
> Fresh is thry river with his lusty strandis
> Blith be thy churchis wele sounding be thy bellis
> Rich be thy merchunatis in substance that excellis:
> Fair be their wives right lovesom white and small
> Clere be thy virgyns lusty under kellis
> London thou art the flour of Cities all.[14]

Dunbar also praised London as a river port describing how 'many a ship ... with top-royall' could be found anchored there. The port of London with wharves lining the river bank from Queen Hythe down to the Pool of London, and the shipyards at Limehouse and Ratcliff with others on the Surrey side, had prospered in the late fifteenth century, with a large proportion of both inwards and outwards bound trade using the river. Even most of those crossing the English Channel at first used river transport by tide barges, going down river with the ebb and up river with the incoming tide, providing a regular service to Gravesend. Travellers then completed the journey to the coast overland through Kent to Sandwich and Dover.[15] There was little doubt as to the primacy of the city in England both in trade and financial matters in general; apprentice records of the city companies make clear how strong was the urge to move to London in many parts of the country. The Vaughans were by no means the only family to do this. Up until the 1520s, however, London and its merchants were not big players in the international money market. The Cely letters have frequent references to the use of letters of credit but in a way related only to the conclusion of individual deals in their case relating to the sale of wool at the Staple in Calais. The brokers or exchange dealers (usually called *wisselers* in the letters) seem to have been in a relatively small way of business. These deals were finally concluded in close connection with the big trade marts in the Low Countries with the majority involving brokers in Bruges rather than Antwerp.[16] Ian Blanchard has described the London bill market at this date as 'characterised by a certain thinness and volatility while the credit system as a whole was both narrow and parochial'. The Crown turned to loans from individual London merchants at times of need but there was nothing like the kind of money market which was carefully nurtured by the kings of France at Lyon based around the great trade fairs held in the city from the mid-fourteenth century. Not until the late 1520s after a period of extreme financial difficulty caused by the intervention of the king in the credit market through his imposition of a system of forced loans did things improve markedly. Loans for commercial purposes became easily available from Italian bankers who congregated at the porch of St Paul's Cathedral or in Temple Gardens. From this point in 1528 the money market gained, a previously unknown flexibility in dealing with the needs of both merchant and king.[17] Financial houses were prepared to do more than just react to fluctuations in trade outside their control. There had, however, been branches of some of the most important Italian merchant houses in London from the fifteenth century. The best known of the early houses is probably the Borromei Bank probably because of the survival of its early records including a ledger detailing business between London and Bruges in 1437–8. It is notable that at that date the London office was subordinate to that in Bruges where all profits had to be transferred. Later in the sixteenth century the Frescobaldi of Florence and the Bonvisi of Lucca did much business in London both with the Crown and with individual traders.[18] Stephen ran into difficulties with the Bonvisi bank branch in London when arranging a loan for Henry VIII in Antwerp in the 1540s.

With regard to its governance, London had had a great deal of control over its own internal affairs since the thirteenth century with authority residing in the Lord Mayor and the Common Council. Much power and prestige also rested in the city livery companies, originally trade and craft guilds like those to be found in any town. By the end of the fourteenth century in London many smaller companies were still little more than associations of artisans and traders though some had charitable and religious aspects as well. Their main aim was to ensure training in their particular craft by way of apprenticeships, control entry to the 'mistery' and maintain the quality of workmanship. In the course of the second half of the fourteenth century and the fifteenth century, however, a select group of these trade associations had developed into the so-called great livery or mercantile companies, including those of the mercers, fishmongers, grocers and drapers. These were also deeply involved in the government of the city as well as the health of their trade. Between 1450 and 1525, twenty-four members of the Mercers' Company, seven members of the Fishmongers', eighteen members of the Drapers' and twelve members of the Grocers' Company held office as Lord Mayor.[19] Earlier in the fourteenth century, by the charter of 1319, the companies had managed to take control of the freedom of the city. Only those sponsored by a company could become freemen, (i.e. citizens) with defined rights and privileges; this distinction could no longer be obtained simply by purchase. By the beginning of the fifteenth century only about 3,000 male Londoners possessed this valuable status out of the population of around 50,000. There were 150–80 members of the Common Council and 25 aldermen. If the wardens of the companies the parish officers and others with some sort of official post are also included in the total, about three-quarters of the freemen were involved in some degree in public life, but, of course, the majority of Londoners was excluded.[20] The leading merchants of the city who were deeply involved in the business of loans to the Crown when Vaughan was royal agent were all involved with the great livery companies and also with the governance of the city. The two Gresham brothers Sir Richard and Sir John were members of the Mercers' Company and Lord Mayors of London in 1537–8 and 1547–8, respectively. Sir Richard put forward a somewhat premature plan for a 'Royal Exchange', or a Bourse in London in 1538 in a letter to Cromwell saying that such building, 'will cost £2000 and more which shall be very beautiful to the City and also for the honour of our sovereign lord the King'.[21]

After 1467 the leading companies took even greater control of city government. Only 'the good men of the common council' with the masters, wardens and liverymen of the so-called great companies could take part in the election of the mayor and sheriffs.[22] The liverymen were the leading and most prosperous members of these companies which, by this date, had established ordinances, often a company hall for meetings and administration, a fraternity for social and religious ceremonies and purposes, and a distinctive robe and hood or livery with its colours changing frequently. Their importance in the government of the city and, more widely, in the government of the country was evident in the way they might be called on to advise or co-operate in such matters as the raising of loans to the Crown or the management of trade. All this was perhaps symbolized in the procession of the newly elected mayor, accompanied by the liverymen of the great companies in their various robes and hoods, to the ceremony at the Exchequer, taking place on every 29 October, at which the new mayor swore loyalty to the Crown. The order of precedence among the companies in the procession was a matter of great importance with the Mercers in the lead in their gowns (of a colour called 'puke' apparently bluish-black by the sixteenth century[23]) ornamented with their cognizance, the maiden's head. No member of the Vaughan clan reached such eminence perhaps largely because Stephen spent so much of his career abroad. London, however, was far from being virtually an independent city-state like some of the most important urban centres in the Low Countries. All the powers of the mayor and Common Council were granted by charter from the monarch and could be altered or even revoked. There was never any doubt as to 'who was the cat and who was the mouse' when it came to the relationship between the Crown and the city. London's privileges had to be paid for; Richard II charged the city £10,000 for a new charter in 1392–7 after the old one had been revoked because the authorities had not kept the peace in London after a disputed mayoral election. It was an obligation as much as a possible pleasure for the city to put on elaborate pageants and processions to celebrate royal marriages or great victories like that of Henry V at Agincourt. Due contributions were expected and almost invariably received to royal demands for loans and other financial exactions.[24]

The wealth of the merchants of the city of London which allowed the liverymen to build their halls, fill them with gold and silver vessels, decorate them with costly tapestries and embroideries and satisfy royal demands for money came largely from the export trade to European markets. The most important were those in the Low Countries. In the fourteenth century this had principally been the trade in the export of raw wool and wool fells (sheepskins) to the cloth-producing towns of Brabant and Flanders. By the beginning of the fifteenth century this trade was tightly controlled and a virtual monopoly of the company of the Staple. This had been established in Calais by the end of the fourteenth century after the town became a possession of the English Crown in 1348. All bargains between Staplers, the members of the company and merchants from the surrounding areas, mainly those from Flanders and Brabant, had to be concluded in the town in accordance with the company's rules. The only major exceptions were direct export to Italy via 'the straits of marroc' (the Mediterranean sea route) and wools from the Borders exported via Newcastle which were considered to be of such poor quality that there was no market for them in Calais. This system had clear advantages for the Crown since it made the collection of the export dues imposed much easier. These duties made up a very important element in the income of the Crown, and the cash flow from this source was also frequently used as the means of repaying loans. It is hardly an exaggeration to say that the Hundred Years' War, the campaigns of Edward III and Henry V, would have been impossible without the existence of this income stream.[25] In the reign of Edward IV the relationship between the king and the company of the Staple, particularly as it concerned the payment of customs dues, was placed on a more considered footing. The company had already lent a large sum of money (around £55,000) to Edward largely to pay for the garrison of Calais and despite repayment via the anticipated revenues of the customs accounts more than half was still outstanding. A deal was negotiated in 1466, later known as the Act of Retainer, by which the company would be responsible for the payment of the garrison and the maintenance of the fortifications of Calais. This was calculated to come to a total of £10,022 6s 8d a year. The company would be reimbursed for this considerable expenditure from the wool customs; if more than this was raised by the duties on wool, the surplusage, as it was called, would go to the Crown. In modern terms, the defence of Calais had been privatized. The system worked reasonably well until the early years of the sixteenth century but this concealed the fact that the wool trade was in decline and had been for some time. The number of Staplers had fallen from a peak of around 400 in the mid-fifteenth century to about 113 in 1517–18.[26] Individual merchants could still trade profitably but the company was no longer the wealthy body it had been as late as the 1480s. By the time Stephen was of age and trading as a Merchant Adventurer, the company of the Staple had been unable to fulfil their obligations in respect of the funding of the defence of Calais set out in the Act of Retainer and were heavily in debt to the Crown. Fortunes in the city of London were now being made by those who traded in cloth or luxury goods rather than those who still loaded their woolsacks on the ships setting out to Calais. Merchants of the Staple often by this also date traded in other goods as well as wool and were members of a variety of livery companies in London, principally the Grocers' and the Fishmongers'.

The cloth trade was not as tightly regulated as that in wool. It was also not so heavily taxed. Denizen merchants paid a duty of 1s 2d per standard cloth exported and at times also a small *ad valorem duty* or poundage. Aliens (except for those coming from towns that were members of the Hanseatic League) paid 2s 9d. This was much less than the combined customs and subsidy on wool which, in the late fifteenth century amounted to 40s on each standard woolsack for denizens and as much as 76s 8d for aliens.[27] The general term for merchants who traded overseas engaged in deals which put their credit and their goods at risk had long been 'venturer' or 'adventurer' with no necessary implication of belonging to any particular organized group.[28] These 'adventurers' came from all over the country, especially towns with a large trading community like York and of course London. In each location they might also belong to a guild or fraternity.

This was the group of which Vaughan and many of his friends and associates were members, although by the early sixteenth century, this loose association of traders had become a much more organized affair. In its earliest days once a merchant was overseas, selling his goods, principally cloth or looking for return cargoes from among all the items on sale, he would naturally tend to join others to form an identifiable group or (to use the usual term at the time) 'nation', the English nation of merchants. An association like this could co-operate in the business of shipping wares overseas and provide support and fellowship in a strange and perhaps hostile environment. It was also important for such a group to negotiate with the authorities in each market, establish terms of trade and hopefully enjoy the privileges that might be available.

Traders travelling to the Low Countries, especially to Bruges, had by the early fourteenth century set up a fraternity with a dedicated chapel to St Thomas Becket in the Carmelite friary in the city. In 1296, they had also obtained a grant from the Duke of Brabant who hoped by this means to lure the merchants away from Bruges to Antwerp. Its terms formed the basis for all the grants of privileges which these 'adventurers' obtained in later years. These included details of the shipping tolls they should pay, if any, and established agreed weights and measures. Rates were set for rents for houses in the host city, and how disputes should be settled. It also allowed the English merchants to hold meetings and control their members punishing them for breaches of their agreements. In 1305 it was also agreed that the 'English nation' might elect a governor to head this association. Over the course of the fourteenth century, mercers based in London came to dominate this group. The mercers had established a virtual monopoly in the import of linen, made in the Low Countries or adjacent German lands into England. This gave them a lever to use when negotiating for trading privileges with the local rulers and provided a strong motive for the 'adventurers' as a whole to elect a mercer as their governor. By the mid-fifteenth century this dominance was also accepted in London where a dispute between the Mercers' Company and the Fishmongers' over the governorship of the adventurers was settled in favour of the Mercers'. In the same way the London Company used its control of the governorship of the adventurers to the detriment of overseas traders from northern towns like York, Hull and Scarborough. By 1485 the problems caused by the establishment of an almost separate group of 'adventurers' in the Mercers' Company, something of a cuckoo in the nest, were becoming plain; this was even more evident since some members of this group were among the richest in the city of London. An agreement in 1486 certified by the mayor and Common Council set up a form of association for the adventurers in London, for both those who were also mercers and those who were not. Lieutenants in London would deal with matters relevant to the group and would communicate with the governor of the adventurers in the Low Countries. Despite this there would continue to be a close connection between the association which could now be formally called the Merchant Adventurers and the Mercers' Company. Accounts of meetings involving the business of the Adventurers appeared in the Acts of Court of the Mercers' Company, with most of them taking place in the Mercers' Hall. Neither this agreement nor the letters patent issued by Henry VII in 1506 established a new 'Company' of the Merchant Adventurers; it was the official recognition of an association of merchants trading overseas which had existed since at least the thirteenth century. Later commentators and historians did, however, interpret these letters patent as the 'foundation deed' of the London Adventurers. In their own eyes, however, as Anne Sutton has made clear, the Adventurers 'were one "nation", one company of venturers who governed themselves whether abroad or in London'.[29]

This 'nation' had its own problems even as the money to be made from the expanding cloth trade increased greatly. The provincial Adventurers resented the way in which the Londoners seemed to be taking over more and more of this lucrative trade. One focus of this resentment was their belief that the Londoners charged excessive prices for their imports from the Low Countries, placing them beyond the reach of their colleagues from outside the city. Another was the entry fee to the fraternity of St Thomas, a great source of support for those trading overseas and more or less essential for those going to the fairs at Antwerp and Bergen op Zoom. The Londoners had raised this to £20 and it took a petition to Parliament to get it reduced to 10 marks (£6 13s 4d). It was in fact the case that between 1490 and 1508 Londoners were responsible for a 46 per cent share of cloth exports. There were also tensions between the Mercers' Company and the Merchant Adventurers, even though many of the most successful Adventurers were also Mercers. Those based for the majority of their time in the Low Countries, particularly Antwerp and the neighbouring town of Bergen op Zoom felt quite able to manage their affairs under their elected governor without intervention from the London mercers. In the summer of 1526 these tensions seem to have reached a peak with a quarrel over the election of the governor between the supporters of Paul Withipoll, a member of the Merchant Taylors' Company, and those in favour of Richard Gresham, one of the leading London mercers. The conclusion of the dispute which eventually led to the intervention of the Privy Council is not clear. What is plain, however, is that after November 1526 there is no regular recording of the affairs of the Merchant Adventurers in the

Acts of Court of the Mercers' Company and their meetings do not seem to have been held, as a matter of course, in the Mercers' Hall. Some of their documents remained in the custody of the Mercers but these were lost in the Great Fire of 1666.[30] The seat of power in the trading association now usually called the Merchant Adventurers of England lay overseas with the elected governor often based in Middelburg or in the house of the 'English nation' in Antwerp. It was not incorporated by royal charter in England until 1564.

London at the very beginning of the sixteenth century was, therefore, still in many ways unchanged from the medieval city. There were few overt signs of the tumultuous changes which lay ahead. Ultimate power lay in the hands of the Crown but the city authorities were well organized and well accustomed to negotiations with the king and the court at Westminster so that friction between the city and the Crown was not a problem. The great livery companies had a firm grip on the most profitable trades and their future seemed assured. Most of the wealth of the leading citizens came from trading overseas with the Low Countries and Antwerp, the leading market both for cloth exports and luxury imports. It is plain that while London had no rival in England, on the European scene it was firmly in the shadow of Antwerp with its trading links all over Western Europe. The city had been in fact outranked by the trading and manufacturing centres of the Low Countries as a whole for some considerable time. Moreover as far as England was concerned trade with the Low Countries was of overriding importance compared with that of other European neighbours. This predominance was to last at least until the mid-sixteenth century.

Vaughan and his fellow merchants in the first two or three decades of the sixteenth century would have found London little changed from the city their fathers had known. The main challenge facing them was the increasing importance of the marts at Antwerp and the growing banking infrastructure centred on the city. Their relationship with the Crown was perhaps of most importance to the members of the company of the Staple because of their obligations regarding Calais. Those in the flourishing even booming cloth trade could be faced with the demand for loans from the king but as trade prospered these could be met.

2

Antwerp at the beginning of the golden age

Antwerp was to be the centre of Vaughan's trading activities and also of his work directly for the king (Figure 2). Here he was following the example of many other English merchants. The attraction of the city to them was pithily expressed in a saying of the time: 'if English men's fathers were hanged at Antwerpes gates their children to come into that towne woulde creepe betwixt their legges.'[1] Its rise to commercial and political prominence was a matter of wonder at the time. In the autumn of 1550, Robert Ascham, the renowned Renaissance classical scholar and former tutor to Lady Jane Grey, set out on a tour to the Low Countries and Germany. He reported on his travels in letters to his friend Edward Raven in Cambridge. In late September he was on his way to Antwerp. After a most uncomfortable night in 'a place of no account', when he couldn't even take off his boots, he arrived in Antwerp and could hardly contain his pleasure at what he found there. 'Good gods' he wrote, it was 'the richest market not only in Brabant but in the whole world'. It was full of splendid and magnificent buildings and in that respect was superior to any other town he had seen.[2] He arrived at the height of what has been characterized as the Golden Age of Antwerp but even fifty years earlier at the turn of the century he would have been impressed by the city. For modern economic historians, it was the cheap money available from the bankers who thronged the city and the relative security of the town which had irresistibly drawn merchants engaged in the expanding trade between England and the Netherland to the new financial and commercial metropolis of the West.

Earlier in the fourteenth and first years of the fifteenth century, Bruges had been the undisputed economic hub of Northern Europe. The rise of Antwerp to primacy in its place was relatively swift and has long been a subject of discussion. The physical evidence of Antwerp's expansion is clear. The population of the city totalled between 7,000 and 12,000 in the late fourteenth century compared with 46,000 in Bruges and 64,000 in Ghent. By 1437 Antwerp had 20,000 inhabitants; there were 33,000 in 1480, 55,000 in 1526 and the population reached an apogee

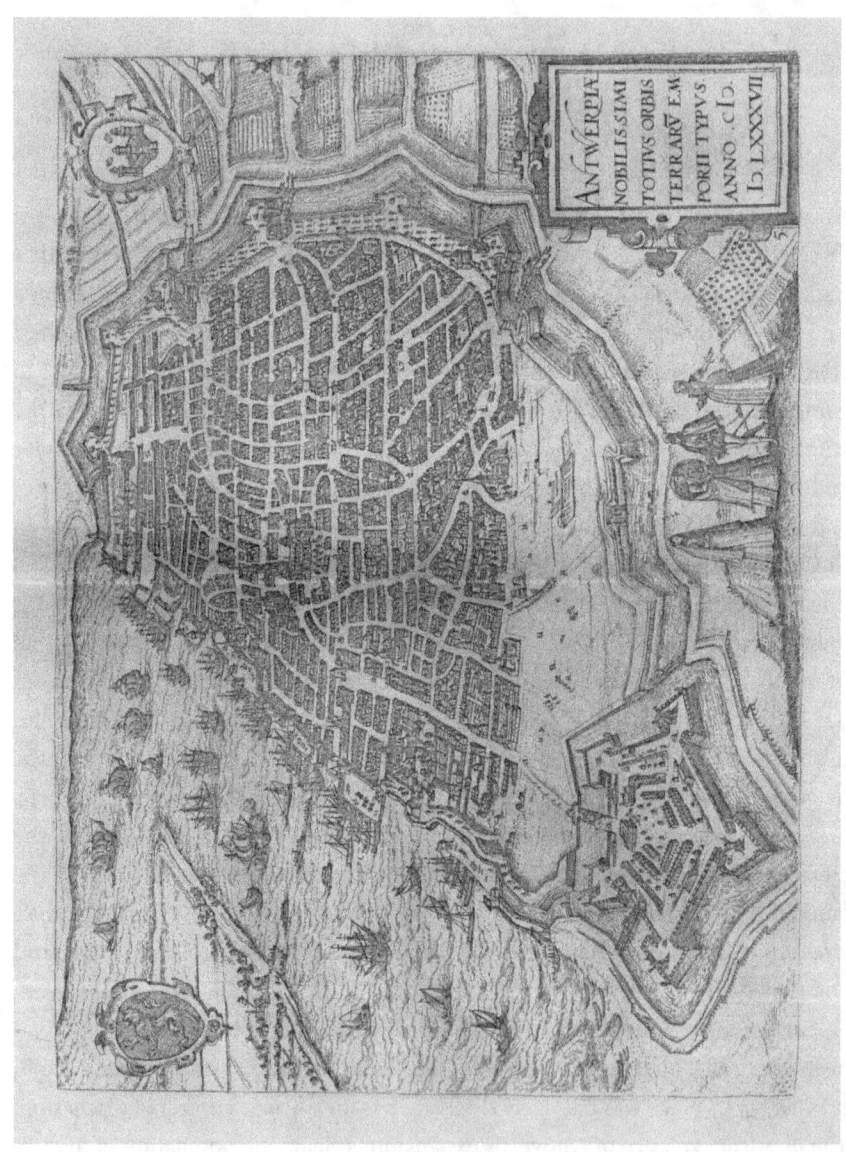

Figure 2 Map of Antwerp c. 1565. Public domain.

of 100,000 in 1565.³ Similarly the number of dwellings in the city as recorded in tax records rose steadily from 2,407 in 1400, 6,153 in 1496 and 7,943 in 1526 to a total of 11,482 in 1568.⁴

Many reasons have been adduced for this growth in wealth, population, trade and general significance. The city was, of course, favourably located in the most economically successful region of Western Europe, the Low Countries, specifically the southern counties of Flanders and Brabant, the most industrially and commercially advanced areas of all. Its position on the complicated system of waterways which made up the deltas of the Scheldt and the Rhine/Meuse as they entered the North Sea had always allowed it some access to seaborne traffic. This access was improved as a result of severe flooding in this area in the late fourteenth and early fifteenth centuries. The increase in the force of currents in the major channels between the islands in the delta caused by the blocking of side channels widened the so-called 'zeegaten' so that a new continuous channel was opened between Antwerp and the sea. This was shown on early seventeenth century maps as the Eastern Scheldt and much improved the means of access to Antwerp, also helped by the permanent inundation of parts of Zuid Beveland in the late fifteenth century.⁵ The channel thus formed was navigable by the early sixteenth century by the largest vessels of the day and also made for easier navigation to Antwerp by smaller craft from the out ports on the island of Walcheren, Middelburg, Arnemuiden and Veere. The city itself was, it is true, situated some way up the river Scheldt and a good distance from the open sea (around 80 kilometres from the coast of the North Sea) but off the wharves of the city, the channel was said to be 375 yards (*c.* ⅓ kilometre) wide, apparently allowing adequate space for the merchant ships of the day to manoeuvre. The map included in Guiccardini's *Description of the Low Countries* published in 1567 shows the city and the river busy with ships as well as the wharves outside the walls.

Antwerp was also well connected to the web of overland routes which had developed in the fifteenth century including that along the valley of the Rhine to Mainz and on to Frankfurt and Nuremberg. Here one branch went north and east to Poland and the Baltic and another south towards Augsburg, and eventually Italy. This was the usual route from the Low Countries to Venice and Milan, crossing the Alps at the Brenner Pass. Another went from the Rhineland to Milan via the St Gotthard pass and on to Genoa. Improvements in the 1480s, like the construction of a road over the Brenner Pass negotiable by heavy wagons as well as packhorses, increased even further the attraction of these routes to merchants.⁶ By the end of the fifteenth century most of the main overland

land routes were also well served by organized companies of carriers. One of particular note was organized by a Genoese, Petrus Gambarus from a base in Luzern providing a service over the St Gotthard pass. Inns along these roads had also been much improved; on the Brenner route travellers were advised in a traveller's guide that there were '*vile gudt herbergen*' including one just below the top of the pass at the tiny village of Sterzing.[7] Brigands and robbers could of course pose a problem, especially in remote areas but rulers by this time including the emperor were making great efforts to ensure the safety of travellers and their goods. River barges particularly along the Rhine/Meuse system were also of great importance. Sea transport as an alternative for valuable goods as well as bulk cargoes like grain and alum was slow with uncertain timings. It could be as dangerous as going overland whether because of the perils of the sea or because of the activities of corsairs. The increasing security of the overland routes was of particular importance to bankers. Although banking instruments increasingly permitted the transfer of funds without the carriage of large amounts of bullion from a banker to his customer this was not always possible to avoid.

At the turn of the century, however, Antwerp, like London, would have appeared as a medieval city still confined within the circle of its walls. These were extensively re-built and redesigned in the early sixteenth century but even the medieval fortifications caught visitors' eyes. A noble Spaniard, one Pero Tafur, on a tour of European courts was particularly impressed with them on his visit in 1438.[8] At this date, however, the construction of many of the buildings which beautified the city by the mid-sixteenth century was either not completed or not yet begun. *Het Steen* the citadel loomed above the city as it had done since the thirteenth century but the cathedral of Our Lady still lacked its tower which was not finished till 1518. The first Bourse or Exchange in Antwerp dates from 1517 but was replaced by the famous New Bourse in 1531. As shown in one of the illustrations in Guicciardini's *Description of the Low Countries*, it was built as a square or large courtyard surrounded by buildings three storeys high with open arcades on the ground level where merchants met and struck their bargains. There were gates on two sides which could be closed when trading was not in progress. On the upper floors were showrooms for luxuries and workshops for artisans. Many other buildings in the city used by traders and merchants date from the same period. One of the most notable was the *Coophuys* or Hessenhuis, the warehouse for the association of carriers who largely controlled traffic on the overland routes to Italy and Southern Germany. Vaughan was of course a frequent visitor to the Bourse and the showrooms of traders in luxuries as we will see. He would not have known the great Town Hall in the Grote Markt decorated in the most admired architectural style, a combination of both late Gothic and Renaissance-inspired motifs since it dates from the 1560s.[9] He would, however, have known and visited the Grote Markt itself and the streets nearby dominated by large multi-storeyed townhouses. These belonged for the most part to the members of the most important partnerships of merchants and bankers, like the Fuggers who carried on the business not conducted at the Bourse from their homes.

Tafur was also not mistaken in lauding the importance of the fairs held in the city itself and the nearby town of Bergen op Zoom for trade in general. In his view, the Antwerp fairs surpassed those in Geneva, Frankfort and Medina di Castilla all of which he had visited. Probably from a date in the fourteenth century, two fairs were held annually in Antwerp; one in early summer at the time of Pentecost, known as the Sinxtenmarkt and the other from 1 October, the feast of St Bavo, known as the Bamismarkt. The fairs at Bergen (called Barrow by the English) were at Easter (the Paasemarkt) and from 1 November known as the Koudmarkt. All lasted from one month to six weeks. They had originally been general markets where local products of all kinds and goods brought in by stranger merchants could be bought and sold. In the course of the fifteenth century, however, these markets became more and more an essential hub for all sorts of international trading and business deals, and crucially the place and time where payments by instalment or as part of deals based on credit were due. The usual credit terms were based on loans 'to the next mart' that is around three months. As these fairs grew in importance and more and more concerned with financial dealings, traffic was gradually drawn away from Bruges which, to that point, had been the principal trading and financial centre of Northern Europe, in one view deserving the title of 'the cradle of capitalism'.[10] Moreover in contrast to Bruges, in Antwerp foreigners traded unencumbered by obstructive rules regarding the conditions of trade that the rulers of other cities introduced to protect their interests and those of their own subjects. The business of exchange was open to all, as was dealing in bills and bullion, for example. If restrictive regulations did exist these were mainly imposed by associations like that of the English Merchant Adventurers not the city authorities.[11]

Benefitting from these advantages, Antwerp began to assert its supremacy over Bruges during the course of the fifteenth century, with a quickening of the process becoming visible in the 1460s. The Merchant Adventurers increased their share of the export of English-made cloth. The banning of the sale of this cloth in Flanders in 1434 to protect the all-important Flemish textile industry had ensured that the Merchant Adventurers based in Middelburg looked for markets including the Antwerp fairs which were prepared to get around the restrictions imposed by the dukes of Burgundy their titular overlords. The authorities in Brabant and Zeeland also granted this group legal and commercial privileges which made their position in these markets more secure as early as 1406. This protection was confirmed in the agreement concluded in the 1460s while their business also improved markedly following Edward IV's devaluation of the pound sterling.[12] At the fairs the Merchant Adventurers could easily make contact with fellow traders from Cologne and from the important merchant cities in Southern Germany where there was a growing demand for quality English cloth. In one view the main reason for both English and German traders to visit Antwerp in the second half of the fifteenth century was to make contact with each other.[13] The resulting trade in the export of English cloth to German cities was a major factor in the prosperity of Antwerp.

Antwerp also became very attractive to merchants from South Germany trading in other highly desirable commodities as well as textiles. It became the favourite marketplace for the sale by these merchants of copper and silver from the newly exploited mines in the Tyrol and neighbouring regions. There was also an increasing demand for the multifarious products of the metal industries of the German lands, including armaments and also more mundane pots and pans. Bullion itself was in demand first because of the rising price of silver at the mints of the Burgundian ruler and second because of the need of the Portuguese for bullion for the purchase of exotic goods in the new markets in the East. It was the ready availability of silver in Antwerp in the 1490s, which made the Portuguese decide to settle on Antwerp rather than Bruges as the site for the sale of all the highly desirable spices and other luxuries coming from their trade with India and the Spice Islands using the sea route established by Vasco da Gama and his successors. Blanchard has also shown that the successful investment in the silver mining boom by South German merchants produced the funds which enabled them to participate so profitably in exchange dealings and international trade and even go some way in the early sixteenth century to satisfy the demands of rulers for loans.[14]

The complex politics of the Netherlands as a whole also worked in Antwerp's favour at the end of the fifteenth century. The Cely brothers' letters make clear how crucial the relationship between England and Flanders was to the conduct of trade at the Staple at Calais. For this to function safely and profitably peace and security between not only the trading partners but also internally in the Netherlands was essential. In February 1487 William Cely, their factor in Calais was reporting anxiously to London that they (Bruges and

Ghent and other towns in Flanders) 'ar utterly determenyd the Romayne Kynge (Maximilan Regent of the Netherlands) schall rewe noo longger amongst them'. He continued, 'and as tochyng making over of mony at Brugys be exchaunge or oder wayis of conveyaunce yn redy mony or ffyne gold ther cen be none tell thys hete (uproar) be over for every man ys yn harnesse (fully armed) yn the market place'.[15] Antwerp, however, was supportive of Maximilian who, in return, urged foreign merchants to frequent the town rather than Bruges. The fact that the ducal court of the Netherlands from this period was based in Brussels also redounded to the favour of Antwerp. There was now a nearby market for all the luxury items Antwerp was only too willing to supply. On the other hand the political capital was not so close to the trading hub that intervention in its internal affairs was easy.

A closer understanding of the rise of Antwerp, at a somewhat earlier date, can also be gained from the 1438 ledger for the Borromei Bank of Florence. This provides an early snapshot of the way Antwerp's importance as an international trading company developed. It shows the partners in the bank actively buying goods at the fairs moving in a circuit from Bruges to Antwerp, Bergen op Zoom and Calais, buying German fustian in Antwerp and Bergen, madder (a fixative used in dying cloth) in Middelburg and wool in Calais at the Staple. In all these towns they could find innkeepers, warehouses and carriers, the necessary infrastructure for their business. Even at this early date partners in the bank travelled to Antwerp so frequently that they rented a house in the town at the cost of £12 14s 2d. They also kept cash accounts in both Antwerp and Bergen which became very active at the time of the fairs when many deals were settled. There was also a lively trade in locally produced goods. The company bought large quantities of fustian, made in Brabant for export often for cash; for example, as many as twenty-seven bales costing £343 1s at the Sinxtenmarkt at Antwerp. This was for despatch to Italy where there was a ready sale of this hard-wearing cloth.[16] For traders like the Borromei, Antwerp had proved to be an excellent base for both financial dealings and trade in commodities. Vaughan and his fellow Merchant Adventurers had similar needs to the partners of the Borromei Bank and by the first decades of the sixteenth century, Antwerp was fully able to meet them.

In the same year, 1438, Pero Tafur also noted in his travel diary another aspect of life in Antwerp. He was fascinated that in the city, monasteries and churches held exhibitions of paintings tapestries and goldsmiths' work for sale.[17] Tafur's mention of the markets for artworks in Antwerp is the first record of what became an increasingly important aspect of Antwerp's commercial life;

the establishment of the *pand* or specialized gallery for the sale of artworks and luxuries of all kinds. That taking place in the monastery of Franciscan tertiaries called the Beghards or Beguines was probably the first to be set up. Since the market was originally held in their cloisters, a *pand* was usually designed on this model as a courtyard surrounded by an arcaded walk with gallery space above. The most important art market in Antwerp in purpose-built premises was established in 1460 on a site belonging to the Church of Our Lady, the *Onser Liever Vrouwen Pand*. There is good evidence of the way it operated and its commercial success from its accounts which survive in a continuous series with few gaps from 1468 to 1560.[18] The Church of Our Lady at this date was in the middle of a very extensive and expensive extension to its fabric. There was already a general market operating in the churchyard during the times of the fairs, and opening the specialist *pand* was probably a speculation to increase the income to the church to pay for the building works. This eventually proved to be a very successful investment. This *pand* was in fact crucial in expanding the market in the Southern Netherlands for the sale of artworks of all kinds which had not been specially commissioned by a patron. It was possible to buy directly from artists and craftsmen producing a wide range of items, including banners and decorations for public displays and ceremonies, as well as religious paintings and portraits of prominent people.[19] In both Brussels and Antwerp painters, sculptors, engravers and even the suppliers of wooden panels for artists and the frames needed for altarpieces and the like were organized into guilds, in this case in both cities with St Luke as their patron saint. The *pand* owned by the Church of Our Lady took advantage of this when, in 1484, the authorities in Antwerp issued a decree that gave this *pand* a monopoly over the sale of 'altarpieces, panels, images, tabernacles and carvings, polychromed or unpolychromed'. Sales would be limited to the 'churchyard occupied by the painters of Brussels and Antwerp' that is the members of the guilds.[20] The income from the rent of the market stalls, set by the length of each, was very important to the church. For the last years of the fifteenth century, the income from the general market exceeded that from the specialized art *pand* but the sale of artwork took off in the first years of the sixteenth century and soon equalled that from the general stalls. Both the demands of the wealthy bourgeoisie of the trading cities of the Netherlands and the conspicuous consumption of the courts of rulers, especially those in Brussels and Mechelen, drove this expansion in the sale of artworks of all kinds. One of the few artists who undoubtedly sold work at the *pand* and who can be linked to a surviving example of his work is Jan Genoots, the maker of a carved wooden passion altarpiece now in the parish church in Münstermaifeld near Coblenz in the Rhineland.[21] This concentration on the sale of artworks became a notable feature of Antwerp with an increasing proportion being made in the city itself as the economy boomed in the sixteenth century. Many of the personal commissions that Vaughan was expected to fulfil alongside his work for the Crown depended for their completion on these markets. By the 1540s the most successful English merchants had their portraits painted perhaps by artists contacted via the *pand*. Thomas Gresham, for example, was painted at the age of only twenty-six by an unknown artist from the Netherlands.[22]

When Stephen Vaughan first visited Antwerp he also found that it was a much livelier centre of the relatively new industry of the printing of books and other items than London. There was both enough money to support an active market in printed items and a relative freedom to produce works of all kinds without much interference for the authorities. The sheer number of books printed in Antwerp in the first half of the sixteenth century dwarfs that produced in any other printing centre in North-Western Europe. A total of 432 were published before 1501 and 2,650 between 1500 and 1539. The majority were pious in nature and included works by, Luther, Erasmus and of course vernacular translations of the Bible not only into English but also into French, German and Danish. The printers in Antwerp were adept in devising various ways of avoiding prescriptions on works judged heretical by the authorities. Merchants like Vaughan were involved in the active market in printed books of all kinds since apart from religious books works of all kinds were to be purchased including maps. The 'runaway success' of the printing industry in the town has been attributed to the way the printers concentrated their efforts on 'diversification, topicality and mass production' in their output which fed into an active export market to England.[23] Thomas More provided an authentic historical background to his satirical fantasy *Utopia* by linking it to his acquaintance Peter Gilles who was the chief secretary of the town. The meeting between Gilles and the supposed traveller to the mythical island is also described as taking place in the Grote Marckt just outside the great Church of Our Lady.[24] For More and his readers no more appropriate place for such an encounter could be envisaged. Antwerp was the centre of new ideas of all kinds as well as a centre of commerce. Vaughan's involvement in the affairs of William Tyndale makes this plain.

By the first decades of the sixteenth century the city had become the European centre of activities now included in the modern term 'financial services'. This was made plain in the Quentin Matsys' painting of the *Moneychanger and his wife* produced in the city in 1514. Ludovico Guicciardini, however, a Florentine merchant and nephew of the political writer Francesci Guiccardini, who lived in the city from around 1542, was the first to write specifically of this aspect of the city's prosperity. In his *Description of the Low Countries and of the Provinces thereof* published in Antwerp in 1567 he included a section called 'A Discourse of the Exchange'. In the 'epitome' of the work in English produced by Thomas Chard this was translated as.

> The Exchaunge consisteth in giuing or receiuing in one place as for example in Andwerp as much money as amounteth to a Crowne, a Ducat or an Angell to receiue or deliver in Italie or in an other prouince as much in valewe which is a goodlie commoditier for traffique.
>
> But rich Marchaunts moued with desire of unsatiable gaine hauing gathered together greate Masses of money doe either by giuing foorth to interest when there is need of money or taking vp when there is no need make money either scarse or plentifull at there owne pleasure & to their owne gaine but to the prejudice of the common-wealth.[25]

It seems that the activities of the brokers, agents, merchants and banks involved in both exchange and loans were not viewed entirely favourably by contemporaries but were certainly helpful not only to 'traffique' or trade but in certain circumstances essential to rulers. The very existence of a system of exchange was not, however, a new development in the middle of the sixteenth century. Italian traders principally from Venice, Florence and Lucca had developed banking methods including the use of letters of exchange to transfer funds from one city to another both nationally and internationally from around the later thirteenth century. A merchant banking network existed linking cities in Northern Italy, particularly Tuscany with the papal court, Paris, Bruges, London and ports around the Mediterranean. In the late fourteenth and early fifteenth centuries, the clearest evidence of the extent of this network is the voluminous correspondence of the Datini company based in Prato near Florence with its associates and factors based all over Western Europe and the Mediterranean. The widespread dispersal and development of business techniques is also made clear by the fact that Pacioli's indispensable manual to double entry bookkeeping was available in print by 1494. The whiff of disapproval attached to this form of business, which Guicciardini displayed, probably originated in the religious and legal prohibitions on usury, the taking of any interest on loans, which were widely supported in the middle ages. A great deal of energy was expended by medieval theologians and canon lawyers in arguments about the validity of these prohibitions and in devising ways in which they might be circumvented without incurring moral and legal sanctions. They had had some success in this endeavour although the practice still encountered some disfavour. By the beginning of the sixteenth century, the main problem for traders was the apparent link between usury and *cambium* or exchange. Dealings in bills of exchange could be and were used as a way of granting credit to traders at a profit. The rates of exchange could be manipulated when a bill was paid to cover up the interest charged on the monetary credit made available by the bill. As de Roover's study of the Medici Bank makes clear the profits of this bank, as of others, were generated not 'from interest on loans per se but from exchange transactions'.[26]

The prohibitions on usury were undoubtedly limited in effect by the beginning of the sixteenth century but the need to circumvent them impinged on the way financial dealings were organized. Perhaps the most obvious effect was the great importance merchants attached to knowledge of the current exchange rates. This included access to any news which might impact on them, like rumours of shipwrecks, wars, alliances and concerns regarding the credit worthiness of individuals both rulers and traders. In London, merchants were anxious at the beginning of every business day to learn the news 'on the street' – that is Lombard Street, the centre of exchange trading. In Antwerp, merchants hurried to the Bourse to pick up the news (or perhaps in reality the gossip) of quarrels between rulers, bankruptcies or similar potential disasters and then returned home to send off a summary of what they had heard to their employers or contacts. There was no mystery about this; 'in large measure upon the movement of the Antwerp exchange depended the fortunes of their trade through that city'. As Blanchard has explained 'throughout the years 1470-1570 mercantile correspondence emanating from Antwerp revealed the intimate connection between the price of money at no western metropolis and the level of commercial activity there'.[27] The fact that the money market in Antwerp could be very volatile and the general dislike of any transactions which could be described as usurious ensured that the market was geared to provide short-term loans, from one fair to the next at the most. It was also the case that the generally accepted interest rate could not be used as a means of controlling the market; the market was 'linked indissolubly' to the rates of exchange with the most frequently traded foreign currencies.[28] The system had grown up to provide credit to merchants trading in commodities. Loans to rulers were difficult to accommodate in this system and might necessarily include physical transfers of bullion or even something akin to barter dealing. All this was not only of concern to English merchants in general but in particular to Vaughan whose prime purpose was to negotiate loans for Henry VIII. The success or failure of his endeavours largely depended on his ability not only to find a willing lender but also to obtain the best terms regarding exchange rates and repayment provisions. The only sure way to obtain the necessary expertise in these matters was by experience of the way the markets worked and close personal contacts with other traders and bankers on the Bourse. The importance of this aspect of his work for the Crown in Antwerp runs though all his correspondence in the State Papers.

Much later, in the 1570s, the famous printer, Christophe Plantin, wrote to Pope Gregory XIII explaining why he had decided to leave his native France and settle in Antwerp in 1549:

> What made me decide this was the fact that in my opinion no town in the world provides more advantages for the profession I wanted to pursue. It is easy to get there, one sees different countries get together at the market; one also finds all the raw materials which are indispensable for my craft; for all professions there is no problem in finding labourers who can be instructed within a short time.[29]

These sentiments would have been echoed by an increasing number of traders and artisans from the beginning of the sixteenth century. Antwerp enjoyed by geography, by chance and by the unforeseen consequences of its lack of protectionist trading practices the circumstances which allowed it to become the dominant commercial and financial centre in Europe at this period.

3

A new century, new rulers and new ways on the money market

For Stephen Vaughan and all others who were merchant adventurers in the original sense of the term (traders overseas), there was a great contrast between the life of a merchant in London and that of a merchant in Antwerp (Figure 3). In London most power and influence in commercial matters were in the hands of the freemen of the city and the corporation many of whom were also in positions of authority in the livery companies. In Antwerp the centre of attention was the Bourse and the business houses of the leading bankers, whether those from Southern Germany like the Fuggers of Augsburg, the Welsers of Augsburg and Nuremburg and the Hochstetters or the Italians including at first the Medici of Florence and later the Bonvisi of Lucca. All merchants trading in Antwerp, however, soon found that the conditions in which they operated and the likelihood of being able to make a profit on a transaction depended very much on the political situation at the time. This was largely dominated by the state of the relations between the three leading rulers of Western Europe, Henry VIII of England, Francis I of France and Charles V king of Spain and later emperor whose domains included not only the German lands and Spain but also the Netherlands and the extensive Spanish Empire in the Americas. The personal rivalry between these three became intense by 1518 when the election of a new emperor was imminent and was further complicated by the upheavals not only in the practice of religion but also in politics caused by the spread of the Reformation throughout Europe. The twists and turns in foreign policy caused by all of this are an essential part of the background of the way the relationship between Henry VIII and the merchant community developed.

Henry had succeeded to the throne of England at the age of seventeen on 21 April 1509. He was handsome, inheriting the athletic martial physique of his maternal grandfather Edward IV, and had received an education influenced by Renaissance ideals. Within two months he had married Catherine of Aragon,

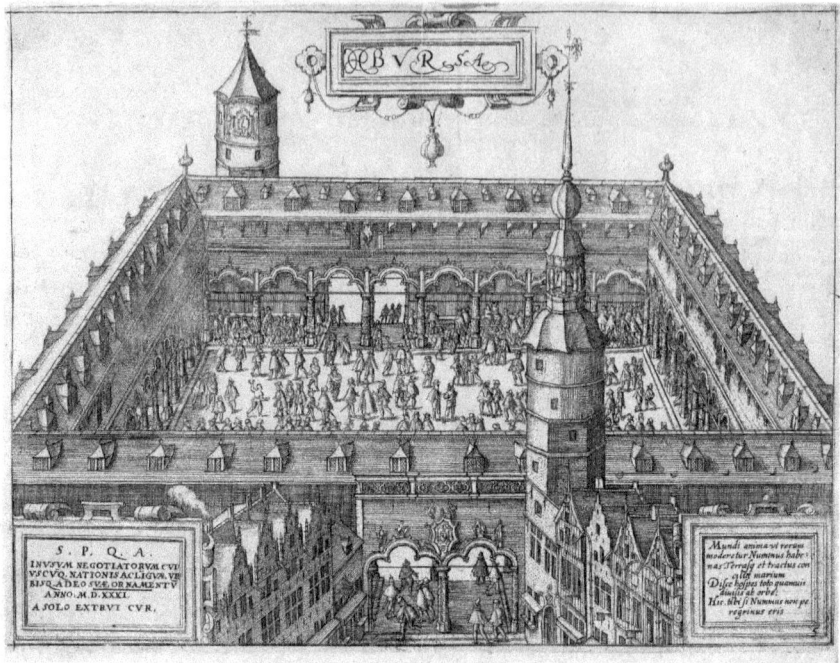

Figure 3 View of the Antwerp Bourse constructed in 1530–1 on the Nieuwstraat from Lodovico Guiccardini, *Commentarii di Lodovico Guiccardini delle cose piu memorabili*. (Public domain).

his brother Arthur's widow who had remained in England after the loss of her first husband. Her nephew, Charles, Regent of the Netherlands from 1506, as successor to his father Philip the Fair, became the king of Spain in 1516. In France, Francis I followed his cousin Louis XII on the throne also in 1516. He was as handsome and as well educated as Henry with an even greater sympathy for and appreciation of the thought and arts of the Renaissance. All three of these young rulers were anxious to make a mark on contemporary life and to promote their own image and that of their realm. There was nothing very unusual in this state of affairs. Rivalry leading at times to conflict had been the norm between European monarchs for much of their history. A new element, however, which became of increasing importance in the sixteenth century increased the likelihood of such conflicts. This was the disruption of the Catholic Church, which had previously met no really effective challenges to its domination of Western Europe, by the ideas on the nature of the Christian religion first associated with Martin Luther. These were first widely distributed in 1517 when Luther's ideas were systemized in his ninety-nine theses said to have been fixed to a church door in Wittenberg for all to see. For traders a further source of disruption was the opening of new trade routes to the East following the successful opening of trading contacts by the Portuguese with India and the Spice Islands. From 1498 when the Portuguese royal factor who controlled the sale of spices from the East Indies settled in Antwerp, this city was the centre of European trade in these valuable commodities. This and the opening of new silver mines largely in Thuringia and Slovakia, controlled by the South German bankers increased the funds available on the money market in Antwerp, something which affected the lives and businesses of all those trading internationally not least those like Vaughan who also acted in the interests of rulers.[1]

Antwerp's successful money market, which had originally developed to serve the needs of merchants and traders especially those trading internationally, expanded rapidly in these circumstances; its mode of operation was by this time well tried and continued to function well even as the traffic in the market prospered. One initial change was that the market was open throughout the year and not limited to the weeks of the fairs. Another was the establishment of a special place where dealings in currency exchange and credit instruments could be arranged This was not a complete innovation. The first such gathering place was in Bruges and called a 'Bourse' from the name of the square in the town where most of the Florentine and Venetian merchants had their houses, and where the dealings in currency took place. By the late fifteenth century, transactions of this nature were more and more also undertaken in Antwerp. Currency traders began to meet daily at *Den Rhijn*, a Gothic building dating from 1485 which became known as the *Beurs* (Bourse, later the *Oude* (old) *Beurs*), adopting the by now familiar term from Bruges. It was soon frequented by traders from all the nations trading in Antwerp, especially those who were in effect bankers. By the first decades of the sixteenth century it eventually became too small for the crowds of merchants meeting there and was replaced by a magnificent purpose-built new Bourse in 1531. The purpose of the gatherings was now not only to conclude bargains but to pick up the latest news of every kind. It was widely accepted that news rapidly affected the supply and price of goods and the all-important exchange rates between currencies. Information of shipwrecks or piracies, of crop failures and gluts, of quarrels between monarchs, was carefully garnered and memorized for the notes which would be sent back as soon as possible to each merchant's home base. The rate of exchange, which was crucial to the profitability or otherwise of any transaction, was extremely sensitive to the latest rumours or whispers on the exchange. As Ian Blanchard wrote, 'merchants at Antwerp watched every movement of the exchange with interest, for upon it depended their very livelihood.'[2]

This was because most international trade in goods involved some element of credit transactions or loans. These were usually for a period either of a month or from one of the great fairs to another, in effect about three months. Crucial to the system was the creditworthiness of those involved, whether individuals or trading companies. This depended on the reputation of the individual or the 'house' to which he belonged. The best way of ascertaining this was, by the beginning of the sixteenth century, summed up by the phrase *'Buone Ditte'* (well-spoken of), that used to describe trading companies with impeccable credit ratings by popular report. Borrowers who could be included in the select group of *Ditte di Borsa* were those held to be solvent and thus 'good' for the sum involved. (The general use of Italian terms indicates which nation's merchants dominated on the exchange in its earliest days.) Some idea of the intensely personal way all this operated, the usual terms of trade and the considerable amount of risk involved can be gained from the surviving records of trading partnerships. For example, the van Molens were a family from Haarlem established as early as 1509 as traders in Antwerp with close connections with merchants in Italy. A letter book in the Antwerp Municipal Archives and other local records give us an unusually vivid picture of the way their business operated. The letters in the book are in Italian and directed to correspondents and merchants in Genoa, Brescia, Venice, Palermo and other cities in Italy and also Italians living in London, Lyons and Cadiz. Some trade was by way of partnerships. In 1532, the van Molens took on a silent partner, their cousin Pieter Waarloos, to share in the profits of the trade in cloth with Bernardo di Zanchi of Venice. This lasted from 1532 to at least 1538, that is after the deaths of both Frederick van Molen and Bernardo di Zanchi. In general the van Molens would have been classified in modern terms as 'risk adverse', preferring to act as commission agents (usually charging a commission of 3 per cent for their services), rather than being personally involved in all the risks of trade on their own account. Bills of exchange tended to come with orders from Italy as the use of a credit instrument avoided the charges incurred (1 per cent to the postmaster of Antwerp) if cash (usually gold coins) was sent instead. The letters talk of shipments delayed by snow on the overland route over the Brenner Pass or of the difficulties caused, for example, by outbreaks of plague in London in 1543 when no ships left the city for Antwerp for weeks. More serious were the difficulties caused by the disruption to trade as a result of rumours of war or even peace between rival states. The trade between Venice and the Ottomans (and thus the price of luxury textiles and spices in Antwerp, whether up or down) reacted very swiftly to either. Even the price of English kerseys rose 15 per cent in Antwerp in the winter of 1540 because of the truce between Venice and the

Ottomans signed in October of that year.³ The letters of Christopher Kurz, sent to his employer Lazarus Tucher of Nuremberg, a merchant renowned for his expert dealing who was also the agent of the court at Brussels on the Antwerp market between 1531 and 1541, show, on the other hand, how someone more prepared to speculate on the extremely volatile Antwerp market for spices went about his business. Kurz claimed that he had an infallible system for foretelling a fortnight in advance what the prices of, for example, pepper, ginger and saffron would be; to do this he employed astrological observations. He explained that he did not follow the 'doctrine' of 'our astrologers aforetime' but sought 'his own rules' which could be applied not only to spice prices but to the rates on the Bourse for bills and whether money would be plentiful or scarce.⁴ His record in making other prognostications does not give much confidence that his system worked. One of his prophecies claimed that the papacy would be extinct by the end of the (sixteenth) century. We do not have similar records for English merchants trading in Antwerp, but these examples illustrate the way deals were organized and concluded and the problems that often arose. They have some similarities with those made or proposed by Vaughan when acting for the king and cast some light on the details of loan finance at this time. It also helps us to understand the circumstances in which Vaughan acted in the 1540s for Henry VIII.

There were in fact some obvious difficulties in using this market and its way of trading for public finance, for providing not credit to merchants trading commodities, but loans to rulers. The private market depended on the known creditworthiness of individuals as we have said; this was not something which could be easily applied to the case of rulers. A ruler's need for money was closely linked to the revenues normally available to him, the prosperity of his realm and the policies he wished to pursue. The state of the relationships with other states was also crucial; in effect, these factors influenced the rationale behind as ruler's need for borrowing. If loans to rulers were undertaken, this inevitably meant the ever closer involvement of the Antwerp money market in politics in general and the prospect of enmity or war between states in particular. This was clear from the second decade of the sixteenth century, and first came to the fore in 1518 when the question of the election of the next emperor arose. The Emperor Maximilian of Hapsburg wished his grandson Charles V, king of Spain as well as the ruler of the Netherlands, to be nominated for election as the next emperor. Francis I of France also aspired to this position as briefly did Henry VIII of England. Frantic lobbying of the seven electors with the power to make the nomination ensued, coupled with the construction of stronger diplomatic links between states by an elaborate series of dynastic marriages involving the ruling families of all those involved. Negotiations with influential German princes to get their support also proliferated. Matters of importance included the fact that the electors were for their part fully aware of the threat posed to the empire in Eastern Europe by the expansion of Ottoman power. There was also a strong feeling among this group as a whole that the emperor should be of German origin. Equally they were not averse to using the opportunity provided by the election to negotiate concessions and benefits from the emperor for themselves.[5] Charles V and Francis I both well understood that each elector had his price and used large sums of money to bribe the electors to obtain their support and that of anyone else with influence. Bribery on the scale undertaken by the rivals for the emperor's crown greatly increased the demand for large sums of money on the Antwerp market throughout 1518–19, with the biggest demands coming from Charles, the Hapsburg candidate. This had a lasting effect on the way the market operated and its development as a source of finance for rulers. One issue was that the primary purpose for raising this money, to influence the outcome of an election, was not the kind of risk that was appropriate for bills of exchange; the outcome was much too uncertain. To collect actual cash in the quantities required was also not easy. Rash promises of payments made by Maximilian in 1518 finally came to a total of 514,000 gulden. In the winter of 1519 the situation was further complicated when Maximilian died with the nomination still undecided. The struggle to raise money intensified with stories of mule trains laden with gold provided by the Fuggers moving through Germany and secret cargoes of gold being hidden on boats on the Rhine. The total committed was now around a million gulden. The immediate situation was, however, resolved in June 1519 when Charles was elected emperor with no dissenting voices.

Political matters, however, continued to influence the money market. At first, despite all the tumult, the market in Antwerp appeared to operate much as usual. Interest rates remained stable or even fell. In 1520 the situation changed. There were problems with the supply of silver from the mines in Central Europe, and, at the same time, the empire moved towards war with France. Charles V at first seemed ready to finance any campaign from grants of taxation, but this and other public sources soon proved to be insufficient. Attention again turned to the possibility of raising loans on the Antwerp market, but the traders there were increasingly reluctant to lend more money to the emperor even at very high-interest rates. By late November 1521 Charles was in a desperate position; his own revenues had been anticipated for two years; the annuities secured on these sources were in danger of going unpaid. There was no other available source of credit except borrowing from the merchants of Antwerp where interest rates rose to 28.32 per cent for three months. (Prior to this crisis public loans were available at the Sinxtenmarkt of 1520 at the unusually low rate of 13 per cent; the rate was normally around 20 per cent for the same period.)[6] Charles' victory over France at Tournai enabled him to survive the immediate crisis by reviving the support of his subjects and their willingness to finance his wars. The events of the next few months, however, made clear that a fundamental change had occurred in the relationship between the Hapsburgs and the money market at Antwerp. Their intervention in the market demonstrated how essential access to this source of finance was to them as rulers, especially in times of war. It was likely in the short term at any rate that this kind of demand was likely to continue and maybe even increase. It also had the effect of raising interest rates for all borrowers, whether commercial or public. To some extent private borrowers had been crowded out by the demands of the emperor with all the attendant results on patterns of trade.[7] The Antwerp Bourse may have lost some commercial traffic as a result, but its position as a source of loans for rulers had been established. This episode was an object lesson in the problems both for the market and for the ruler concerned of using loans raised on the Bourse for funding a government in time of war or any other emergency. Vaughan would face similar difficulties in the 1540s when a servant of Henry VIII, who like Charles V, was in desperate need of liquid funds to finance warfare.

What mattered above all when seeking to raise loans for a ruler and trying to find bankers prepared to undertake the risk was to provide some security with regard to repayment. For example, what was the nature of the royal revenue pledged for this purpose? How effective was the system of collection? Since so much weight was placed on an assessment of the would-be debtor's individual circumstances and the effectiveness of his government, each loan was usually negotiated separately with approaches to individual banks or business partnerships. Clearly this was easiest for those who made frequent requests for loans and had an established pattern of repayments secured on known revenue sources, like the rulers of the Netherlands. Newcomers to this market, like Vaughan in the early 1540s, had to make personal contacts, fully understand the way the Bourse operated and be very up to date with all the gossip and news of the day, especially with regard to wars and the relations between rulers. It should also be remembered that though modern scholars have calculated and charted changes in interest rates in Antwerp and other financial centres, this was not done in a clear and transparent manner at the time. The teaching of the Christian church was firmly against the charging of interest on a loan as we have seen; any such transaction might be accounted usurious and therefore a sin. The most important factor in negotiating any loan in Antwerp and elsewhere for a ruler was, as in the case of commercial deals, the rate of exchange between the currencies involved and how this could be managed to ensure that the lender might make some profit. Merchants at the time spoke of the supply of money being restricted or being easily available (*strettezza* or *larghezza* were the terms used again, reflecting the original Italian dominance of the money market). This also applied to loans for rulers. Although these became much more common in the sixteenth century as de Roover has explained, they were not really part of the usual operation of the Bourse. Each required lengthy personal negotiations, perhaps lasting for weeks with the leading members of the small minority of banking partnerships which could make available the large sums required.[8]

These were the requirements faced by Vaughan and his colleagues as agents for Henry VIII when the English monarch finally turned to Antwerp to raise funds. English monarchs had, of course, borrowed money from overseas creditors in the past. Both Edward II and Edward III had had a long-standing relationship with Italian financiers, especially the well-known partnerships of the Bardi and Peruzzi. These loans were largely secured on the profits of the trade in raw wool. Loans like this had, however, largely ceased during the fourteenth century, when the Italian creditors of the English monarch failed, and the kings of England had to seek loans from their subjects. These loans were largely secured for payment either on the revenue from customs duties, that is on export trade, or on that from taxes granted by Parliament. The creditors could be individuals. A good example is the immensely wealthy Cardinal Henry Beaufort, bishop of Winchester, who loaned large sums of money to support the policies of his cousins Henry V and Henry VI. For example, he lent over £27,000 to the government of Henry VI between May 1442 and August 1446 including £22,000 from April to July 1443. The great majority of this money was secured on the customs revenues, although loans from July 1443 were also secured on the value of a 'rich collar' and other jewels. Beaufort's own access to funds probably came not only from the wealth of the bishopric but also from his participation in the wool trade.[9] Other loans were requested throughout the fifteenth century from the city of London as a whole, from the livery companies, the company of the Staple with its monopoly of the sale of wool via the Calais Staple[10] and from individual merchants. The source of revenue most often used to repay these loans was again that from the customs. It is also the case that there was no element of hidden interest in these loans. Even if the arrangement was designated a loan rather than a benevolence, a compulsory gift to the Crown with no prospect of reimbursement, the money was repaid with no additional monetary advantage to the creditor.¹¹ The inducements offered were benefits like licences to export goods without paying the relevant duties or obtaining the favour of the Crown in other ways.

Historians for the most part agreed that, once on the throne, Henry VII was focussed on becoming solvent.¹² Much careful research has been undertaken to show how this happy state was achieved in view of the fact that he was almost alone among English monarchs after the Conquest in fulfilling this ambition. Henry VII was in fact characterized by contemporaries as a ruler who was both rich and careful with his wealth. Reports from ambassadors from Venice, Spain and Milan commented on this. The Milanese envoy wrote in 1499, 'he (Henry VII) has upwards of six millions of gold and it is said he puts by annually 500,000 ducats which is of easy accomplishment for his revenue is great and real not a written schedule nor does he spend anything'. The Spanish ambassador drily stated in 1509, 'if a gold coin once enters his strong boxes it never comes out again'.¹³ Henry achieved financial stability during his reign by using all the methods available to an English monarch in a coherent and sustained manner. One important tool employed by the king and his closest advisers was the widespread use of bonds and recognizances. Fees were charged for setting these up and also fines for breaches of their terms. The system was both highly beneficial to the king financially and was also a way of maintaining law and order throughout the realm. (bonds often included an obligation for example that to keep the peace.) It has been claimed that this was a 'national policy for royal finance and justice based on centuries of private transactions between parties and the various remedies at law afforded to them'¹⁴, which worked well and was well accepted by the king's subjects. More controversial at the time was the king's recourse to benevolences and loans. The best documented of these attempts at raising money for the Crown is the loan demanded in 1496 to finance an army to oppose a threatened invasion by the Scots. Fabyan in the Great Chronicle of London describes the process in a vivid passage.

> Upon the Sunday ffolwyng the mayer his brethir being at paulis as they custumably use cam unto theym from yhr kyng. In message sir Reynold Bray wyth other of the kyngis counsayll, Shewyng thet the kyng deyrid to boroe of the Cytesyns xMli, wherof to gyve an answer the mayer desyrid Respit till the Thursday ffoluyng, At which daye was assemblyd at Guyldhalle the common counsayll and thidir cam the fforenamyd sir regnold Bray with other of the kyngys counsayll at which daye with grete submission & prayr made unto theym to be good meanys ffor the Cite unto the kyngys gracs, The comuns lastly grauntid to lend unto the kyng MMMM li which of his grace was well and thankfully takyn.¹⁵

As is perhaps implied by Fabyan in his Chronicle but not clearly stated, considerable moral pressure to contribute to this loan was applied by the commissioners who toured the country armed with assessments of the wealth of individuals and corporations. Negotiations about the actual sum to be contributed (as happened in London) were possible but a straight refusal was difficult despite pleas of poverty. Faced with a request for £40, Lady Elizabeth Elmys of Henley on Thames promised £5; she was summoned to 'apere by fore the kynges counsel by fore Candelmas' to explain herself and thereupon offered twenty marks (£13 6s 8d).[16] This loan (unlike the non-repayable benevolence) was repaid relatively quickly for the most part by March 1498. It was, however, deeply unpopular as contributions were expected not only from the good and the great but also from relatively humble artisans and traders. It was one of the triggers for the Cornish rebellion of 1497, and this perhaps made the king and his council reluctant to use this procedure again.[17]

Henry VIII was, therefore in an enviable position for a young monarch on his accession in 1509. He was rich, personable and facing what looked like a stable situation both in his own realm and in relations with other European states. The alliance with Spain was quickly re-invigorated by his marriage with Catherine of Aragon, the widow of his late brother Arthur. As an ally of Ferdinand of Aragon, his father-in-law, Henry was soon involved in a war with France, something which appealed to his desire to acquire a reputation for successful military adventure. Despite having begun his reign by arresting and then executing the two men, Edmund Dudley and Richard Empson, blamed by contemporaries for Henry VII's policies which successfully extracted money from 'noble men bothe spyrtuell and temporal and to othir wythowth mercy or pyte',[18] Henry had no need for extra resources for the campaigns of 1512–13. He spent £960,000 on military purposes in the years 1512–14, as recorded in the payments books of John Heron for 1509–15. It did not even cause any financial problems when the House of Commons agreed to provide only £126,745, in tax receipts (which had of course to be collected) when asked to grant £600,000 for the proposed invasion of France. 'Henry VII's treasure provided his son with the means to seek out Lancastrian glory abroad and royal pageantry at home.'[19]

He was even in a good enough financial position from around 1515 to offer large subsidies to Emperor Maximillian to assist him in his campaigns against France. There was no need for loans to provide these. Problems arose not in finding the money but in laying hands on the actual cash required. The despatches of the unfortunate ambassadors whose task it was to set up these subsidies and arrange for their payment make clear the difficulties in arranging this kind of money transfer even with the support of the most prominent merchant bankers of the time. No involvement was required by English merchants. This was the first attempt by the English Crown to use the Antwerp money market and the services of the merchant bankers operating there for the purposes of advancing a political aim, the support of the war aims of the emperor. At first the Florentine partnership of the Frescobaldi was used, but they were soon proved not to have the connections in Antwerp which would permit them to lay their hands on the sums of money, almost all in cash, required. William Knight, the ambassador to the Netherlands wrote to Wolsey in February 1516:

> Fokers [Fugger], refused to take it in crowns of the sun, at 39 stivers apiece, and preferred it in nobles at 10s. Understands from him that the Frescobalds would pay by way of Lyons and Italy, but thinks they will find great difficulty. Wolsey will see by this that the King makes the exchange, and pays the interest himself, and the advantage will go to his enemies.[20]

By 23 April, Richard Pace, the prominent humanist who was also in the king's service as an ambassador and who was in fact with the Imperial forces in Italy, wrote to Wolsey despairing of the situation:

> Left Lodi for Bergamo on the 15th to recover as much money of theirs as is retained in Brixia [Brescia]. The Swiss will wait there six days for the King's money, which has not come according to Wolsey's letter of 22 March. Thinks Wolsey is deceived by the merchants, as the whole was in Flanders 20th March. The 25,000 florins in Brixia were provided by a merchant in Augsburg, factor to the Friscobalds. The Swiss say the Friscobalds have been corrupted by French money. Wolsey's proposal for the Swiss to invade France must be set aside for the present, as the Emperor's delays have spoiled the expedition. The Pope, the Florentines and the Genoese will not assist till Milan be won. The Emperor must be spoken fair. So oppressed with sorrow and disappointment, doubts if he shall ever see Wolsey again.[21]

The use of the systems developed by merchants for money transfer and loans was the only one available to rulers. They had no alternative but to use the expertise of bankers like the Frescobaldi, the Fuggers or the Hochstetters, because they alone could provide access to funds on the scale required. Only these and similar partnerships had sufficient experience of the way exchange operated not only in international commerce but also in loans to rulers. William Knight, also the bishop of Bath and Wells, and Richard Pace, a noted author and friend of Erasmus, were both highly educated, respected diplomats and royal councillors. Neither, however, had any background in commercial dealings and tended to be both highly suspicious of merchant bankers and at something of a loss when dealing with problems like those mentioned earlier. Even if not looking to raise loans in Antwerp, it was clear that Henry VIII needed to have in his service men who knew the customs of the Bourse and had personal and business connections there. It was essential for the king and his advisers to have access to this powerful source of intelligence and gossip. Men like this were, of course, most likely to be found among English merchants conducting business there, probably among the members of the Merchant Adventurers and the associated Mercers' Company.

Thus, even before there was any need for loans, Henry VIII and his councillors developed strong connections with men who could supply the need for agents with experience of Antwerp and its markets. Among the most prominent were Richard Gresham and John Hackett. Gresham, born in Norfolk around 1485, was apprenticed to the London mercer, John Middleton, and made free of the company in 1509. By 1517 he was well established as an enterprising and successful merchant trading not only at the Antwerp fairs but also investing in trading voyages to both the Baltic and the Mediterranean. In 1526 he and his brothers were caught up in the dispute with Charles V which resulted in the arrest of English merchants, including Richard and his brothers, together with the impounding of their cargoes of cloth at Nieuport, an outport for Antwerp in 1526. His close relationship with the Hochstetter banking family in the 1520s had both personal and commercial advantages, since Joachim Hochstetter, who also had a successful business in trading grain for English cloth, was able to secure his release from arrest on this occasion. Gresham was equally happy to act for Wolsey on personal commissions like helping in the decoration of Hampton Court. In October 1520 he informed Wolsey that he had measured '18 chambers' at the palace and had ordered hangings for them in Antwerp at a total cost of 1,000 marks (£666 13s 4d), a considerable sum.[22] Further help was given to Sir Robert Wingfield, the royal ambassador to the Regent of the Netherlands, with a loan of £5. As the latter explained to Wolsey, he had been left 'moneyless' and on the verge of selling his plate in order to live.[23] Later in the 1530s when no longer so active personally in trade, Gresham and his brother John were heavily involved in managing the transfer of money to the Antwerp market for Henry VIII. It was this experience of trade both in commodities and on the money market which lay behind his proposal to Cromwell that there should be a 'goodely Bursse in Lombarde strette for marchauntes to repayer unto. I doo suppose yt wyll coste ii m li and more wyche shalle be very beautyfull to the citti and alsoo for the honor of our sovereign lord the kinge.'[24] He like his colleagues was well aware of the advantages which accrued to Antwerp from the existence of the Bourse there and the gap in English trading systems which the lack of such a facility in London revealed.

Apart from the help that the grandees of the city's trading community were able to offer to the Crown, there was a clear need for locally based experienced traders to act for the Crown. In this role Sir John Hackett proved to be equally, if not more useful both to Henry VIII and his councillors and ambassadors in the Low Countries as the Greshams. Hackett was Irish being born in Waterford, but he lived for most of his active life in Middelburg, in Zealand, well placed for trade with Antwerp and Bergen, and much used by English Merchant Adventurers as their base. William Knight wrote to Wolsey in September 1523 explaining how the Regent of the Netherlands, Margaret of Austria, had suggested to him that Henry VIII needed, 'on[e] ther on his behalf to see the disposicion of his money' (that offered to Charles V). In Knight's view such a one should be, 'a gentleman of Ireland called Jhon Hackett'. Hackett could speak Latin, French, Spanish, Dutch and Italian as well as good English and 'is wele accepted her with all the best'. In January 1525 Hackett had been appointed by John Hewster, the governor of the Merchant Adventurers since 1515, as his lieutenant in dealing with the authorities in Middelburg to serve when Hewster himself was absent in Bergen or Antwerp.[25] Hackett's reputation as a skilled negotiator perhaps originated in this first position of influence. He seems to have been elected governor in Hewster's place shortly after this initial appointment as Hewster had died. He was enrolled in service to Henry VIII as an envoy to the court of the Regent Margaret at Mechelen in April 1526.[26] His service as governor of the Merchant Adventurers has been described, somewhat disparagingly, as that of a diplomat who was a useful man to the company rather than that of a successful merchant but it is the case that his expertise in commercial matters was as useful to the Crown as his detailed reporting of all the court gossip regarding the political situation in the Netherlands and elsewhere.[27] He was a personal friend and colleague of Vaughan and may in fact have acted as his mentor since their careers followed a somewhat similar trajectory.

Hackett's usefulness as a source of intelligence emerges clearly from his frequent letters to Wolsey and other prominent courtiers as well as the king himself. In July 1526 he was explaining to Wolsey the need for him to communicate confidential information to him in cipher form 'wheder hyt be trywe or not your Grace ys descressyon sall calculi the raysson'. He was also buying artillery and gunpowder in Antwerp for the Crown as well as getting a licence for the Merchant Adventurers to export 'towssyns of bowstavys'.[28] More technical was his long letter to Brian Tuke, French secretary to the king, in September 1526 which goes into some detail about the difficulties on the Antwerp exchange caused by the political situation at the time. The Hochstetters had made clear to him that interest rates were rising fast and on the exchange, 'owr Ynglys grotres that were wont to go here for 5d ob. and vid now they go for vid ob. and in sum other for viid Flemysh.'[29] Further letters from the same period make plain the difficulties caused for traders, whether in goods or on the money market by Charles V's decrees re-valuing gold and silver coins. It was impossible to conclude any bargains because 'they [Antwerrp dealers] wold not cum here to no condision of tyme nethyr pryce of the interesse tyll they knowe what payment they shall ressew'.[30]

As well as the repercussions of the war between the emperor and France on trade, Hackett was also drawn into the growing religious upheavals of the early days of the Reformation. He was himself a strong supporter of the old ways and in 1527 informed Wolsey that he thought that it would be difficult for the Regent and her council to prevent the spread of 'the secht Luterien' in her lands; 'the kanker sall wycz soo gret that hyt salbe hard to bryng al to a good end.'[31] By the next summer he was actively attempting to prevent copies of the New Testament printed in Antwerp being exported to England and pursuing their printer Richard Harman in the courts in Antwerp. Nevertheless by December 1533 Hackett supported the royal divorce and could write to Cromwell roundly abusing the pope for his decision on this matter. The pope was 'unwourdy' and activated by 'mallice and inquyte agence against the lawe of God and all beyngnyte'.[32] By the following October Hackett was dead leaving his affairs in the hands of Stephen Vaughan, a clear indication of the close bonds between them.

The Crown not only needed but profited greatly from the services of merchants who acted as ambassadors or other diplomatic envoys. They were an indispensable source of intelligence, could be relied upon to perform tasks of many kinds and as became clear in the 1540s understood the financial market centred on Antwerp better than any other royal servants or councillors. Stephen's own career in this role to which we will now turn was based on the secure foundation of the reliance by the English Crown on the work of his predecessors. It was also made necessary by the growing dominance of the Antwerp market and the network of trading links of which it was the centre, in the economy of Western Europe at this time. Less obvious at the start of Stephen's career was the role which the increasing cost of warfare and the need for fresh sources of money was to play in his affairs.

4

Stephen Vaughan

His family and youth

We do not know where the Vaughan family lived when Stephen was a child. If the family was already living near Cheapside this was a district much favoured by those dealing in cloth of all kinds. The Mercers' Hall was at the eastern end of the street and many of the wealthiest merchants as well as the lesser traders owned property in the area.[1] The home of a family like the Vaughans provided a reasonable standard of comfort. It would have had most if not all windows fully glazed. There might have been an internal privy but more certainly several chambers and a parlour and perhaps a counting house. There would also have been adequate furniture, cooking equipment, napery and tableware. A surviving inventory of the goods of a mercer living in Ironmonger lane in 1551 implies a fair degree of comfort in a well-furnished house.[2] The whole area in the fifteenth century had been known as the Mercery because of the way members of that company clustered in the district. Stephen may have been one of the earliest scholars at the newly re-founded St Paul's School but there is no clear evidence of this.[3] If so, he would have been part of one of the first groups of 153 'children' enrolled each year under the new statutes. He would also have been a schoolfellow of William Paget, his later colleague although somewhat older than him. The curriculum set out in the statutes would not have been, on the surface, very suitable for a boy aiming at a mercantile career since it was heavily biased towards the learning of Latin and studying humanist views on written style in this language, with books by authors lauded by Erasmus and his followers set for the children to study. However, Stephen was clearly not without an education. By the time he was an adult he had enough Latin to read diplomatic documents written in that language even if he was not sufficiently proficient as a young child to fulfil the requirements for entry into the lowest class at St Paul's School.[4] By the time he was an adult with a family of his own he was also enthusiastic about the benefits of humanist education and

Figure 4 Hof van Liere, the English House of the Merchant Adventurers, now part of the University of Antwerp. Public domain.

made every effort to provide this for his own children.[5] He wrote a good hand (many of his surviving letters are holographs) and had no problems with the intricate calculations involving discounts and varying exchange rates needed by a merchant trading internationally at this time. He was certainly fluent in Spanish. (In 1530 he was present at a meeting between Catherine of Aragon and the Imperial ambassador Chapuys for the sole purpose of monitoring their conversation in Spanish so that the king's advisers could be sure of its content.)[6] He lived for long periods of time in the Low Countries and other areas speaking Low German dialects or Flemish so we can presume he had no difficulties in conducting business for himself or the Crown in the local vernacular. English was not widely spoken in these areas. He was less secure in the German spoken in Saxony as emerges from his letters. Vaughan may have been unsure about his own mastery of French since in 1529 he asked Thomas Cromwell for help in getting hold of the best available book on learning the language.[7] Some years later, however, he felt he had managed well when negotiating in that language, which was that spoken at the court of the Regent of the Netherlands. He was also, as an adult, an avid reader of the polemical and religious texts of the day well able to form his own opinions and express them with vigour as much of his correspondence shows.

After his school days, a boy like Stephen Vaughan would have expected to be apprenticed to a member of a craft or trading company and to have joined that company when his apprenticeship was completed. Stephen did not, however, join his father as a member of the Mercers' Company. This may be because his father, Richard, at the time when Stephen would have been an apprentice, was in considerable difficulties over his business affairs. Around 1518-24 Richard was involved in a complicated deal over the supply of kerseys to another London merchant, John Parnell. The deal included a complicated barter swap with woad being supplied to cover the cost of some of the kerseys. The deal went wrong leading to a series of legal actions in Chancery. Unusually the litigation was instigated by Richard's father, Geoffrey acting as plaintiff, not by Richard himself leading to the possibility that Richard was incapacitated in some way. The final result, however, was that Richard Vaughan was declared insolvent.[8] A later compilation of the laws of the Company of Merchant Adventurers, dating from 1612, specifically excluded from membership all sons or apprentices of bankrupts.[9] Even if not a regulation of either the Mercers or the Merchant Adventurers when Vaughan was a young man the stain of family insolvency was perhaps enough to prevent him from joining his father's livery company. All manner of business and bargains in this period was based almost entirely on trust and confidence in the worth of trading partners so the loss of one's good name was a little short of a disaster especially commercially.[10] Stephen in fact became a member of the Merchant Taylors Company and was probably able to enter this company through the good offices of his grandfather Geoffrey Vaughan. Unfortunately many of the apprenticeship records of this particular company and all the details of the admission of its freemen are lacking between 1493 and 1562 so there is little surviving evidence of when this might have occurred. Geoffrey is listed as Master of the Company in 1520[11] and in 1538, both Stephen and Geoffrey appear in a list of freemen of the city of London sorted by the livery company to which they belonged. This list was compiled after a proposal put forward by Richard Gresham who was Lord Mayor in that year. Each company was expected to supply the names of the wardens, those in the livery and those who were 'freemen being householders' (or journeymen) who were expected to supply one or more sets of armour and weapons (known as 'harness') to defend the city. Stephen appears in the warden's section of the list for the Merchant Taylors, rather lower down the list than Geoffrey Vaughan.[12] Geoffrey was certainly a member of the Merchant Taylors' Company by 1509.

An agreement dated in that year concerning those involved in bonds of over £600 includes him described as a citizen and merchant tailor of London.[13] Geoffrey also appears as a donor to the company in an inventory of its effects dating from 1512. He presented eighteen new cushions to the company when he was a warden; these were embroidered with the arms of the donors held by angels; they cost £7 14s 10d, thus were undoubtedly luxury items probably embroidered with extravagant amounts of gold-work.[14] The standard of embroidered textiles expected by members of the Company is exemplified by the surviving elaborate and beautiful funeral palls or 'herse cloths' used at the burial of liverymen.[15] By 1520, as Master of the Company, Geoffrey was one of the city's grandees.[16] He was obviously in a better position to give his grandson a good start in a mercantile career than the child's father.

Membership in this company may also have had another unlooked-for advantage for Stephen. Thomas Cromwell was also a member. This membership is confirmed by the record of a case concerning a debt in the Court of Common Pleas in 1523 in which Cromwell was described as *civis et mercator scissor* (citizen and Merchant Taylor) of London.[17] It is possible that Cromwell met Vaughan at some gathering of their joint guild and was attracted by the young man's energy and intelligence. Another link between them might have been through the Welsh community in London. Cromwell's sister Katherine had married Morgan Williams, the son of William Morgan ap Howell of Newchurch, Glamorgan. The Williams family had much the same social status as the Vaughans and retained close enough connections to Wales for their son Richard to be born there. This child was in fact brought up by Cromwell with his own son Gregory and eventually adopted the surname of Cromwell himself. It is not fanciful to suggest that Vaughan was another young man of Welsh origin taken under Cromwell's wing. The early warm links between the two are evidenced in their letters even though those surviving are mainly concerned with public affairs. Several of Vaughan's letters, especially one from 1528, from Stephen to Cromwell mention Cromwell's mother-in-law, Mercy Prior, on this occasion calling her, 'after you my most singular friend'.[18] This lady lived in Cromwell's house at Austin Friars with her second husband, said to be a shearman whom Vaughan may have met in the course of trade or again at livery company events. There is no doubt that this friendship was a deciding factor in Stephen's early career and determined the way in which it ultimately developed.

Cromwell and Vaughan may also have been drawn to each other by sharing similar religious views, something which became of increasing importance in their lives as of those of many other Londoners in the religious turmoil of the first half of the sixteenth century. By the end of the 1520s, in MaCculloch's view, Cromwell had a 'discreet but decisive and effective commitment to the forces of religious reform'.[19] He sees Vaughan, in his prime, on the other hand as, 'much less inclined than his old master to dissembling his vigorously evangelical opinions'.[20] Since both made their careers in close contact with the king and his court at a time when the religious beliefs and allegiances most in favour with those in power were ill-defined and shifting, it is not surprising that Cromwell, in particular, has also been described as a Nicodemist, prepared to hide his own views in order to conform with official religion.[21] In the 1520s, however, before the full extent of the future upheaval in the church and its practices was visible, Vaughan as a young man may have been one of the so-called 'brethren', evangelicals with whom Cromwell had much sympathy. Among the members of this informal group were scholars like Miles Coverdale, who was responsible for the first printed English Bible. In 1527, when based at the Augustinian Priory in Cambridge under the tutelage of Robert Barnes, later a Protestant martyr, he wrote to Cromwell beseeching him, 'for the tender love of god and for the fervent zeal that you have to virtue and godly study' to send him books he needed for his studies.[22] The import and distribution of controversial and heretical religious books mostly from the Low Countries was one of the most successful tactics to spread the new learning used by the Brethren as a group.[23] With his involvement in the Netherlands as a Merchant Adventurer, Vaughan was well placed to help with the import of books. He was commissioned to obtain books of all kinds for Cromwell. He certainly knew those prominent in the business of printing, publishing and distributing controversial religious texts as his involvement with Tyndale in the 1530s testifies. Some other young men who were later identified as convinced Protestants were in Cromwell's service from the early 1520s. One of the most prominent of these was Ralph Sadler, later a highly successful diplomat and administrator for Henry VIII.[24] Vaughan worked with Sadler in 1527–8 when both were employed in the complex business of taking possession of the goods, premises and other assets of the group of religious foundations which were dissolved in order to provide the endowment for Wolsey's great legacy projects, Cardinal College at Oxford and another Cardinal College, a new grammar school at Ipswich. The closeness of their association with Cromwell even though relatively young and inexperienced at the time is emphasized by the fact that both were named as executors in the somewhat premature will drawn up by Cromwell in 1529.[25] Stephen and Sadler in fact remained friends for the remainder of Stephen's life since he left his old friend a ring in his will.

Vaughan's share in the work, undertaken to establish the legal and financial basis of Wolsey's new educational foundations, provides the first clear evidence of his activities as a young man. In April 1523, a chatty letter from Cromwell to a fellow Merchant Taylor, John Creke, about his experiences in the Parliament of that year concludes with the news that 'Master Vaughan fareth well'.[26] This may refer to Geoffrey Vaughan rather than Stephen but provides evidence of Cromwell's contact with the family. Moreover, Cromwell also mentions another Merchant Taylor, Master Muncaster in this letter. William Muncaster died the next summer leaving legacies to both Stephen Vaughan and Cromwell, as well as several other fellow liverymen; £10 to Stephen Vaughan and £6 13s 4d to Cromwell, 'for his pains taken with me in his sickness and to be good unto my wife in her causes'.[27] Stephen would have been by this time established in the livery company as a friend and a colleague to be favoured in this way. The Company of Merchant Taylors also had many links with trade with Spain especially the port of Seville. Such well-known traders as Thomas Bridges, Thomas Thorne and possibly Roger Barlow were all members of this company.[28] Both Creke and Muncaster traded with Spain and it may be that while acting on their behalf that Vaughan learnt Spanish. The association with Cromwell is also clear with the added suggestion that Vaughan was involved in Cromwell's legal practice, able to supply helpful advice if not more direct help. Both Cromwell and Stephen were involved on Muncaster's behalf in litigation with Creke who was Muncaster's factor in Seville. Stephen would have been about twenty-three or twenty-four at this time, possibly with experience of trading overseas; perhaps in Spain as well as in the Low Countries.[29]

Another aspect of the work Vaughan did for Cromwell in London and its environs was rather different. Wolsey's great new foundations at Oxford and Ipswich were to be supported by the lands and incomes of a collection of religious houses, destined by the cardinal for dissolution. The legal aspects of this process were both complex and time-consuming. By 1524 Cromwell had made a reputation for himself as an astute and hardworking lawyer in London well versed in the complexities of conveyancing in this period. He had already carried out a few commissions for Wolsey and his close associates, including Thomas Heneage. At some point in the first half of 1524 around July, Cromwell entered Wolsey's service initially for the express purpose of ensuring the timely and legal suppression of some twenty-nine religious houses (notionally all with less than seven inmates) to endow the new colleges.[30] Probably within a year Vaughan was in Cromwell's service to assist with the work on this project.

Vaughan's role, along with a group of other young men, was to ensure the accuracy of the details relating to the landed property of all these houses. This was no mean task since it involved not only an accurate survey of the lands but also a precise account of the forms of tenure of the occupiers of the lands and the amount and nature of their rents and other payments due to the new owners. The title to the lands of each house had been determined by a series of inquests but detailed information was needed to back this up. Stephen was particularly concerned with the property of Lesnes Abbey near Erith. This small house of Augustinian canons had been in a bad way for some considerable time; it had only five residents apart from the abbot in 1525 when formally dissolved, and had suffered from debts and bad management since the early fifteenth century.[31] It had, however, some potentially productive properties making it highly suitable for the endowment of Wolsey's colleges. Stephen's task along with one Richard Swift was 'to view, mete, butt and bound' the lands of the house. This meant that all the landed property had to be inspected, then measured correctly and all the boundaries clearly marked and established. This entailed involvement with the manorial court and all the various tenants of the lands to establish the terms of their leases and the amounts and nature of rents. Vaughan and Swift ran into trouble over extracting this information at Lesnes. None of the tenants could or maybe would inform them about the quit rents in place. One Pemsey (Vaughan called him 'perverse Pemsey' in his report) was suspected of trying to defraud Cromwell about some lands about which he alone knew the status. An assessment of the manor ('a book of sesse') included 600 acres of Thames side marshland but Pemsey spoke only of much less. Only Pemsey knew the true position and influenced the tenants so that the court would not assist Vaughan and Swift. In exasperation Vaughan complained to Cromwell that people in this area and also in Plumstead where Lesnes had further property were so obstinate that it took four days before he could find anyone to show them what lands in Plumstead belonged to the manor of Fulham which they needed to identify.[32] 'Nether by prayer ne money can we west them otherwise then it shall please them.' Vaughan and Swift also found a more serious situation in Dartford where they left, 'sondry parcelles of londes unsurueyed by reason we can have no man to lede vs to theym as there they dye of the pestilence dayly'.[33]

The level of detail required for the assessment of the assets of the dissolved houses is exemplified by a surviving 'book' for a group of properties in Northampton which runs to 140 folios all in the hand of one of the assessors except for a small section.[34] The problems with the Lesnes marshlands along the Thames were eventually resolved; in September 1526, £10 was paid to one John Abell for 'thassesse for the marisshe of Liesnes'.[35] Abell eventually leased these marshes and Vaughan delivered the money paid to Dr Stubbs in York

Place,[36] at this date still Wolsey's London residence. Apart from this time-consuming surveying work, Vaughan also seems to have worked for Cromwell in his London office compiling reports of the overall progress of the work on the dissolved houses and also giving him family news (they 'praye for your sauf retorne' he ended one letter), as Cromwell travelled around the country on Wolsey's business. Vaughan was in charge of the quantities of paperwork that even this small-scale dissolution of religious houses produced and often items went missing like that listing the sale of items from Bromehill Priory in Norfolk[37] and papers relating to the abbot of Bruern near Bicester. These could be found neither in Cromwell's counting house nor in his own home. In the case of the Bruern Abbey lands, Vaughan felt obliged to pursue the former lessee into his parish church. He wrote that he had found him at evensong and was told that 'he was disposed to serve God and could not attend to such matters there'. Vaughan replied tartly that 'sith it was his mind in such place to serve God that better he could not serve Him than with restoring the right unto his brother whom he had wrongly defrauded'.[38] The wide-ranging nature of Vaughan's responsibilities is further emphasized in the same letter when he relates how after a violent robbery at a house very near Cromwell's in Austin Friars, he took pains to put a chain on the gate 'that no man not well known may enter'. He finished this particular letter by informing Cromwell, who was in Oxford, of the latest news in London about the French invasion of Naples and the fact that the level of the market in grain would be affected by the arrival of two hulks in the port of London with more expected. Clearly his duties, often called 'writing' in Cromwell's accounts, were more like those of a modern personal assistant.[39]

During much of 1527 and the first half of 1528, Vaughan was travelling in England on the business concerned with the dissolved religious houses, but he also briefly went to the Low Countries on business for himself and for Cromwell in December 1527.[40] This was the beginning of a period when an important part of his work consisted of fulfilling all manner of personal commissions for Cromwell in the Low Countries, including picking up potentially valuable information. In August of the following year when once more in Antwerp, his main task for Cromwell was to find a large iron chest for the safe keeping of his papers and deeds. Finding an item like this should not have been difficult given the number of skilled artisans working in the town. Chests of high-quality workmanship would have been found in the general market of the Church of Our Lady or one of the workshops in the streets nearby. The commission was to prove more of a burden than Vaughan originally imagined. The first one he found was expensive (£8 Flemish) but 'strong and cleanly made' and would last a good hundred years. Vaughan wrote that he would wait for Cromwell's agreement before buying it but was confident it would be satisfactory. In the rest of this letter written from Antwerp in August 1528 Vaughan mentions his personal problem over some financial dealings with the Clarenceux king of arms which had been brewing for some time. He then gives Cromwell the latest news about the exchange rates on the Bourse (25s Flemish for 1 pound sterling) and a hint about a possible profitable trade in cheese.[41] By December of the same year he was still trying to conclude the business of the chest. He had had no indication from Cromwell about the price and was not hopeful of getting a reduction. Desperate for some communication from Cromwell, and perhaps to remind his close ties to the family, Vaughan finally asks to be commended to Cromwell's mother, 'after you my most singular friend'; this time he was writing from Barrow (Bergen op Zoom) the base of the Merchant Adventurers.[42] It is no wonder his letter is rather plaintive; he had already written in October saying he now had the keys to the chest but still no certain news that Cromwell agreed to the bargain.[43]

Vaughan was, however, not only concerned with the demands of Cromwell, his close but domineering friend and mentor. He was also trading in cloth and other goods on his own account as a Merchant Adventurer and fully involved in the affairs of the company as a whole. With his focus now firmly on what was happening in Antwerp, on the Bourse and in the business world, he may not have been fully aware of the way things were developing in England, especially of course for Cardinal Wolsey and his confidential servant, Thomas Cromwell. When Vaughan left England in 1527, and also in the late summer of 1528, Henry VIII's passion for Anne Boleyn and his determination to have his marriage to Catherine of Aragon annulled was still a secret from most people. Cardinal Campeggio, the pope's special legate, did not arrive in England until 9 October 1528 to hold a special court which was intended to deliver a verdict on the validity of the king's marriage.[44] If Vaughan returned to England in the spring of 1529, as was his declared intention in the letter written in December 1528, he would have found that Wolsey's position as the king's closest adviser was looking increasingly insecure with, of course, consequences for Cromwell and perhaps ultimately for himself. Cromwell's position and that of Wolsey were made much worse after Campeggio adjourned his court from Blackfriars to Rome in April 1529, having made no decision on the king's Great Matter. This was now unlikely to be settled speedily. Uncertainty about his personal safety may lie behind Cromwell's decision to make a will in July 1529. (At this time it was more usual to draw up a will when death seemed imminent not when in full health, as Cromwell was in the summer of 1529.) This will made clear to any unfriendly reader that Stephen was close to Cromwell. He was left with a legacy (100 marks, £66 13s 4d) and more importantly named both as an executor and as a personal servant.[45] He would not have been able to deny this connection if it ever became possibly dangerous to be too close to Cromwell.

Vaughan was probably in London when the will was drawn up but his safety and career were also threatened in another way as he explained in a letter again written from Bergen op Zoom on 3 August 1529. A row over the fees paid to him by the Company of Merchant Adventurers based at Bergen had blown up because he had been voted a fee of £40 per annum by the assembled merchants for his work on their behalf, while the governor had only been voted £20. Vaughan claimed that the governor out of pure malice had 'procured the lewdest woman and harlot in the land' to accuse him of heresy.[46] The governor in question was probably Paul Withipol, a fellow Merchant Taylor, who had allowed his chagrin at being offered a lower fee than Vaughan to overcome the usual loyalty between members of the same company.[47] Withipol had apparently written to the bishop of London seeking to start an inquiry in London which might end in Vaughan's imprisonment for heresy. Vaughan had, however, found witnesses ready to deny the charge and had got his accuser to deny she knew him or anything about him, finishing his report to Cromwell with the words, 'there is a place of justice where I could be right well avenged were it not that God willed me to refer the same to him'. Fortunately the accusation was disproved. Just over two weeks later Vaughan wrote further still smarting at the governor's spiteful behaviour but seeing him as an old man, 'meter to sit by the fire and dally with children than in a council house to govern a multitude'. Happily he could also report regarding commissions fulfilled for Cromwell, including the purchase of a dining table with a border, 'wherein is set out certain Scripture in the Greek, Hebrew and Latin, the neatest piece of work that I have seen'.[48] Despite all these problems, Vaughan had made another successful expedition to the alluring workshops of Antwerp to buy an example of the skilled workmanship on view. He also seemed to have scotched any accusation of heresy.

By the end of October, however, Vaughan had no illusions about the dangers which threatened his friend and master. An anguished letter from Antwerp makes this very clear. He had been concerned about what was going on when he was last in London but was afraid to say so. Now he writes how worried he is; he is 'more thristye to know your state and more greedy to show you, if it were possible by works how much it coveteth me to serve you'. His only consolation is that he thinks, 'you are more hated for your master's sake than for anything which I think you have wrongfully done against any man'. In his opinion, Cromwell's truth and wisdom will preserve him from danger.[49] A modern observer may think it was Cromwell's political skills and known administrative skills which allowed him to escape the opprobrium heaped on Wolsey by the court and transfer easily to the king's service while still helping Wolsey as far as was possible. By January Vaughan could write from Bergen about his pleasure at receiving news from Cromwell and that his master 'now sailed sure in a safe haven' protected from danger. 'A merry semblance of weather often thrusteth men into dangerous seas not thinking to be suddenly oppressed with tempest when unwares they be prevented and brought in great jeopardy'; this would not be Cromwell's fate. With some relief Vaughan turned to bring his master up to date with the latest rumours going around in Antwerp and once more asked to be commended to Cromwell's mother-in-law.[50]

Stephen Vaughan was still of course very much Cromwell's servant but as his master steadily advanced at court he was also drawn much closer to the centre of affairs and ultimately into direct royal service. In 1530–1 he was still acting as the agent for the Merchant Adventurers in their dealings with the authorities in the Low Countries whether the court of the Regent in Brussels or Mechelen or the local magistrates in Antwerp. At the same time he was actively trading on behalf of Cromwell more as an opportunistic trader in general goods rather than specializing in the export of English cloth like his fellow adventurers. As well as this he also kept Cromwell abreast of the news on the street or more likely on the Bourse, whether commercial or political, and at times fulfilled particular commissions like that for the iron chest. It is hard to be sure of his movements between cities in the Low Countries and his home in London. Our evidence is primarily his correspondence with Cromwell and this of course gives only an intermittent snapshot of his whereabouts. There is enough, however, to gain an overall understanding of his activities. He was clearly at home in the Low Countries, particularly the business world of Antwerp and Bergen and also was well received at the Regent's court. At times his various roles were hard to reconcile; in June 1530 he was wearing himself out with the Merchant Adventurers' problems at the same time trying to find a particular illustrated book (*Cronica cronicarum cum figuris*) for Cromwell at a reasonable price in Antwerp. He himself could not get back to London as the governors of the Merchant Adventurers refused to allow it.[51] Some months later his letter of 30 November 1530 makes the same point about the multifarious nature of his responsibilities. He had arrived in Mechelen the day before and had found 'Lady Margaret' (the Regent) on the point of death. The emperor (Charles V) would be there by the early spring and was plotting to make his brother king of the Romans (his likely successor). The countryside was badly flooded. Trading in 'spermaceti' (wax from the heads of whales; used in ointments and perfumes), bought for Cromwell, was unlikely to be as profitable as anticipated. The globe ordered by Cromwell would be delivered with this letter; in his view; 'it was singular good piece of work'. Finally he went back to his own problem about money owed to him by Clarenceux, king of arms which had still not been paid and once again asked to be remembered to Cromwell's mother-in-law.[52]

Stephen had established a pattern of travelling between London, Bergen, Antwerp and Mechelen, acting for two employers; on the one hand, Cromwell, as his agent in both business and as a source of reliable information about the political situation in the Netherlands and on the other, the Company of Merchant Adventurers as a political agent dealing with the court of the Regent and as head of their English house (trading centre) in Antwerp. At the end of 1530 he was also put under considerable additional pressure by a new commission which came directly from Henry VIII. At this time, Thomas More now chancellor in the place of Wolsey saw it as one of his main aims to stop the import of heretical books and their spread within England. He also wished to find and root out groups of dangerous heretics spreading ideas of religious reform in England. He had initiated the issue of a royal proclamation in June of that year which named several publications which had been condemned by bishops and divines from the universities as particularly pernicious. The proclamation also declared that new translations of the Bible into English 'would tend to the increase of error'. New translations would only be permitted when, 'in the future the people abandon their present perverse opinions'. Authorized translations would be undertaken by 'great learned and Catholic persons'. All other translations must be delivered up to the bishop or parish priest on pain of being brought before the king's council. The books banned by name included William Tyndale's *The Obedience of a Christian Man* while his translations of the Bible were those, from More's point of view, most full of error.[53] More had in fact earlier directly attacked Tyndale in his *Dialogue Concerning Heresies* published in June 1529.

Tyndale himself had been out of England since the spring of 1524. He had initially settled in Cologne and devoted his energy and skills to the translation of the New Testament, producing an early version in 1526. John Hackett, newly appointed the English ambassador to the court at Mechelen writing from Antwerp to the king, expressed his determination to prevent this publication reaching England as early as November of that same year.[54] In October 1528 Tyndale published *The Obedience of a Christian Man*, banned by name in the proclamation. This laid down that he and many other English supporters of Reform supported two fundamental ideas; the supreme authority in the church was the Holy Scriptures: the supreme authority in the State was the king. It is widely believed that Anne Boleyn brought the second of these ideas to the attention of Henry VIII.[55] By the spring of 1531, the king's Great Matter, the invalidity of his marriage to Catherine of Aragon, seemed to be bogged down in endless inconclusive arguments among scholars and churchmen in Rome and elsewhere. The king's mind, influenced perhaps by Cromwell's leaning towards the ideas of the evangelicals, began to consider whether approaches to the Lutheran German princes, linked in the Schmalkaldic League from February 1531, might be more inclined to help him find a way out of his marital difficulties than other European rulers.[56] The idea of approaching English Reformist exiles in the German lands in the hope they might be able to support this initiative may lie behind Vaughan's somewhat enigmatic remarks in a letter sent to Cromwell at the very end of 1530. He writes: 'I have not greatly learned any assured knowledge concerning such matters as pleased your mastership somewhat before my leave taken to common me of.'[57] By the following January his commission was clear, to find Tyndale and encourage him to return to England. On 26 January 1531, Vaughan felt able to write to the king with news of his progress in this matter, having taken the precaution of sending a draft to Cromwell beforehand for his approval. He reported that he had written to Tyndale at three locations in Germany where he had some hopes of making contact with him but despite promises of safe conduct Tyndale was not prepared to make the journey to England. As Vaughan told Cromwell, 'he (Tyndale) daily hears news which frightens him.'[58] This was not surprising taking into account the vigour of the campaign More was mounting against reformers in England at the same time. The draft sent to Cromwell makes clear Vaughan's trepidation in writing to the king on so sensitive a matter. He asks Cromwell to make sure that the king got the letter at a time when he could look at it at once and Cromwell could 'excuse any faults therein'.

The matter was not, however, to be left there. Vaughan became more and more involved in the affair. His opinion of Tyndale as an inspired translator and skilful polemicist went up as the two had more contact. It was, however, the case that despite the cautious nature of his approach to the king, Henry VIII did not share Vaughan's opinion of Tyndale or his latest work. This became very clear in mid-April after Vaughan had sent the king a copy of Tyndale's answer to More's attack on him which Vaughan had in fact laboriously copied for this purpose by hand as the printed copy was so poor. This took up no fewer than three quires of paper for the whole work so was no mean task. Vaughan nevertheless hopefully suggested that this piece, 'will better like you than some other of his works'. He also told the king of his meeting with Tyndale which reads like something out of a modern spy novel. Stephen was told that 'some unknown friend wished to see him' outside Antwerp. At the meeting place Tyndale gave his name and a robust defence of his views. He was a true subject of the king and his warnings against Wolsey were justified as the king had later agreed. Having access to the Scriptures in a tongue all could understand would 'open men's eyes to their own wickedness'. He, however, would not dare to come to England as he believed the English clergy would declare any promises made to heretics invalid, including any promise of protection from accusations of heresy. Tyndale then left Vaughan clearly afraid that Vaughan would try to follow him.[59] Vaughan had no intention of doing this but was left with the impression that Tyndale would not listen to his advice because 'he greatly suspects me'.[60]

Cromwell wrote back to Vaughan almost immediately after the king had seen the book, explaining how the king had received it. His reaction was not what Vaughan had hoped for. The book 'was filled with seditious and slanderous lies and fantastical opinions showing therein neither learning nor truth'. Vaughan was to have nothing more to do with Tyndale and to stop urging him to come to England. If Tyndale was in the country, he would probably do what he could to infect and corrupt the whole realm. Cromwell strongly advised Vaughan for his own benefit and safety to show 'no favour love or affection to neither the said Tyndale nor his works'.[61] At this point in 1531 Cromwell was rising in the king's favour with his energies concentrated on finding academic support for Henry's case for the annulment of his marriage to Catherine of Aragon. The last thing he wanted, we may presume, was the presence of Tyndale in the country since he was clearly deaf to any ideas of moderating his views for political advantage and only too likely to enrage the king.[62]

Writing in May 1531, Vaughan accepted Cromwell's admonishments diplomatically calling them his 'friendly and rather fatherly writing', but he was not put off meeting Tyndale again and urging him to return to England.[63] Another latter of the same date records how, at this later meeting, he told Tyndale that the king would be very pleased if he could moderate his views a little. Tyndale with tears in his eyes seemed willing to accept this provided only that 'a bare text of Scripture' was allowed to be distributed in England. The chances of this seemed remote to Vaughan. By the summer he was complaining to Cromwell that 'he (Tyndale) always sings one note',[64] and 'uses so rude and simple a style nothing seeking any vain praise and commendation'.[65] But even so Vaughan did not give up his hopes that the king himself would come to appreciate Tyndale's works better than academics and scholars did and would thus support his views.

At the same time, during 1531-2, as well as dealing with these delicate negotiations relating to religious affairs, Vaughan was becoming more and more drawn into royal service as a source of political and commercial information and as a suitable person to undertake special commissions for the king. His letters concerning Tyndale also contain accounts of the news current in Antwerp, sometimes answering direct queries from the Crown. He was specifically asked to report on the way Charles V was raising money in his various dominions for a possible war with France and the friction this was causing between Spain and the Netherlands. In a letter of May 1531, relating to these queries, Vaughan felt compelled to point out that he was 'a common servant to a multitude' (the Merchant Adventurers) as well as concerned in royal affairs. He was thus forced to travel continually between Barrow (Bergen op Zoom), Antwerp, Brussels and Ghent and could do with some more money for expenses. His closer involvement in royal affairs was recognized in July when he was appointed a 'writer of the king's books' with a stipend of £20 a year.[66] It has been pointed out that Vaughan over the course of his whole career 'received but a minor share of the official spoils commonly parcelled out to ministers of the crown in the political grab bag of the day',[67] but this grant did go some way to improve his finances. Royal indifference to the financial strains experienced by royal servants serving abroad was nothing new in the early sixteenth century. It was a common plaint of most envoys.

A further major problem for Vaughan dealing with all his various responsibilities to the Crown, Cromwell his personal friend, and the Company of Merchant Adventurers was also the uncertainty and unreliability of communications between the Netherlands and England. While Vaughan kept a close ear to the ground regarding developments in the Netherlands, it was conversely hard for him to get good information of the state of affairs in London. Getting letters, some of them highly confidential, from Antwerp to London or the reverse depended very largely on informal ad hoc arrangements, not on any regulated postal system. All this became a real issue in November and December 1531. Two letters to Cromwell sent more or less simultaneously on 14 November reveal how nervous Vaughan was about the perceived lack of letters from London which he believed had led to the view in some circles that he was neglecting his duties. This was far from the case. These letters also reveal how deeply he felt about reformed ideas in religion and his hope that Henry VIII might come to understand them better if he was better informed. He devised elaborate schemes for sending Tyndale's new work on the first Epistle of John to Cromwell as well as a book by Robert Barnes. Barnes was a Cambridge theologian who had been driven into exile in Wittenberg by the hostility of Wolsey and was widely considered to be a Lutheran. The book in question was his *Supplication,* newly published in 1531; this put forward his support for the idea of royal supremacy, an idea which also found favour with Tyndale as well as Vaughan. Stephen's fervent postscript to the letter to Cromwell, claiming, 'how good a deed should you do to help Dr Barnes to declare the opinion of his book before the King, that men might be suffered to hold them for good' concludes, 'Behold the signs of this world would be wondrous' and reveals his own opinion on this matter. Cromwell probably found more interesting than these religious concerns the report that the Flemings were hostile to the king's desire for a divorce and the news of ships docking from England with cargoes of foodstuffs in contravention of a royal decree.[68]

Some six days later Vaughan was still worried about the delivery of his letters having sent them by different couriers including 'a haberdasher living on the hill going up from New Fyshe Street' whose name he didn't know. He was, however, on this occasion concerned with intelligence from the emperor's court and Cromwell's personal business deals. These had perhaps been neglected by the overburdened Vaughan. The consignment of spermaceti, which he had undertaken to sell for his master a year ago was still in its boxes with a hard crust 'as black as coal' but he had found a possible purchaser in London. Finally on 9 December in a long letter to Cromwell Vaughan makes explicit the worries that had clearly been on his mind much earlier but which he had not spoken of openly. He had at last found letters from Cromwell waiting for him at the English house in Tournai. These confirmed the rumours he had already heard. George Constantine, another exiled reformer who had recently returned to England,[69] had been arrested by Sir Thomas More in his drive against perceived heretics in England and under heavy duress had accused Vaughan of Lutheranism. Vaughan was extremely disturbed by this news. First, in his mind it was completely unwarranted; Vaughan was not and never had been a member of what he called the sect of Lutheranism. He believed fervently in the divine origin of royal rule and saw himself as absolutely loyal to the king and bound to his service and obedient to his edicts. Second, he was also as deeply convinced of the pre-eminent position of the Scriptures in teaching religion. He did not trust 'in the learning of any earthly creature'. In his view 'God's learning cannot deceive'. He did not blame Constantine for his accusation because 'these punishments' (the use of such instruments as the rack inflicted by More's agents on the wretched

Constantine) 'will make a son forget his father and mother'. In his agony of mind he continued, 'I hear I have lost a most dear friend and special good master in you (Cromwell) and that you have excused yourself to the King for ever having advanced me as you are greatly deceived in me. This was reported to me from my Lord Chancellor's mouth.' He would, however, remain loyal to Cromwell. 'Nothing can turn me from you to whom I owe so much.'[70]

After this long and heartfelt emotional outburst Stephen turned to a description of Charles V's procession in Tournai and the successful conclusion of negotiations regarding the taking of English vessels by pirates from Holland. He also promised to deal with the spermaceti before he left the country. His final remarks are of more importance. Constantine had escaped from prison in London and reached Antwerp on 6 December; in the future Vaughan would have nothing to do with him or those with similar beliefs. He would, in fact, copy the low profile displayed by Cromwell in religious matters. By the end of the month Vaughan was back to business, concentrating on matters to do with the all-important cloth trade between England and Flanders. Antwerp was full of rumours that the emperor had embargoed the trade something that had grave consequences not only of course for the Merchant Adventurers but also for royal income from customs duties. Constantine's accusations still rankled however, and he was well aware of how he could be harmed by any 'evil disposed person in England who may perchance spit out any venom against me'. He will in the future keep well away from religious exiles and those who 'have so corrupt a mind, evil a conscience or so little understanding as it seems they would I have'.[71]

Vaughan had in fact much on his mind apart from his deeply held but also personal religious views at this time. He was clearly strongly attracted to Reformist ideas, particularly the idea that the Scriptures alone were the gateway to truth but at the same time he accepted that Henry VIII had authority in such matters by virtue of his position as a ruler sanctioned by God. Apart from the strong possibility of these views leading to the holding of simultaneous but contradictory beliefs, Vaughan was in danger of being pulled in several directions at once by the conflicting calls on his professional expertise and loyalty to his various masters and employers, the king, Thomas Cromwell and the Company of Merchant Adventurers. There were also issues with his family responsibilities in London. In Bergen op Zoom in early 1532, Vaughan had been acting as a mentor, to one of Cromwell's young personal servants, Thomas Avery, probably teaching him about business methods and the merchant's world. Vaughan regarded this young man as 'the first-fruit of my rude education'. His return to England had to be arranged while Vaughan was also still trying to unload the boxes of spermaceti on some unlucky buyer. Ruefully in one letter he moaned that the spermaceti had put him 'to more pain than anything else I ever had to sell'.

In between his business trips to the Netherlands and all the errands for Cromwell, Stephen also had to deal with important changes in his private life. Many of these changes demonstrate how intertwined the various aspects of public and private life in the sixteenth century were. Vaughan himself was now at one and the same time a servant of the king, a close associate of the most powerful of the king's advisers and prominent in the foremost trading association in the country. In the relatively small society of London at the time he was persona grata at court, well thought of as a businessman, and friendly with a wide range of people of some reputation. Much the same could be said of his life in Antwerp. His personal contacts at the court of the Regent of the Netherlands, on the Bourse and in the markets as a whole were of immense importance. He was not unusual in this; this tangled web of personal connections of all kinds was a particular feature of life at the time.

Probably in the last days of 1532 or early 1533, he married Margery or Margaret Awpart. She was the widow of Edward Awpart a London merchant and member of the Girdlers' Company who died in June 1532. Like Stephen, Margery came from a Welsh family, the Guinets or Gwynedds. At the time of the marriage she lived near Cheapside in a property called 'The Three Legs' leased from St Bartholomew's and had five small children. It would be only too easy to see this as a marriage bringing some degree of wealth to Stephen in return for security for Margery and her family. It is likely that the relationship was more personally important than one based only on financial considerations. Since Stephen lived in the same area it is likely that they were at least friends before she was widowed. After the marriage, the family probably continued to live in The Three Legs. In 1536 Vaughan himself took a new lease on the property from St Bartholomew's and also extended his holding into two shops and a cellar next door.[72] Stephen was also concerned about promoting his new wife's interests. His connections allowed him to establish his new wife in the household of the queen. In May 1533 he wrote to Cromwell asking for a position in Anne Boleyn's household for his wife, implying that Cromwell in fact knew her well;

> I am informed that the Queen intends to have a silkwoman to trim and furnish her Grace with such things as she shall wear. If you will recommend my wife to the place you will bind us both. You know what she can do. I suppose no woman can better trim her Grace.[73]

This was no sinecure, nor was it unusual for a silk-woman to have friends among the Merchant Taylors since their crafts were related. Margery clearly had full command of the skills of a silk-woman well able to create fashionable and elaborate trimmings for the queen's extensive and expensive wardrobe. Vaughan fully appreciated his wife's skills and was anxious that his wife's work should be properly appreciated. A matter of months later he complained to Cromwell that although his wife had 'devised certain works for the Queen' these were 'neither seen nor was she thanked for them'.[74] If Cromwell did intervene on her behalf, it clearly worked because after Anne's execution when her household accounts were settled Mrs Vaughan was recorded as being owed £68 4s 1½d.[75] More light is also thrown on Stephen's family responsibilities by the mention in the same letter to Cromwell as that complaining of his wife's treatment in the queen's household that he wanted to make sure that the 'last year's stipend' should be paid to his father 'whom I cannot see lack'. Richard Vaughan, perhaps with some long-standing disability, had not recovered from the financial difficulties he suffered in the 1520s.[76]

Moreover, Stephen's marriage and that of his sister Mawdlyn at much the same time, firmly linked him with a circle of prominent London families with connections with trade and the governance of the city of London. His brother-in-law, John Guinet, was particularly close to Stephen finally being an excecutor of his will and responsible for the provisions made for Stephen's children after his death.[77] Guinet was probably much the same age as Stephen and of Welsh origin, in this case, Caernarvonshire.[78] After taking orders he made a name for himself as a composer of church music and received the degree of Doctor of Music from Oxford in 1531. His supplication for the degree claims that he had composed 'three masses of five parts and five masses of four as also certain symphonas, antiphonas and divers songs for the use of the church'.[79] Only one example of his work, a song, survives in an incomplete version but he seems to have had a role as a musician and chaplain at St Alban's Abbey. He later held livings including those of St Alban's Church in Luton and St Peter Westcheap in London as well as that of St Beuno's Church in Clynnog Fawr in Caernarvonshire in Wales. There is no doubt that he held fast to the old ways in religion and was prepared to defend them in print, vigorously attacking the views of John Frith, a friend and ally of Tyndale, who suffered martyrdom at Smithfield for his heretical views on the Eucharist.[80] This, however, does not seem to have detracted from his friendship with Vaughan. It is clear from Vaughan's letters that Guinet lived with his sister's family at their house near Cheapside, the 'Three Legs' and was happy to look after correspondence and the like for Vaughan during his periods in the Low Countries.

Vaughan's sister, Mawdlyn's first husband, was William Pratt, a liveryman of the Grocers' Company, and the stepson of Sir Christopher Askewe, Lord Mayor of London in 1533–4. Sometime after his death in 1539 she married his former apprentice, Thomas Lodge, and set up a house with him in the parish of St Michael's Cornhill. She and her husband were also close to Stephen, who used his brother-in-law as a confidential agent in the Netherlands in 1545 when he was deeply involved in the affairs of the Crown.[81] Lodge was also described as his 'trustie friend' when named as one of the overseers of his will in 1549 although Mawdleyn had died in 1548. Lodge's later career makes clear his drive and intelligence. He was prominent in city affairs as master of the Grocer's Company, and as an Alderman and eventually Lord Mayor in 1562–3. He also invested actively in new trading ventures like the Muscovy Company and early voyages to the Guinea Coast.[82] All this and the fact that he also survived financial and legal problems in his later years demonstrates the vigour and enterprise of the merchants of the city of London, a group in which Stephen Vaughan and his family were now firmly embedded with contacts by marriage and business. Stephen, however, at first through his links to Thomas Cromwell and later through his links with other prominent courtiers was increasingly involved in the service of the Crown rather than his own business affairs or being involved in the governance of the city. It is to this aspect of his work that we now turn.

5

Vaughan as a diplomat

In retrospect, it is clear that the commission from Henry VIII to approach Tyndale marked a turning point in Stephan Vaughan's career (Figures 5 and 6). After this event he was drawn ever closer to the court and to the service of the Crown at a time when the political situation in England itself and its relations with other polities in Europe were changing rapidly. Diplomacy now dealt with differences in religion and commercial conflicts as well as issues relating to the prestige of states and rulers and ultimately questions of war or peace. Especially in England, as the nature of diplomacy changed, it became more organized and more broadly based. At the beginning of the reign of Henry VIII there were few, if any, 'career diplomats' (to use a modern term) in the service of the Crown. Ambassadors and others empowered to negotiate with foreign powers were usually appointed on an 'ad hoc' basis as and when needed. This system was continued into the 1520s but by the end of the following decade, the ambassador resident abroad, often for quite long periods, usually accompanied by a suite of servants or agents, whether clerical or lay in status, had become a permanent part of the system of government. In this respect England was finally following the example of Venice and the empire and their long-serving envoys at foreign courts. Eustace Chapuys, the ambassador of Charles V to the court of Henry VIII from 1529 to 1539 and from 1540 to 1545 is the most prominent and influential example.[1]

Leading clerics, many already embedded in royal service, had been prominent as envoys overseas for the Crown for much of the thirteenth and fourteenth centuries. In the fifteenth century, it has been calculated that some 27 per cent of those sent overseas between 1422 and 1461 were in orders. Henry VII continued to employ a similar group of clerics, either bishops or those with close personal relations to the Crown, on important diplomatic missions. This group included Christopher Urswick, the dean of Windsor and confessor to the king's mother Lady Margaret Beaufort, Richard Foxe the bishop of Winchester and William

Figure 5 Hof van Savoy, at Mechelen the residence of the Regents of the Netherlands. Public domain.

Warham the archbishop of Canterbury from 1502. Henry VIII similarly used the services of Stephen Gardiner, Cuthbert Tunstall and Edmund Bonner, all of whom eventually became bishops, of the sees of Winchester, Durham and London, respectively. All served initially on diplomatic missions with a particular purpose but in the 1530s Gardiner was appointed ambassador to France and remained there for three years. He was succeeded by Bonner on the same terms. Over a third of the members of missions sent overseas between 1540 and 1547, whatever their rank, were still clerics despite the increasing prominence of laymen close to the Crown[2]

To some extent this was due to their sound understanding of Latin, used in, for example, the wording of treaties and other formal communications. Some also had knowledge of civil law, as well as canon law, a useful diplomatic tool in much of Europe. Particularly after the breach with Rome, the predominance of clerics as ambassadors, however, gradually gave way to the much greater employment of men from the gentry and nobility. What they may have lacked in fluency in Latin and legal expertise was made up by their knowledge of courtly life and manners and experience in royal service. They could fit seamlessly into the elaborate social rituals of foreign courts and could, by their very presence, if sufficiently eminent at home, flatter host courts overseas. Wolsey had used his apparent magnificence and the opulence of his train

Figure 6 Stephen Vaughan's coat of arms. Permission granted by the College of Arms.

of servants as a diplomatic tool to overawe even the court of Francis I but most clerics including modest men like Thomas Cranmer, sent on diplomatic missions before becoming the archbishop of Canterbury, could not operate in this way.

It is also the case that some rulers were reluctant to receive envoys of less than upper gentry status seeing this as a form of disrespect. This was particularly the case with Charles V and Francis I. At the beginning of his career before his ascent to high office, Thomas Wriothesley, even though he was the son of the York Herald William Wriothesley and had studied at Trinity Hall Cambridge, felt slighted by imperial officials when on a mission to that court in 1538 with Stephen Vaughan. He wrote indignantly to Cromwell, 'some of them begynne foolishly to talk of me as marvelling that his maiesty would send so meane a man as I am to mayne so greate a mater', unjustifiably calling him a man of 'no estimacion'.[3] It is the case that more noble envoys were sent by Henry VIII to the Imperial court than to any others.[4]

This reliance on clerics and noblemen did not mean, however, that there was no place for merchants and those of similar status as envoys for Henry VIII. Especially in the Low Countries where many of the issues causing problems between rulers concerned commercial matters, envoys, agents or ambassadors (the term used might change) who understood local trading conditions and conventions were essential. Thomas Spinelly, a Florentine from a well-known merchant family, probably first served Henry VII in negotiations of this kind and also as an invaluable source of information of events in the Low Countries and elsewhere. His uncle Philip Gualterotti was head of the largest banking house in Antwerp and had access to the best and most up-to-date information and gossip on both political and commercial affairs. From 1509, Spinelly also served Henry VIII in the same capacity and eventually became the accredited resident ambassador of the English Crown to the court of Charles V. He died in the early 1520s, by this time referred to in letters as Sir Thomas Spinelly.[5]

Their connection with the markets of the Low Countries and the merchant community was equally a crucial factor in the careers of other merchant diplomats. John Hackett originally from Waterford in Ireland was based in the Low Countries from the beginning of the sixteenth century. At first, around 1500, he was living in Bergen op Zoom, the base of the Merchant Adventurers, and working in the wool trade in the service of Philip Gualterotti, Spinelly's uncle. In 1522, Sir Robert Wingfield recommended him to Wolsey as the king's solicitor or agent, describing him 'as the myetest man I knowe for such an appointment'.[6] He was given an even more glowing recommendation in 1523 when William Knight wrote to Wolsey declaring that Hackett would be 'much more mete to do singulier service than Sir Thomas Spynelly was'. One particular benefit expected was that Hackett was not only on good terms with 'all the best' but also was a considerable linguist knowing, 'langages Latyne, Frenshe, Spaynyshe, Dowche and Italian and good Englishe'.[7] By May 1526, at the latest, Hackett was established as the envoy of Henry VIII at the court of Margaret of Austria, the Regent of the Netherlands. From the body of his letters to Wolsey and those in his service like Brian Tuke, the cardinal's secretary, it is easy to see how useful Hackett was, passing a stream of informed local gossip and information back to the English court. In September of that year he sent the first reliable news of the outcome nearly three weeks previously of the Battle of Mohacs and the considerable list of slain among the nobility of Eastern Europe, an event which gave the Ottoman Empire control over much of the area. Later in October he kept the English court informed of the progress of Charles V's campaign in Italy and the sack of Rome by his unpaid troops. At the same time he was hunting for possibly heretical books in English in the bookshops of Antwerp so that they could be impounded and burnt and negotiating terms with Margaret on the trading conditions of the Merchant Adventurers. It is notable that a lot of his information came from contacts in the merchant community like news that the French Duke of Bourbon had come 'owte of Myllan half dysesperat with suche men as he had and has bett the Venyssians owte of ther fyld and has the victory of them'. All this 'att after dynar' from 'a marchand man cum from Andwerp'.[8] Some of this intelligence was perhaps no more than hearsay, but it certainly helped Wolsey keep his grip on foreign affairs to the benefit of Henry VIII's standing in Europe.

Some of his effectiveness as an ambassador also seems to have been due to the close personal relations he managed to maintain with Margaret of Austria and her court up to her death in January 1531. Stephen Vaughan his close friend and colleague referred to this in a letter to Henry VIII advising that Hackett should be reappointed to his post in the Netherlands.

> His Grace shall not be prouvyded of a man that more substancially shall handle his matters in these partie this xl yeres no one that shall do more in these parties then he and excedyngly well enterteyned and beloued with all the great men of these parties which he hathe purchased with his wisdom his getyll humanyte and great cost and charge and peradventure to his Highnes letle knowen.[9]

Hackett then represented Henry at the court of Charles V until his own death in October 1534. During all this time he regularly and diligently reported on the situation, in the Netherlands and at the courts of Mary of Hungary, Margaret's successor, and Charles V, directly to Henry VIII and to Cromwell. His reports range widely over the whole field of the relations between states and rulers including guesses at the intentions of the Ottomans in Eastern Europe and the tangled relations between, for example, Denmark and the Hanseatic towns. He reported apparently verbatim conversations usually in French with his contacts and even Mary of Hungary herself. In April 1533 when the marriage of Henry and Anne Boleyn became officially acknowledged, the way this outraged the emperor and his supporters was made plain. Hackett had already had some word privately from England of the 'grete kloude which is likely to be a grete storm when it falleth'[10] that was overhanging the country. He was summoned to see Mary and asked if he had any news from England. Hackett said no and then endured a hostile interview which began with her giving him 'a loeke as too [though] that she showld merwell there of' and continuing coldly, 'jay des nouulles qui ne me semblent point trop bonnes',[11] that is concerning the marriage. Hackett had had no official 'briefing' as it were at this point and defended Henry as best he could.[12] In another letter he made clear to Cromwell, from information from 'a secret friend' that there was fury in Brussels that Catherine of Aragon was being badly treated, 'not like a kynges doghter neither lyke an Emperors awnt'.[13] There is little doubt that Hackett's reporting and intelligence allowed Cromwell and the king to understand the way Charles and his court viewed events in England and the continuing comings and goings at the court; something no other source of information could provide.

John Hackett also became something of an expert in the negotiation of agreements concerning the conduct of trade between England and its major markets in the Netherlands. That trade relations were an important part of the role of the English envoy to the court of the imperial Regent of the Low Countries had been the case for many years. Since the mid-1520s Hackett had been deeply involved in problems of this kind. One source of disagreement was the interpretation of the Magnus Intercursus of 1496 which had granted English merchants extensive trading privileges including the exemption from local tolls and the right to sell cloth retail. Hackett in 1526 writing to Wolsey called this 'the intretenaunce of owr intercowrs'.[14] There were also more 'domestic' problems concerning things like the salvage and recovery of English merchants' goods after a shipwreck or quarrels about the value of promised discounts and the like which placed English merchants at a disadvantage in Brabant. Hackett asserted that the only response to his complaints to the Lords of the Council in the Netherlands was 'fayre wordes' and little action.[15]

In matters of this kind when Vaughan was in the Low Countries, he co-operated with Hackett. Stephen had in fact been involved in keeping Cromwell informed about commercial problems in this region from the beginning of his entry to Cromwell's service. In the summer of 1528, for example, he told Cromwell that 'the slack trade is owing to the abundance lately coming and to the war between Gelders and these parts'.[16] By December 1531 he had access to better information and was able to report the important news that 'the Hollanders had bannysshed Englishe clothes out of theyr contrey'. He also passed this unwelcome intelligence on to Hackett in Brussels though on this occasion Hackett 'neuer knew ne harde of any suche thing'.[17] By February 1532, however, a copy of the imperial decree to that effect became available.[18] It then became the duty of Hackett and others to negotiate on this matter with the emperor's commissioners who were (or so Vaughan alleged) 'the polytikist fellows in all this londe'. In his view only an experienced diplomat like Tunstall the bishop of Durham could cope with them even though Paul Withipol, a prominent Merchant Adventurer, was part of the delegation and 'hathe studied our entercourses here and knowyth more than any merchaunt longyng to all th'Advenrurers'.[19] Vaughan continued his own involvement in this matter reporting in March that the emperor was inquiring throughout the Low Countries about 'what greffes they fynd ageynst the merchanttes of Englond and ayenst any liberties to them graunted in these parties'. All of which would be 'layd sore to the charge' of the Imperial commissioners. Damaging allegations about the 'false packyng of woolles' and 'false making of clothes' were included.[20] The English delegation met the imperial commissioners armed with a long and inclusive list of points to make and arguments against the demands and complaints of the imperial commissioners drawn up by the king's advisers. These varied in importance from a stout defence of the privileges of the city of London to bald statements that the imperial claims were not true. As far as the Merchant Adventurers were concerned the English delegation was instructed to claim that 'pryvate agreements and orders between the companies of marchaunts at what days to bye and selle cannot be drawen to appertaune to the treatyse between princes ne any publique contract canne take awaye any private pollicye'.[21] No definite conclusion was reached in these negotiations but the cloth trade in fact flourished greatly in the next few years leading to the conclusion that the matters were probably quietly shelved as prosperity increased in both realms.[22] Before the negotiations began Vaughan had written an analysis of the problems in the cloth trade at this time in a book (unfortunately not surviving) which he sent to the king. His view was that the Merchant Adventurers and clothmakers should forcefully remind the Netherlanders of the advantages which they gained from the trade with England. How in fact Flanders gained 'more profit from us than any other country' in view of the purchases our merchants made of 'linen cloth, St Thomas Worsteds, says, buckrams, Bruges satins and other things'; all for 'ready money'. In fact if the Flemish merchants' unreasonable demands were granted and this trade ceased 'they should in short time bring our heads under their girdles'.[23] It had always been clear that, it was to 'Cromwell's advantage to have one of his long-time friends and agents so well placed in the single most important company in the English economy'.[24]

Stephen Vaughan was finally also recruited by the Crown as a diplomat in direct royal service overseas rather than as the useful confidential friend and agent of Thomas Cromwell in the early 1530s. His first mission, undertaken at very short notice, shows how these two roles were at times so intertwined as to be almost indistinguishable. In the beginning of 1532 events in England were making it more and more apparent that it was Henry's firm intention to marry Anne Boleyn. Henry's foreign policy was dominated by the need to find support for his Great Matter, that is the legal process to annul his marriage to Catherine of Aragon to clear the way for a new marriage to Anne Boleyn. Henry had been hopeful of support from Francis I for some time and this wish lay behind the signing of a treaty that summer which promised England aid from France if Charles V attacked the country. In the autumn preparations were going ahead for a meeting at Calais in October between Henry and Anne with Francis I to consolidate their alliance. This was envisaged on a scale which almost attempted a re-run of the enormous display of the Field of the Cloth of Gold in 1520. Anne herself was granted the title of Marquis of Pembroke by the king. In early September, Stephen was sent by Cromwell to Windsor to show the king and his new consort the design of a jewelled chain ordered for this occasion which was to be set with diamonds emeralds and rubies. The 'lady Marquess liked it well' he told a probably relieved Cromwell.[25]

The meeting of the two kings in October was in fact accounted for a resounding success. It was lauded to the English reading public in Wynkyn de Worde's *The Maner of the Triomphe at Caleys and Bullen* published as rapidly as possible in the first months of 1533. In early December, however, Stephen was despatched on an urgent mission to France. Thomas Cranmer, the archbishop of Canterbury elect since the death of Warham, his predecessor, in the summer, was making his way back to England in a leisurely manner after a diplomatic mission to the court of Charles V. Stephen was commissioned to find him and get him back to England as soon as possible. What lay behind the need for the utmost haste which saw Stephen riding to Dover through the night immediately after seeing Cromwell? He arrived in Dover at 5.00 am but by 7.00 am had hired a boat and was en route for Boulogne.[26] He was in Paris within three days after walking 12 miles from the coast at Whitesand Bay, where his vessel landed, through snow and ice to find post-horses at Boulogne. Even when he had secured horses there were problems; near Amiens he suffered a heavy fall on the icy road injuring his leg, which delayed his arrival in Paris by half a day.[27] It seems very likely that Anne who, it was strongly rumoured, had finally given way to Henry's ardour after the excitement in Calais, thought herself pregnant.[28] Cranmer needed to be canonically installed as an archbishop acceptable to the pope in order to pronounce the divorce with due solemnity. Stephen, bruised, battered and despondent, wrote to Cromwell from Paris that 'he had heard nothing of the man [Cranmer] during his journey'.[29] There seemed to be no firm news of him in Lyon but Stephen followed a possible trail to that city and four days later was able to report to Cromwell that Cranmer was in fact in the neighbourhood. He finished this latter by declaring dramatically that 'I will conduct him in safety or die by the way'. Cranmer, however, was not disposed to rush back to England and wanted to make only 'small journeys'.[30] The pair eventually reached England in early January. Henry and Anne were married in secret on 24 or 25 January while Cranmer was finally formally consecrated archbishop on 30 March 1533.[31]

By the end of May the breach with Rome had been enshrined in statute law and its consequences made plain. The Act in Restraint of Appeals, abolishing the legal powers of the papacy in England and therefore its ability to pronounce on the validity of Henry VIII's marriage to Catherine, was passed in the first week of that month. On 23 May, Cranmer at the end of proceedings in his court declared that this marriage was against the law of God and therefore had always been of no effect. Catherine would henceforth be known as the Princess Dowager as the widow of Arthur, Prince of Wales. On 28 May the earlier secret marriage of Henry and Anne was validated. The following day Anne was crowned queen of England in an elaborate ceremony. News of these events was received with consternation in most European courts. As we have seen, Hackett's graphic reports from the court of the Regent of the Netherlands left little room for doubt at the anger in Brussels.

Vaughan who had returned to England with Cranmer, was now deeply occupied with Cromwell's concerns. In the late spring of 1533 he was involved in getting intelligence for his master, probably of the organization of local opposition to the king's policies.[32] In June, however, he was again recruited for another overseas mission as an envoy for the Crown. The primary purpose of this journey was to try and obtain the support of the Lutheran princes of the empire for Henry's remarriage and the total rejection of the ties binding the English Church to Rome. Vaughan was accompanied at the beginning of this mission by Christopher Mond or Mont. Mond came from Coblenz but entered the service of the English Crown in 1527. He was a doctor of civil law, fluent in English (one of his first known jobs was as the translator of German texts to English for Cromwell) and was granted denization as an Englishman in 1431. He was in modern terms a skilled and professional diplomat while Vaughan at this time was still an amateur in this field, uncertain of his command of the necessary languages and somewhat unused to the formalities of foreign courts.[33]

This can be seen in the early letters sent by Vaughan to Cromwell reporting on this mission. The first letter from Calais and the second from Antwerp are a confused muddle of gossip and rumours, sound intelligence and his concerns for his own affairs, particularly those relating to his wife. He had good information about the activities in the Netherlands of those opposed to the king and his Great Matter. Friar Peto, the Provincial of the Observant Franciscans in Greenwich, already known to be hostile to the king's policies, was busy stirring up trouble in Antwerp largely by distributing books attacking the king like that said to be written by John Fisher, the bishop of Rochester. Vaughan had no patience with dissident clerics, seeing them all as traitors who in his view deserved to be put on the rack so that their plots could be discovered. His views were shared by Cromwell, who wrote to the king advocating the same treatment for the Greenwich friars. In a calmer mood Vaughan then turned to the vexed question of his own remuneration for the mission. It was not sufficient to cover his costs, including the provision of horses and the payments to couriers. Not only did he lack money but his wife was not being paid by the queen; she should have, 'her fee [as the queen's silk-woman] or else she had better keep sheep for any gain she will have'. Concerning the main business of his trip abroad he reported that he would leave for Cologne on the following day (4 August). As the last shot he warned Cromwell that friars might try to slip out of England in laymen's clothing.[34]

By the end of the month Vaughan had reached Nuremberg where he and Mont separated; Mont set off for Bavaria while Vaughan travelled to Saxony. At the duke's castle in Weimar he faced problems although cordially welcomed at first. The apparent issue was that Vaughan had intended to 'deliver an oration' to the duke in French and Latin explaining his mission. It then transpired that the duke understood neither of these languages but would receive written copies of his speech. Two hours after these had been delivered to the duke, Vaughan received a reply; the duke saw no need for a resident ambassador from England in his court. Such a change in established custom was inadvisable. Vaughan felt unable to press matters further and did not think it expedient go on to Hesse or Lunenberg to present the same request from Henry VIII to their princes. In his report he put his finger on the real reason for this brush-off by the duke. Neither he nor in all probability the other Lutheran princes were prepared to offer any support to England in face of the emperor's hostility to Henry's treatment of Catherine.[35] This impression was emphasized in Vaughan's later report to Cromwell from Cologne. Although the Duke of Saxony 'is the chief maintainer of Lutheranism he will not embroil himself in any fresh difficulty especially as the King has repudiated Katharine which affects the Emperor'.[36] As Vaughan put it in a letter to Cromwell, 'here is thonely thing whiche I undoubtydly thinke ferithe the Duke and makithe hym not so hardy to receive the Kynges agent.'[37]

By the end of October Vaughan was back in Antwerp, still smarting from the apparent failure of his mission to the Lutheran princes. Perhaps in some relief he turned once more to the activities of Peto and his supporters, characterizing the friar as a 'tiger clad in a sheepskin' and 'a perilous knave'.[38] Personally Stephen was in a bad way. He felt ill briefed by Cromwell, had lost his horse and moreover was very short of money and not in the best of health. With real bitterness he wrote, 'those who serve least, I see, are often best rewarded'. He even lacked responses to his reports because the couriers had not been paid to deliver them. It was in this frame of mind that he turned on Cromwell in the same letter and castigated him for something which might seem to us to have had little immediate relevance to his current situation. He unleashed a torrent of abuse on Cromwell because he intended to make Roland Lee the bishop of Lichfield and Coventry. MacCulloch sees this as evidence of Stephen Vaughan's propensity for self-righteous ranting.[39] Vaughan calls Lee 'an earthly beast a mole, and "a papist an idolater"'[40] and describes bishops in general as full of 'tyranny, falsehood and untruth against God, prince and man'. Vaughan was undoubtedly jealous of Lee gaining major preferment while he, as close a friend of Cromwell as any man, languished in Antwerp, desperate to get home to London. Vaughan was undoubtedly sincere in his own religious beliefs and despised Lee's tepid traditionalism but this outburst was more an expression of depression and a feeling of being overlooked that anything else. In his usual swift change of subject he ends this letter by making sure that Cromwell knew that John Hackett had sent him a silver inkhorn as a gift along with letters from his fellow envoy Christopher Mont. Within three weeks Vaughan had calmed down; he now had the king's permission to go home and return to one of his usual tasks for Cromwell and apologized for being unable to find the books he (Cromwell) wanted.[41]

Vaughan was probably back in London by Christmas 1533. There is little correspondence with Thomas Cromwell, the prime source for his activities, for most of 1534. This may have been caused by the anger aroused by his emotional explosion over the advancement of Roland Lee. It seems more likely that in this tumultuous year in public and religious affairs in England, Vaughan was content to keep a low profile devoting himself to his own business and his family. It is very probable that his eldest child was born at this time. He was also perhaps appeased by his appointment as a Chancery clerk in the office of dispensations and faculties in absentia which improved his financial position. John Hackett's reports from the Netherlands to both Thomas Cromwell and the king make very clear how confused and stressful life was for an English envoy overseas in the aftermath of the breach with Rome. Hackett was faced with defending Henry's position, for example, as set out in the pamphlet *A Glasse of the Truth*, from courtiers in Brussels appalled at the pope being called 'a bastard and symonakre'.[42] It is very doubtful that Vaughan was disappointed when he was not included in another diplomatic mission from England to the princes of the Schmalkaldic League which was sent overseas in January and was as unsuccessful as the approaches made by Vaughan and Mont the previous year. In England Cromwell's focus was on the Acts of Parliament necessary to establish the legal basis of the new regime for the church and his own advancement to the post of royal secretary. As the year progressed, the situation in both France and the territories allied to the emperor became even more complex from the English point of view. Hackett faithfully reported back much of the news from this part of the world to the king and Cromwell including developments in the Baltic and Denmark where Lubeck was attempting to intervene in the succession to the Crown. There was also great alarm at the rise of Anabaptism among communities in the Netherlands and Northern Germany and the establishment of an Anabaptist regime in Munster, something regarded as abhorrent almost universally by other rulers.[43] Even in France, the hopes that Francis I might support English policies were dashed by Francis' response to the affair of the Placards on 16 and 17 October 1534. Documents supporting radical reform of the church and the Reformist theology of the Eucharist appeared in public places, including the king's apartments and prompted a harsh reaction, including the execution of the supposed perpetrators.

Vaughan was, however, drawn back into Cromwell's service overseas by an unforeseen turn of events only ten days after the disturbances in France. Hackett died at Douai on 27 October 1534, having made his will the day before.[44] He had fallen ill about a week earlier and despite consulting the best doctors nothing could be done.[45] His careful diplomacy and agreeable character had served Henry VIII well but clearly his death left a gap that needed filling and the state of his affairs, not least the whereabouts of his private papers, needed to be ascertained and made secure. Thomas Leigh, a merchant of the Staple who had been Hackett's factor and man of business as well as also working for Cromwell since at least 1528, set off from Antwerp to Douai immediately on getting the news of Hackett's death to 'gytt in to myn hands or ells put them in the best surety I can' all 'such wryttynges with all his other rekenynges'.[46] By 6 November, however, Vaughan was clearly in overall charge of tidying up Hackett's affairs. Leigh had reported to him from Antwerp that he had taken steps to ensure that the doors to Hackett's chambers were sealed by the town authorities as were his 'chests and male'. By the beginning of December, Vaughan, writing from Brussels to Cromwell, could assure him that Hackett's 'books lettres escriptes and wrytynges' had been burnt.[47] There was no possibility of leaks. He could now turn his attention to the disposal of Hackett's worldly goods, including a quantity of plate, some of it left to individuals in the will, and the settling of his accounts.

It is possible that the concern over the security of Hackett's papers may have been occasioned by events in Denmark. The king, Frederick of Holstein, had died in 1533, leaving his successor to be elected. The city of Lubeck had decided views on who should be chosen. The likelihood of trouble over this increased when Frederic's son (not Lubeck's choice for the position) was chosen as successor by the Estates of Denmark in July 1534. The newly elected Christian III in many ways seemed to be an obvious ally for Henry VIII; he was a convinced reformer and fully supportive of the break with Rome. Henry VIII, however, had been making tentative moves to support Lubeck's position and their opposition to Christian largely because Henry believed the Lubeckers were hostile to the emperor. In the ensuing civil war in Denmark, Henry made efforts to support the city and had even toyed with the idea of becoming a candidate for the Crown himself. Thomas Leigh had in fact been in touch with the leaders in Lubeck, Hackett, the king and Cromwell over this matter for some time. By the late autumn of 1534, it was becoming clear that Lubeck was unlikely to prevail in this conflict and that Henry and Cromwell had backed the wrong side. It would not have been a good idea to allow the extent of these negotiations to become public when the situation in Denmark was so uncertain.

Vaughan also became directly involved in the business of Denmark when, at the beginning of September 1535, he received letters from Cromwell entrusting him with a delicate mission to this country. He was ordered to take ship thither with one companion, Christopher Morris, carrying the enormous sum of £5000 in bullion keeping it 'with you as closely as ye can so as no man know of it but yourself and such as ye dare trust'.[48] On arriving at the castle of 'Werberge' the money or as much of it as they needed was to be handed over to Edmund Bonner and Richard Cavendish the English Ambassadors to Christian III. These two had been in Denmark since late July or early August, attempting to negotiate some kind of peace treaty. It is not made clear why they might need so large a sum. Plausibly it might be to hire mercenaries if some more direct intervention in the Danish civil war was contemplated. Arranging Vaughan's journey soon ran into problems. Some of the crew apparently deserted, delaying their departure despite a royal ship, the *Sweepstake* being commissioned to undertake the journey, to ensure that the money was conveyed 'in the secretest maner' possible. After his initial doubts about the mission, Vaughan was also assured that he would be adequately recompensed for what was in effect a dangerous voyage into a war zone, given the situation in Denmark between the rival contenders for the throne. He would receive a daily payment or diet of 13s 4d for three months a total of £56; this offer came after what had been a somewhat acrimonious correspondence between Cromwell and Vaughan over his efforts for the Crown and his finances.[49] This was finally concluded by Cromwell offering some effusive assurances that his services 'towardly preparation and good hart' had met with 'condign thanks' from the king himself.[50] Vaughan's plan was to leave England by sea around 13 or 14 September sending Cromwell a final letter on 10 September tying up lost ends on Hackett's estate and relaying some of the latest news from Flanders. Stephen also mentioned relying on his wife to look after any letters that come in and to deal with the auditing of his accounts. However late in the evening of the 14 September, fortunately before he embarked on the *Sweepstake* the whole mission was cancelled. All the money was returned to Cromwell immediately. A week later William Gonson in charge of the king's ships sent all the victuals bought for the voyage to another group of king's ships bound for Bordeaux.[51] No reason was given for this abrupt change of plan, but it probably related to changes in the situation in Denmark.

Stephen remained in London. The year 1535 had not been an easy year for him. He had been unwell with a fever in the summer[52] and had suffered the personal blow of Tyndale's arrest by the Imperial authorities in July. Tyndale had been sheltered in the 'English house' in Antwerp, the base for English merchants trading in the city but had been lured from his sanctuary by one Harry Phillips, supported by those hostile to reform in England. Vaughan was the official head of this house and although not in Antwerp at the time objected strongly to the arrest as did many of his colleagues.[53] Vaughan felt this situation was aggravated by the lack of an envoy of Hackett's experience in the Netherlands as he pointed out to Cromwell. The Merchant Adventurers claimed it infringed their privileges, guaranteed by charter, which included freedom from arrest by the local authorities in Antwerp. His personal relationship with Cromwell had clearly deteriorated with possible adverse effects on his prospects and finances at a time when, with a young family, his needs were increasing. One unlooked-for consequence of the proposed Denmark expedition, however, was that it seems to have restored the good opinion which Cromwell had of his efforts for him personally and the Crown. There was now no impediment to him continuing to act as Cromwell's personal assistant and also for the Crown in a range of matters as before.

In early January 1536 Vaughan was offered a new commission which confirmed his close ties to Cromwell. He was deputed to go with Ernest Chapuys, the emperor's ambassador in England on a visit to Catherine of Aragon at Kimbolton in Huntingdonshire where Henry had required her to reside. Chapuys, as the ambassador of the emperor and also as a close friend of Catherine, had always done all he could to oppose Henry's policies and to support Catherine, always the rightful queen in his eyes. He had maintained a close connexion with her by frequent letters and as well sent reports of her treatment by Henry to the emperor. The king and Cromwell had for their part previously done their best to make contact between the two difficult and to prevent Chapuys from visiting Catherine in person. In July 1535, for example, such a visit had been aborted at the last moment by direct order of the king and in fact, on the journey to Kimbolton before he was forced to turn back, Chapuys had encountered Vaughan whom he described on this occasion as a 'fine galant'.[54]

The journey to see Catherine in January was overhung by the knowledge she was in very poor health. Chapuys set off with a large suite including some who had been in Catherine's service in the past. This was largely because, as he reported to the emperor, he was full of fear of the possible reports sent to Cromwell and Henry by 'a friend of Cromwell's' included in the party. This friend was Vaughan whom Chapuys called the man 'that secretary [Cromwell] had sent to accompany me, or rather to act as spy on my movements and report what I might say or do during my visit'.

Once at Kimbolton and in the presence of Catherine he reported to Charles V that he at first spoke of her health:

> After this I entreated her to take courage, and do her best to get well. If not entirely for her own sake, I said she ought at least to consider that on her in a great measure depended the union, peace, and welfare of Christendom, To enforce which, I made use of several arguments. as previously preconcerted between her and myself, through the intermediary of a third person, all this being said aloud that the guide I have alluded to, and several others present at the interview, might, if necessary, report our conversation, and my words be the cause of greater care of her.[55]

Stephen's own report of this visit which occurred a matter of days before Catherine's death was presumably made to Cromwell orally. There is no written record. The visit was an indication, however, of the degree of trust once more enjoyed by Vaughan. By February 1536, Vaughan felt sufficiently secure to take on a new lease from St Bartholomew's Priory in the city of the family home in the alley off Cheapside called *The Three Legges*. He also took over the leases of some additional adjoining shop property from a mercer who had lately died. The rent of the house, £6 13s 4d, was now affordable and moreover, the lease described him as Stephen Vaughan, a gentleman,[56] an acknowledgement of an important step up the social ladder.

Shortly after this he was ordered to return to the Netherlands where he could be of most use both to Cromwell and the king, noting with approval on the way there the good progress being made on the harbour works at Dover, a pet project of the king.[57] Once back in Antwerp he was engaged as before in keeping tabs on dissident friars and monks and retailing rumours of the state of relations between the French king and the emperor. His news made few waves in London where the court was becoming more and more embroiled in the conspiracies which finally brought down Anne Boleyn. In April it was probably a forlorn hope to write that Tyndale might be saved from his likely execution if only Cromwell would get the necessary letters authorized by the Privy Council. This plea and his complaint about the food available in the Netherlands, which Cromwell apparently liked, fell on deaf ears. He wrote plaintively, 'the diet of this country "dymysseth my health greatly. Yow thinke I am in Paradice and I thinke in Purgotorie; purgotorie I fynde it".[58] In May he was finally given leave to return home.[59]

He would have found both London and the country in a somewhat nervous state. The lingering effects of the Pilgrimage of Grace made for public unease. Vaughan's careful recording of the presence of any dissidents in the Netherlands before he left for home was both clearly understandable and necessary. The mood perhaps lightened in the autumn with rejoicing over the birth of Prince Edward on 12 October 1537 but this was followed twelve days by the disaster of the death of his mother, Jane Seymour. The position of Cromwell, as the king's principal minister, fortunately seemed secure despite the unrest in the country, with support for at least a moderate degree of religious reform still evident. In these circumstances Stephen resumed his former position as one of Cromwell's confidential private secretaries. This was not, of course, an official appointment but the nature of his work can be deduced from the traces left in the State Papers. There are no letters between the two from the spring of 1537 till October 1538 probably because they were in regular, if not daily, contact in Cromwell's main place of business, the Office of the Rolls in Chancery Lane, if not at court.

Documents in Vaughan's hand and mentions in documents by others make clear that Vaughan was involved in many aspects of Cromwell's multifarious business for the Crown at this period. He was involved, for example, in setting out the strategy for the defence of the Scottish border,[60] keeping an eye on the intentions of the Ottomans and noting any news of their possible preparations for a campaign in Italy, possibly against Naples.[61] He translated from Latin official documents about a possible general council of the (Catholic) Church,[62] (a move of some concern to Cromwell), and had some involvement in the arrangements for the execution of the leaders of the Pilgrimage of Grace.[63] Returning to something he had been involved in as a young man, he also had some responsibility for the taking down of monasteries and other religious houses now going forward at some speed. The fate of the important and wealthy monastery at Abingdon was overseen by Richard Rich. Rich specifically asked that Cromwell put the details of the process in the hands of Vaughan.[64]

His involvement in work for Cromwell and the king probably prevented him from spending much time on his other activities as a merchant and as a leading member of the Company of Merchant Adventurers. Despite this, the likelihood is that, even though based in London at this time, he remained a valuable link between the Adventurers and the king's most important minister. Personally Vaughan enjoyed one of the few periods of his married life when he was able to spend some time at home. His frequent mentions of his wife in his letters and her evident responsibility for his affairs in London when he was overseas, suggest a close relationship. The household also included at times her brother John Guinet, a priest and a composer of some reputation. Guinet was a strong upholder of traditional religious beliefs. He wrote a vitriolic pamphlet in 1536 against the view of John Frith, later a Protestant martyr and it casts some light on Vaughan's disposition that this did not prevent the two from being good friends.[65] Vaughan was prepared to lobby for Guinet to be given some preferment by Cromwell, recommending him in strong terms and claiming that Cromwell would never repent it if he was offered a position.[66] By 1538 Stephen's family included three young children with the youngest, his son, also Stephen, born in the autumn of 1537. His two daughters, Anne and Jane, were probably around four to seven years old. Of all the changes in life in London at this time one would have been particularly pleasing to Stephen and his wife. This was the licencing in August 1537 by the king of the so-called Matthew Bible. This was printed in Antwerp and largely based on the translations of William Tyndale. For it to appear in London with the words, 'set forth with the kings most gracious lyc-ce' appearing on the title page must have gladdened Stephen's heart. The absolute necessity for the Scriptures to be available in English to all was one of the basic tenets of his religious beliefs along with his support for the royal supremacy.

By the summer of 1538 the question of foreign policy and in particular the question of possible alliances with foreign princes had once more also come to the fore. This was clearly linked to the issue of the possible remarriage of the king. It was not perhaps a matter of urgency as there was now a male heir of undisputed legitimacy but it was again open for discussion. Should the old way of using alliances based on strategic marriages be followed? Did this necessarily imply a foreign bride for the king? MacCulloch sees most of the proposals put forward as having an element of fantasy on the part of the king's advisers remarking that 'it would be tedious to follow the twists and turns of Henry's unrequited courtships in 1538'.[67] One possible thread of this policy however came to concern Vaughan directly. This was the scheme to link Henry's desire for a treaty of friendship with the emperor with a proposal for two marriages, one for himself with the widowed Duchess of Milan, the emperor's sister, and the other between the Lady Mary and Don Ludovico of Portugal, Charles V's nephew. Behind this plan was a fear that Charles V and Francis I seemed to be moving towards a policy of mutual cooperation rather than hostility, something which would leave England dangerously exposed. Opposition to Henry's religious policies overseas was also increasing following the campaign being energetically conducted by dissidents like Cardinal Pole, particularly dangerous because of his Yorkist blood, and the dismay of many both at home and abroad at the attacks on shrines with European reputations like that of Thomas Becket at Canterbury.

Cromwell evidently felt that a mission to the court of the Regent of the Netherlands, Mary of Hungary, also Charles V's sister, might help move the proposal for dual marriages forward. Henry's intended bride was in fact living at Mary's Court which might also help progress the wooing. Vaughan together with Thomas Wriothesley were commissioned to present the king's suit to the Regent and, via her, to the emperor. Stephen's own qualifications for this mission were clear; he knew the region well; he had contacts at court and was fluent in the local vernacular. An additional problem which Vaughan was uniquely qualified to deal with, however, emerged as the mission was being set up. John Hutton, the governor of the Merchant Adventurers who had been acting as an ambassador to the Netherlands died on 5 September 1538.[68] This seems to have been unexpected and weakened the English diplomatic team. Hutton had established good relations with the Regent Mary and was not afraid to face her anger when he accused her of aiding Henry's opponents including Pole.[69] It also meant that Stephen was expected to deal with matters like the safe return of

Hutton's widow to England and the problems caused by Hutton's debts as well as the delicate mission which was his primary concern.[70] He went over to the Netherlands shortly after Hutton's death to make the necessary arrangements for the security of his papers and the payment of his debts but still found time to have a preliminary meeting with Mary of Hungary on 26 September. The Regent was cordial but also seemed in no hurry to advance matters; tactics which became increasingly familiar in the days ahead.

Thomas Wriothesley, who was deputed to accompany Stephen, was also in the service of Cromwell, having previously been close to Stephen Gardiner, the bishop of Winchester. He had some legal training, having been admitted to Gray's Inn in 1534 and also had some experience of overseas missions for the Crown. In 1530 he had been appointed to a clerkship in the signet office and had recently come to royal attention as the supervisor of the taking down of the shrine of St Swithin in Winchester cathedral. There were few signs at this date of his success as a politician which would eventually earn him a peerage as Earl of Southampton and the office of Lord Chancellor in Henry's last years. He left England after Stephen, landing at Calais and then, travelling via Dunkirk and Nieuport, reached Antwerp. His first letter to Cromwell mentions that he had forced himself 'into a great sweat' the night before but woke feeling well.[71] This was not the case. For the remainder of this mission Wriothesley was suffering from a bad bout of quartan ague or malaria with a four-day cycle of one day of high fever followed by three of lassitude, exhaustion and depression. This did not of course bode well for the success of their mission.

He and Vaughan eventually met on 2 October in Antwerp, but, in accordance with protocol, had to wait there to be summoned to the Regent's presence. Despite this, Vaughan and Wriothesley had no initial cause for complaint about the way they were treated by the authorities in the Netherlands. Their letters make it clear that they were shown every courtesy and solicitous enquiries were made concerning Wriothesley's illness. On the other hand, the Regent and her advisers proved to be masters of delaying tactics. The excuses varied. The Regent needed to consult further with her council; she had not yet had full authorization from the emperor to proceed with the negotiations. She was imminently intending to travel to Valenciennes or elsewhere. The long report sent back to London by Vaughan and Wriothesley as early as 6 October included details which would appear in very much the same terms in others sent to the king or to Cromwell between this date and the spring of 1539. Before their first meeting, however, the two were most hospitably entertained. One of the Regent's servants made sure they had a suitable lodging and escorted them to the court with horses provided with 'velvet saddelles and harnises'. When they entered the Queen Regent's presence they were impressed by her apartments and pleased to see the Duchess of Milan was present. She was apparently 'a godly personage of stature higher thenne eyther of us, a very good woman's face and competently faire but very wel favored a lytle browne'.[72] In the actual interview Vaughan and Wriothesley pressed for clarity and some evidence of a desire to conclude matters hinting at their knowledge that the emperor was simultaneously in friendly discussions with Francis I.[73] The Regent listened but agreed nothing even finding an excuse for not writing directly to Henry. Vaughan and Wriothesley were mollified by a present of wine after the interview was over but in truth they had no progress to report.

For most of the winter of 1538–9 Vaughan and Wriothesley earnestly sought further interviews with Mary of Hungary following her court from place to place despite Wriothesley still being in poor health and with very little to show for their persistence. They travelled from Antwerp to Valenciennes, on to Cambrai, and eventually to Brussels; this was a total distance of around 300 kilometres, all undertaken on horseback in winter. Their efforts to offer hospitality to the queen's counsellors in return also ran into difficulties. When entertaining Don Diego de Mendoza they could only offer 'as good cheer as we could' as their 'stuff and plate' had not reached Cambrai as the baggage cart had broken down 'two leagues out of the town'.[74] At one point they also ran out of money and Stephen had to undertake a hurried journey back to Antwerp to obtain more cash.[75] They also could not ignore the fact that Mary recently had a long and cordial meeting with Francis I and that simultaneous negotiations were going on between the emperor and his envoys and the French king.

As time went by at first the Netherlanders continued to be cordial. Wriothesley told the king how her grace (the queen) was 'tender to us' and suggested that should avoid any 'molestious' route to Brussels.[76] Wriothesley was even offered the services of the queen's personal physician. (if her phesityan or any thing in her house might doo me any pleasure, she badd me use it boldly.)[77] In London, the king and Cromwell were clearly anxious to push forward the marriage plans and that for a treaty of friendship. Sir Edward Carne was sent over from England to strengthen the delegation as early as mid-October.[78] Carne, a distinguished civil lawyer, was needed to draft any treaty but was also a skilled negotiator on good terms with both Cromwell and the king.[79] He had the experience of negotiating overseas, having spent four years in Rome as a royal proctor and excusator in the case of the divorce of Henry and Catherine. In Brussels, however, his presence made little difference. The delays continued and by 20 November Vaughan was able to report that since their recent meeting with the King of France, 'they (the Netherlanders) proceed coldly with us.' He concluded that he feared, 'on this matter we shall find them more subtile than trusty'.[80] In his opinion, the problem was that the Regent was relying on the views of counsellors who were very close to the French court. It was also the case that some at the court in Brussels now believed that 'religion was now extinct in England, that we had no mass that saints were burnt and all that was holy subverted'. No definite answers were given to their proposals with the excuse that all decisions must be deferred to Spain to Charles V himself, something which might well take a considerable time.[81] Henry had already sent Thomas Wyatt and Philip Hoby as envoys directly to Charles V but despite a brief note from Cromwell advising them to 'call upon the Emperor to send full instructions into Flanders for the expedition of the matters there', no movement in the negotiations on these matters occurred.[82] By 1 January 1539, Wriothesley was clearly exasperated by all the delays and looking for a way to withdraw from them. His report of the meeting with the Regent and the full council of that date clarified the stalemate which had overtaken the negotiations. Wriothesley's summary of Henry's position on the matter made plain that the king was 'out of affection to the Emperor' but, willing to forget the coldness he had met with, could tolerate no more delay because of his age and because of the pressure to re-marry from his own council. There had to be a conclusion to the matter.[83] Wriothesley's private note to Cromwell on the same date rather surprisingly puts forward the idea that the Duchess of Milan had an 'inclination to the King and would in fact make him a suitable wife given her good nature and virtue'.[84]

At this point Wriothesley and Carne hoped to be able to leave for England within a few days. Stephen, however, had been appointed formally as the accredited ambassador to the court of Mary of Hungary shortly after Hutton's death in October and would be expected to remain in Flanders. The expectation of an early departure for home for his colleagues soon proved to be a forlorn hope. Relations between the two envoys and the court worsened significantly. They were not given leave to depart and there were fears a scheme was afoot on the emperor's side to keep them and Vaughan in the country almost as hostages until Chapuys, the Spanish ambassador to Henry VIII, who wanted to leave England, was safely in Brussels. It was suspected that the emperor was using a rumoured ban on English ships leaving ports in the Low Countries to exert pressure on England.[85] Vaughan's first task as ambassador was to deal with the problems for merchants caused by Charles V's ban. Cromwell had picked up the news that the emperor had forbidden all foreign ships to leave ports in his realms around about the beginning of March. At first Vaughan was unable to find out if English vessels were covered by this blanket ban. For the next two days, this was still uncertain and more worryingly Wriothesley reported to Cromwell that, 'all men believe war must follow'. It was not until the imbroglio over the departure of Chapuys from London had been sorted out that English ships were allowed to leave port and the crisis abated. At its height Vaughan heard rumours of a squadron of ships being prepared for attacks on English shipping in hope of 'fatt bote' (booty)[86] and reports of a Flemish pirate with a black galley who was preparing to cruise off the mouth of the Thames to take English shipping.[87] A note from Ralph Sadler to Cromwell after receiving a report from Vaughan speaks of 'the Emperor's ingratitude and the cankered hearts of his people' and the need for musters to be taken to assemble a defence force. Beacons were to be made ready on the coasts to warn of an approaching invasion.[88] Fortunately tempers soon cooled somewhat and on 19 March 1539 Carne and Wriothesley were given leave to depart by the Regent while Stephen Vaughan was left to reside in Brussels. The departure of his two colleagues had been held up while elaborate arrangements were made for the safe departure of Chapuys from England.[89] At this juncture there was no real substance to the fears of war. After their safe departure, Vaughan's attention could now be concentrated on his need to serve the interests of the king. His colleague Wriothesley returned to England to hear the welcome news that he had been elected to the new parliament as one of the knights of the shire for Hampshire nominated by Cromwell himself. Bishop Gardiner and other traditionalists were furious at his election but the support of Cromwell had carried the day.[90] Cromwell's policies especially his support for an alliance with the German Lutheran princes still seemed to be in favour with the king, policies long familiar to Vaughan. Stephen would also have received the welcome news at about this time that his application for a Grant of Arms had been successful in time for him to display his coat of arms as an ambassador at the Regent's court.[91]

By late May the feared crisis seemed to have evaporated. Stephen was able to tell the king that the forces gathered during Lent by the emperor, perhaps in anticipation of the outbreak of hostilities feared earlier in the year, had been dispersed and were in fact causing mayhem in the countryside in the northern Netherlands.[92] By July relations were considerably more relaxed and Vaughan could turn to the purchase of munitions for the king in the German lands including cannons, armour for men and horses and gunpowder. He had been assured by his contacts that the emperor had been advised not to make war on England until Imperial control had been re-established over England's friends in

German lands including Cleves and Denmark. This was to ensure in any conflict that England would be isolated and without allies.[93] At this time, however, it almost seems as if it was Vaughan who was isolated; there is no indication in the sources that Vaughan was aware of how the political situation and the jockeying for power in the king's council were developing at the English court. Cromwell was ill with ague in the early summer which probably reduced the correspondence between the two. Vaughan seems to have had little recent knowledge of the hostility developing between Cromwell and the Duke of Norfolk. He would, however, have been fully familiar with the policy, still being actively promoted by Cromwell with the king's approval, to seek closer alliances with the Lutheran princes of the empire, including the Duke of Cleves, to counteract any unfriendly actions of the emperor. By the autumn of 1539 a match between the king and Anne of Cleves, the duke's eldest daughter, was being energetically pursued. All seemed set fair for this to happen and the necessary marriage treaty was signed on 6 October. In London this was accounted as a triumph for Cromwell's approach. The elaborate new decorations of the ceiling of the chapel at St James's Palace incorporating the monogram HA and the names of the duke's territories were a physical expression of this success and the benefits which were expected to flow from it.[94]

Stephen was at this point directly involved in the matter. First of all he had to maintain the often difficult and slow communications between Cleves and the court in London.[95] Next he was involved in planning Anne's journey from Cleves (now Kleve) near Nijmegen, close to the frontier between the German lands and the Netherlands, to Calais and across the sea to England. As early as 19 October a safe conduct for the bride and her extensive train through the Netherlands was granted[96] but by 9 November there were concerns that the emperor himself was intending to come to Brussels because of fears of the effects of 'the confederacy between the King and the Almayns' leading to the possibility of 'some displeasure against the King'.[97] Two weeks later the news was better; Vaughan could assure Lord Lisle, the governor of Calais, that the Regent intended to make sure the Lady of Cleves was well treated in the emperor's dominions until she reached the Calais Pale.[98] She was expected in Antwerp on 2 December and would be in Calais six days later. In early December Anne in fact spent some time in the city resting from the earlier stages of the journey. She was accommodated at the English house at Antwerp where Vaughan and the Merchant Adventurers laid on entertainment for the party. It was said to be as great a spectacle as the 'joyeuse entrée' of the emperor.[99] The size of the party is made clear in an anxious note from Nicolas Wotton to Cromwell; 88

persons were expected to cross from Calais with Anne while a further 263 with 228 horses would only come as far as Calais. There was also some worry that the marriage customs common in German princely households might be ignored. These included the giving of a 'morning gift' to the new bride and *bruidstuckes* (presents of clothing and jewellery) to all the attendants.[100] After a sumptuous welcome to Calais, the bride faced appalling weather on the Channel crossing. Nevertheless all seemed well until the complete collapse of the marriage project after the first informal meeting of the king and Lady Anne at Rochester. This disaster was not foreseen by any least of all Cromwell. As for Vaughan he had no reason to suspect that all had not gone well. On 15 January 1540 about a week after the marriage ceremony had taken place he finished a letter with the latest news of the emperor's doings with the words that he had received Cromwell's letter about the wedding and was glad 'that Cromwell found his judgment true of the Queen'.[101] The implication was that this was favourable in contrast to Henry's horrified reaction to his new queen, news of which had not yet spread beyond the king's confidants.

Unlike the moment when Wolsey fell, when Vaughan was in close contact with Cromwell, Vaughan probably heard few whispers in Brussels of the way Cromwell's enemies were inciting the king's rage against him during the spring of 1540. He certainly committed nothing to paper apart from routine diplomatic reports. When the news finally reached Brussels of Cromwell's execution and the king's remarriage to Katherine Howard, both on the same day, 28 July 1540, Vaughan would have had every reason to fear that he too might be an object of the king's wrath. He was someone after all who was known to be Cromwell's servant and close friend although also in the king's service. This was, however, not to be the case. He, like other close colleagues of Cromwell, did not suffer directly from his mentor's catastrophic fall from grace. In some ways the most important part of Vaughan's career was to be in the years after Cromwell's death when he was the servant only of the Crown. These were the years when his career developed a new momentum and national importance when all the experience and expertise he had acquired earlier was put to good use in the court of the Netherlands and the markets of Antwerp.

6

War with France

Despite the shock of Cromwell's precipitate fall and execution, it must at first have seemed to Stephen that business as usual was the order of the day (Figures 7 and 8). In early June 1541, he was once more commissioned to travel to the court of Mary of Hungary in Brussels to negotiate in a quarrel between the Merchant Adventurers and their counterparts in Antwerp and other Flemish towns over alleged changes in the way trade between them was conducted. From Vaughan's point of view this would have seemed like a further recurrence of the arguments over the interpretation of the terms of the *Intercursus Magnus* of 1493, and other regulations governing the trade which had occurred at regular intervals in the intervening years. Stephen Vaughan himself would have recalled his involvement with John Hackett in a dispute of this nature in 1532. In the past, however, these commercial quarrels had often been used as something of a proxy for political disputes between England and the empire. It soon became apparent that this was also the case in 1541.

Vaughan was commissioned to act with Sir Edward Carne, who had been his colleague in the abortive discussions in 1538–9 regarding a possible marriage of the king and the Duchess of Milan. Both men had the advantage of knowing the style of negotiation to be expected at the court of the Regent as well as having personal contacts with many of her advisers. Their earlier experience would have prepared them to expect no quick solutions to any problems but rather delays and time-wasting, and the avoidance of any definite conclusions. The problem this time ostensibly related to an English Act of Parliament passed in 1540 called innocuously enough *Concerning Strangers*.[1] This was intended to gather together all the earlier legislation regarding strangers (foreigners or aliens) resident in England, especially those engaged in any form of trade or business. The preamble to the Act declared that all sorts of useful regulations had been 'infringed frustrated and defrauded' by means of letters patent obtained by the 'craftie sutis inventions and practisis' of foreigners who had obtained letters

Figure 7 William Paget first Baron Beaudesert. Public domain.

of denization. These had the effect of removing all the legal distinctions between aliens and 'Englishmen naturally borne within the "Kinges Graces Dominions"'. To remedy this situation the new Act laid down that, from the first of September next, all the legislation regarding aliens would apply to all 'strangers' irrespective of any letters patent they might have obtained. All letters of denization would in the future include a proviso that all relevant laws had to be obeyed. The Flemings saw this Act as a direct attack on their trading privileges in England and when no concessions were offered, prevailed on Mary of Hungary to issue a decree forcing English merchants to use Flemish ships to carry goods being exported to England. Such a decree would gravely hinder trade and decrease its profitability. The result was fury in both merchant communities.

The pair received their instructions on 6 June.[2] They were instructed to push the line that the Act was merely a piece of legislative tidying up and contained no new provisions which could justify the difficulties and unjust treatment of which English merchants had lately and loudly claimed to be the victims. At the same

Figure 8 Mary of Hungary sister of Charles V, Regent of the Netherlands. Public domain.

time Chapuys, who had recently returned to London as the Imperial ambassador, was warning Mary in despatches that the matter should be treated with caution.³ He advised her to 'make the English ambassadors understand that besides my not being well acquainted with the mercantile affairs of the Low Countries' (a blatant lie in the opinion of Chapuys' modern biographer) 'I showed myself to be a little partial to this king'.⁴ He suggested to her that the dispute could be used as a lever to move England towards an alliance with the emperor, for example, by removing a tax imposed on English merchants in Antwerp as a reward for their co-operation. Vaughan and Carne reached Brussels three weeks after receiving their instructions on 26 June; not till four days later were they presented at a formal meeting with the complaints against the statute which was, or so it was said, so weighted against the interests of the Flemish merchants. The Flemings' case was that English merchants in the Low Countries were treated more favourably than any other nation while in England Flemish merchants faced grave problems made worse by this statute.⁵ The deadlock between the two sides soon became apparent but there were, as Chapuys had hinted, issues of somewhat greater importance behind all this bickering. These related to the rivalry between Charles V and Francis I, between the Habsburgs and the Valois, which had dominated the relationship between France and the empire since the 1520s. The hidden question, behind the negotiations over such relatively trivial matters as to whether Henry had unjustifiably stopped the export of wood, victuals and other things from England to the Low Countries, was what was Henry's attitude to France? Was the real stumbling block preoccupying the advisers to Mary of Hungary the fear that Henry was no longer in favour of an alliance with the emperor but thinking of reinvigorating his links with France?

In the 1530s and 1540s the political situation in Western Europe had changed significantly from that in the first decades of Henry's reign. Under Wolsey's influence Henry had moved from adopting what might be called the traditional attitudes of English monarchs to France, exemplified in the war of 1512–13, to the policies laid out in the treaties of 1527 which established 'Perpetual Peace' between the two realms. Since that time relations between England and the two major European powers, France and the empire, had been complicated by the king's Great Matter, his divorce, remarriage and the breach with Rome. Neither the emperor, appalled at the insult to his aunt Catherine of Aragon, nor Francis I, wary of the forces for church reform evident in France, were prepared to support Henry in these matters and even seemed prepared at times to threaten hostile action against England. Thomas Cromwell, a firm friend of reform, had made efforts to get the support of the German Lutheran princes, particularly those who were members of the Schmalkaldic League, a policy that could be seen as unfriendly to their overlord the emperor. The collapse of this policy following the failure of Henry's marriage to Anne of Cleves and the execution of Cromwell had left Henry in a somewhat awkward position intent on exploiting any hint of a split between Charles V and Francis I. At the same time as Vaughan and Carne were in Brussels, Henry's ambassador in Paris was putting forward the idea of a marriage between the Lady Mary and the Duke of Orleans. Stephen Gardiner was also at the emperor's court actively promoting the idea of an alliance with the connivance of Chapuys and Mary of Hungary. Vaughan and Carne were in the middle of a tangled web of diplomatic double-dealing of which they were only partially aware.[6]

From the start their own negotiations were not fruitful as their first report made clear; the atmosphere was not cordial with the English apparently stating that Henry would think himself 'very evil handled' if the Netherlanders tried to introduce new matters into the discussions. In a later private conversation with one of the Regent's advisers at the house of the Duke of Arskott, Vaughan and Carne became suspicious of what the emperor's real intentions were; this gentleman seemed to the English envoys to be unduly interested in matters like the new fortifications being built by Henry at Guines in the Pale of Calais while the Regent had refused to continue supplying war materiel to the English.[7] A meeting on 6 July was no more productive. When Henry had read the reports from Carne and Vaughan on these meetings, he responded with new instructions which were couched in rather more hostile terms. He wrote that Mary on Charles' behalf may have stated that the emperor supported the *Intercursus* but the actions of the pair 'show the world that they esteem not our amity' and 'in that case we will so provide that they shall shortly see that in their doings they had neither that consideration of us that reason would have required ne that regard to their own pacts that appertained'.[8] The two envoys were then faced with the familiar delaying tactics of the court of the Netherlands; they were told no meetings were possible because the Regent was hunting, or because she was visiting friends. It seems the exchanges became quite heated at one point with Vaughan and Carne using 'undiplomatic language'.[9] Chapuys later complained to Henry that the pair had accused the emperor and his sister of being '*levem and inconstantem*' (not serious and untrustworthy).[10] It seems clear from their report that the English envoys felt they were being fobbed off with weak excuses for delays while one of the emperor's captains was telling them stories about the French king hiring ships and men in Friesland 'to go as he thought against England'. The confusion only increased when Chapuys in London not only complained about the language used by Vaughan and Carne but also pressed for a new trade agreement and 'stricter amities' with the emperor. New instructions from the king sent to Carne and Vaughan at the end of August ordered them to apologize for their language but also to make clear that in 'this desire for a new intercourse the King thinks they press him unduly'.[11] The two were now being more or less ostracized by the court at Brussels. Rumours were still current about the purpose of the forces being collected in Friesland. Vaughan had been compelled to go to Antwerp to try and find out what was going on 'for here no gentleman of the Court from whom they might learn news have come to dine, sup or talk with them, which is otherwise than it was wont to be'.[12]

Matters did not improve and by October the negotiations were completely stalled with neither side prepared to alter its attitude. Vaughan and Carne could not leave Brussels until given leave by the king and were forced to kick their heels in the city until they were allowed to set out for home in January 1542. The annoyance generated by this incident continued for some weeks. As late as May in the same year Bishop Bonner, reporting to the king concerning his negotiations with Granville the emperor's adviser returned to the subject of the unfriendly handling the two had received from the Regent.[13] This was excused by Granville, the emperor's closest adviser, because of the original accusation that they had been rude to Mary of Hungary. Despite this squabbling the question of how to improve the relationship friendship between Charles V and Henry was clearly the real object of the discussions. Charles V's own report to Chapuys in London written on the same day as Bonner's makes clear his real aim; Chapuys was to 'induce Henry to take the Emperor's part against France'.[14] There should be no quibbling over the wording of any treaty with no 'word perverted in the transcriptions or translations a thing in which the English are not overscrupulous'.

It was not until almost a year later that negotiations between Henry and Charles V finally moved on considerably. Although there were still echoes of the old commercial arguments, the focus was now firmly on possible English involvement in an invasion of France in alliance with the emperor. The discussions on this matter reached the stage of being occupied with details like the likely availability of wagons to transport the large amounts of supplies needed, and the state of the fortifications of the French towns on the border with Flanders. Henry needed to despatch further envoys to Brussels to discuss matters like this. This group included Thomas Seymour and, once more, Edward Carne. As he reported to Mary of Hungary, Chapuys was pleased that Stephen Vaughan was not to be included this time; the two named would, he said, be 'more dexterous and modest' than he was.[15] Stephen was not, however, in any disfavour because of the way his last commission to the court at Brussels had turned out. He had returned to his work as a clerk of the faculties and in November 1542 had received a grant from the Crown of the reversions and rents of a large number of leases on the site and buildings of the hospital of St Mary without Bishopsgate (St Mary Spital) on the edge of the city. This included a 'mansion' which would be for his own occupation. There were also some properties in Shoreditch. The total annual value of the rents included in the grant was £131 9s 2d, a welcome addition to his income.[16]

Moreover, Stephen's apparent exclusion from diplomatic negotiations in the Low Countries and with the emperor was to prove only temporary and from his point of view allowed him a welcome breathing space to attend to his own affairs. In the summer of 1543 the treaty committing England and the empire to a joint invasion of France was finalized and signed by Henry and Charles V. This abandonment by Henry of a position of either friendship with France or some form of balancing neutrality in England's relations with the two major

European powers had been the subject of long and difficult negotiations between Henry and Charles. The negotiations had largely been conducted by Stephen Gardiner on the one hand and Chapuys working with Mary of Hungary and Granvelle, the emperor's most prominent adviser on the other. Henry's desire for the alliance had been strengthened by the renewal of the close ties between France and Scotland, always regarded as dangerous for England.[17] This was especially the case when war with Scotland was imminent as it was at this time. In confirmation of the new treaty a small force of English troops under John Wallop in fact went to Flanders to assist the emperor in July 1543. The logistics of any campaign also continued to be under much discussion bringing to the fore questions of the manpower and war supplies available in England and of course the issue of how any campaign would be financed. Henry had begun his reign as a wealthy monarch, able to indulge his desire for glory on the European scene because of the treasure accumulated by his father. By 1544 this hoard was largely exhausted along with extra funds coming from the dissolution of the monasteries and other religious foundations and the sale of much of their land, something Vaughan was much aware of through his work at the Court of Augmentations.

Richard Hoyle's calculation of the yield of taxes in 1543–5 revealed that lay subsidies produced £408,642 in these years with a further £59,000 from two grants of fifteenths in 1545. When arrears were finally collected in the reign of Edward VI the total from both lay and clerical taxes, loans and the 1545 benevolence came to £1.037,854. An account of the total cost of warfare between 1539 and 1552 made in the last year of the reign of Edward VI stated that £2,145,765 of this expenditure had been incurred in the reign of his father. This included the costs of fortifications on the Scots border and in Calais and what were called 'sea charges during the wars'. Manoeuvres like the debasement of the currency in the 1540s, which was highly profitable to the Crown, had some effect on improving the financial position of the king, but it is clear that warfare in the 1540s was very expensive and strained the resources of England to the utmost. Hoyle claims that war taxation was, even if only for relatively short periods, 'extremely burdensome', especially for the land-owning classes at this time.[18] Even if all the money needed to wage war successfully against France could have been eventually raised by Henry VIII from his ordinary resources and from taxation there was still an important problem regarding 'cash flow'. Taxes came in slowly and irregularly. Continental monarchs increasingly waged war using professional mercenary troops. Their commanders had absolutely no inclination to wait for their pay and were fully conversant with such matters as the going rates of exchange between currencies which might affect their value. They expected, and often seem to have received, cash on the nail; if it was not forthcoming they always had the option of withdrawing their services and even enrolling in the forces of the opposite side, potentially disastrous for a campaign. If Henry was going to be involved in warfare as an ally of the emperor it was clear he too would have to employ mercenary forces. The normal way of recruiting an English army via voluntary levies was simply not suitable for recruiting either the numbers required or professional fighting men like gunners, pikemen and cavalry. Stephen's expertise and experience of the way the loan market worked in Antwerp and of the whole system of international finance thus became of great importance from the early months of 1544, first of all as de facto paymaster general for the mercenaries and later as the essential middleman for the king in the process of raising loans on the market.

In the early months of 1544, the State Papers are full of letters and reports from the Privy Council, its most prominent members like Petre, Paget and Wriothesley and ambassadors like Nicholas Wotton at the emperor's court, regarding preparation for war with France. One document sets out all the arrangements necessary for the campaign with estimated costs and provisional sources of finance. The document seems to have been drawn up by Richard Riche, not only a privy councillor but also the chancellor of the Court of Augmentations, and a colleague of Vaughan's at this time. He estimated the total cost of preparation for the first three months of the forthcoming war at £250,000. He also calculated that taking into account all the money rapidly available, there would be a deficit of £116,000 'for the supplement whereof these means be devised'. His list of 'means' included £50,000 to come from the sale of lead (stripped from the roofs of dissolved religious houses), £10,000 in loans from merchants and 'by the practice of Mr Vaughan' £20,000. Probably even before he had left England (the precise date of this document is not known) Vaughan's responsibilities were under active discussion.[19]

The first mention of the departure of Stephen and his colleague Thomas Chamberlain comes in a letter from Paget to Lord Hertford dated 11 March.[20] Paget reported that the two would leave for Flanders the next day and had been instructed to arrange with de Buren, a leading mercenary captain often employed by the emperor, the hiring of an extra 2,000 footmen at the king's expense. The envoys' help was urgently needed; Wotton wrote from Speyer, where Charles V was based, on 19 March in some confusion. He needed to try and contract for another 1,000 horses for the king but could find no captain who would agree to the pay on offer and was very uncertain about the rate of exchange. Were fifteen batzes (the coinage current in Germany) worth 2s 6d or 3s 1½d? Or 20 or 25 Brabantine Stuvers?[21] The answer to this conundrum was urgently needed to assess accurately the sum needed in sterling. Vaughan and Chamberlain received their instructions at much the same time that Wotton wrote of his difficulties to the king. These made clear that they should not be inflexible about the pay of mercenaries but should follow the lead of the emperor; they should also ensure that the location of musters and all other arrangements with captains being hired for the king should be clearly set out. All this should be relayed to Wotton. The king also informed them that £5000 had been sent to the factor for the Fugger Bank to cover immediate expenses. It was also their duty to find out what the emperor intended and 'where he intends to march forward'. The last point of all hinted that the process of hiring mercenaries for war outside the English realm was something of which the Crown had little experience. Vaughan and Chamberlain were to try 'to get a true example of the ordinances whereunto the Almains both horsemen and footmen be usually sworn' and sent it back to London.[22]

The pair of envoys reached Bruges on 19 March and had to track de Buren down to his castle at La Noye; the negotiations began a couple of days later in a merchant's house in Antwerp.[23] It was very soon apparent how tortuous the whole process would be and how expert mercenary captains were in driving hard bargains. They knew from bitter experience how to deploy the threat that they would not serve at all if the conditions were not to their liking. There were also inevitable delays in making bargains when it was necessary first to report to the Crown in England or to Wotton with the emperor and then await a reply. All this took days if not weeks no matter how hard the couriers rode, and inexorably drew out the making of any decision. It was not until 13 April that one *Christophorus De Landenberga lata Landenberg ad Schamberg* (as he was formally called) issued a receipt for the conduct money of 1,000 horsemen, their 83 wagons and 4,000 foot soldiers, received from Stephen Vaughan, to cover their journey to the place of muster.[24] To get to this point Vaughan had had to travel to Speyer to speak with Wotton and Landenberg in person and on to Frankfort to arrange the payment with the bankers. Chamberlain remained in Brussels busily collecting intelligence for the king, including the titbit that Charles V had just received 'a million and half in gold' from the Indies. It had not been easy to conclude the contract. Landenberg had claimed at first that he had been misled about the exchange rate for his fees and about the mustering place. At one meeting he arrived in an 'exceeding heat'; he claimed Vaughan had 'used deceit with him' and a 'shouting match' ensued. In the end Landenberg calmed down and saw reason, particularly about the mustering place although Vaughan's view remained that Landenberg was a 'hasty fellow'.[25] Nevertheless it seemed that Landenberg had finally agreed to be paid in money 'current in France at the present value'. The conduct money was in the end delivered to Landenberg in Speyer not in the Low Countries because, as Vaughan wrote to Paget, 'so stately captains or rather froward be here in these parts it is very dangerous of carrying money by the ways'.[26] Large amounts of cash in bullion were a tempting target for any band of armed men encountered on the road. The difficulties in obtaining and transporting large amounts of ready money were a continual problem throughout the whole period of the war.

This was not the end of Vaughan's troubles with money for mercenaries, however. He also had to provide funds for another captain hired by Wotton, one Hans van Sickyngen who despite his red face so 'fiery and garnished with rubies as it may well appear that his mother never taught him to water his wine' was very well recommended by Granvelle. The problem here was that this captain expected bonds backed by leading towns in Germany as surety for his fees, a usual practice in the empire but not something the English had ever formerly been expected to provide. Moreover it was not clear what coinage he would accept in payment. In the end Vaughan managed to raise at least some of the money needed from the bank of the Sorers at Frankfort which satisfied van Sickyngen's demands.[27]

After successfully concluding this arrangement Vaughan hoped to take passage back to England to take up the business of his office in Chancery as clerk 'of all confirmations licences and faculties'. His appointment was confirmed by the Crown on 12 May. There is, however, no clear evidence that he ever made it back home to London on this occasion.[28] On 1 May he was still in Antwerp, begging for leave to go home as he had many things to do there. He had come from Speyer, where he had been arranging the musters of the mercenaries and pointed out that those commissioned to take them should be wary of 'the many crafty shifts made especially about the carts'. They also needed a good interpreter whose expertise was in German someone like Vaughan's former colleague the 'honest and trusty' Christopher Mont.[29] Besides the tricks and general untrustworthiness, in his view, of mercenary captains, there was also a general problem about the method of paying these men. As well as the considerable difficulties in getting hold of sufficient ready money in the coinage demanded by the captains, arguments over the level of payments seemed never-ending. Established 'customs of the trade' made life difficult for newcomers to this market like the English. One such allowed for the number of 'pays' to be higher than the number of men actually present. De Buren, for example, claimed that the emperor 'has but 400 [men] but allows them 500 pays'.[30] There was also much argument about the level of what was called 'entertainment' (victuals and other supplies) to be provided.

All these negotiations could become quite heated and further trouble was encountered with Landenberg despite the signing of the initial contract with him. Thomas Palmer one of those commissioned to take the musters of his men in June wrote to the council that 'the Almains swear that they will hew Mr Vaughan in pieces' largely because he had reprimanded Landenberg for speaking 'somewhat roundly' to him.[31] This may all have been one of the misunderstandings due to the language problem since, in a later letter to Paget, Vaughan denied that Landenberg himself had made such a threat and stated that his troops were well armed and using the king's preferred colours of white and green. This letter, however, also made clear that disgruntled mercenaries could easily become violent if not paid on time and thus could pose a threat to the surrounding civilian population, all of course subjects of the emperor. He had begun to think it would be best to dismiss Landenberg and his men from the king's service quietly but as soon as possible. Landenberg's demands for more money, however, did not cease; at the same time the commissioners for the muster claimed that he was not providing the forces agreed. A particular point at issue was the lack of barded horses included in his forces, that is, those equipped with full (and very expensive) horse armour, although this had been precisely specified in the original contract. This proved to be the last straw for his would-be employers and Landenberg was let go from royal service in mid-June.[32] The main reason for the trouble with Landenberg may well have been that, as Paget said, German captains were playing the market to their own advantage because this was 'their fayre time' while the English lacked 'the advantage of proximity and the network of acquaintances' which allowed both France and the empire to operate with much greater success in the market for mercenaries.[33]

By this time Vaughan himself had more urgent business to deal with than this haggling and bickering. He was fully involved in complex negotiations relating to the arranging of loans for the Crown on the Bourse at Antwerp. As these got underway, it became apparent that he faced new problems outside his previous experience as a diplomat or intelligence agent for the Crown or as a private merchant. First of all it was true that lending to monarchs was no new thing for the members of the Bourse; Charles V in particular had long made use of its services in this respect. The highly successful banking partnerships of the Fuggers from Augsburg had been involved with lending to the emperor since the 1490s, often in conjunction with that of the Welsers originally from the same town. A 'balance sheet' for the Fugger business in 1539 shows a total of 293,700,000 maravedis owed by the emperor to the Fuggers. Their willingness to be involved in state finance came from their extensive network of connections in the financial markets in both Antwerp and Lyon and also, most importantly, their intimate knowledge of the credit worthiness of the emperor and the finances of his extensive realm. The Fuggers and the other banking houses in Antwerp had no such clear view of the reliability of Henry VIII as a debtor nor of the resources of the English realm as a whole. The realization that Henry was seeking loans in the market before hostilities had commenced against France led rather to the fear that the English had already run out of money. Stephen needed help from someone experienced in dealing with the large banking houses and on the Bourse and for this he took the decision to use the services of Gaspar Ducci as his broker.

Ducci came originally from Pescia and had at first links with merchant companies in Lucca before moving as a young man to the branch of the Nobili company in Antwerp. He was never a member of any of the main Florentine partnerships and thus worked usually as an agent in the markets of Antwerp for a wide range of both Italians and Germans. Vaughan probably got to know him around 1540 when Ducci had become well known for acting as an agent in both commercial deals in cloth and other commodities and complex financial operations on the exchange and loan market on the Bourse. Ducci was not, however, regarded favourably by all his contemporaries; he was described, for example, as 'an ill-conditioned intriguer and quarrelsome fellow' in a complaint over a deal to the local magistrates in Antwerp in the 1530s. It was also widely believed among the business community that his activities relating to exchange dealings had led to the ruin of the agent of the king of Portugal in 1540.[34] Because of this he was officially banned from the Bourse for three years. Despite this, however, he managed to build up a very close relationship with the court of Mary of Hungary and with the emperor himself raising large loans for them at a reasonable rate of interest. In this way he ensured that he became the chief financial agent of the government of the Netherlands on the Antwerp Bourse and also undermined the hold that the Fugger Bank had established on the financial markets in Antwerp much to their displeasure.[35] Vaughan undoubtedly realized the value to the English Crown of these links and also appreciated that he needed access to Ducci's expertise in the operation of the financial markets in Antwerp. As he reported to the Privy Council, Ducci was a shrewd but crafty man who always drives a 'hard bargain'. He might be 'indeed a fox' with a 'wily head', but as Vaughan explained, 'it was difficult to borrow money on the Bourse without his assistance'.³⁶

The first clear indication that Vaughan's responsibilities in the Low Counties would extend far beyond those of the harassed paymaster of demanding mercenary contingents came in May 1544. Mary of Hungary reported to Chapuys that Vaughan had visited her at court and had explained to her considerable surprise that Henry VIII needed to raise a loan on the market in Antwerp. Mary was not pleased with this at all. It would 'impede the Emperor's affairs'. As far as the emperor himself and his sister (Mary) were concerned they had the first call on the funds available in Antwerp and had no wish to see another borrower enter the limited market for state loans. Chapuys was asked to find out if any other envoys had been inquiring about loans to the English king. If Henry needed money he should 'levy in his own realm'. The implication was that while being co-operative on the surface Mary would do her best to scupper English attempts to borrow on the Bourse.³⁷ Vaughan was clearly not deterred by any difficulties she raised in relation to the loan proposed. On 4 June he wrote happily to Wriothesley and his colleagues stating that the deal for a loan of 100,000 crowns would be available within a matter of days, with a further 100,000 by 12 July had been all set up by Ducci. The only problem was that neither Staplers nor Merchant Adventurers were acceptable as sureties but Italian merchant houses in London like Vivaldi would do. Ducci just needed a few words of encouragement from the king and 'then would work with a galloping pace'.³⁸ Less than a fortnight later the deal began to fall apart. Vaughan's optimism was shown to be naïve. The English Crown had thought to provide the necessary sureties by sending over letters of credit drawn on the London branch of the Bonvisi bank. Although Antonio Bonvisi, the head of the business in London, originally from Lucca, had been resident in England for many years and had been involved in trade and financial dealing with both Wolsey and Thomas Cromwell, it was a mistake to rely on him in these circumstances. The merchants approached to accept the bills 'sang all one note taught by the elder bird Bonvice' (Antonio). The London branch, these merchants claimed, was now dissolved and Antonio himself was no longer in charge. In this case sureties provided by this branch were not acceptable. The Antwerp house of the branch of the Welser partnership based in Nuremberg would only take up one-third of the amount already requested (100,000 crowns), as would the Vivaldi and the Bonvisi in Antwerp. Vaughan kept his nerve in this situation, arguing that he could get the total needed by accepting the plan of dividing the sum needed into thirds. The only problem remaining was that new letters of credit must come from London backed up by a procuration in

Latin certified by a notary. The money would be for nine months at 10½ per cent interest in Flemish money.[39]

Again despite appearances this was not the end of the matter. In another letter written just a day later on 18 June Vaughan had to tell the chancellor and his colleagues that as usual, the devil was in the details. The king's possible merchant creditors were insisting on manipulating the exchange rates between English and Flemish currencies to their advantage, explaining that they were only applying the rates usual in loans to the emperor. The validity of the letters of credit he had just received was also too short, six months rather than nine. As he said, the 'merchants look narrowly to the wording of the bills' and, not surprisingly, would not accept this. It is a sign of English inexperience in raising loans like this that this requirement was not understood in London from the outset. Sir Richard and Sir John Gresham both were involved in the London aspects of these negotiations but had apparently not questioned the six months validity of the letters of credit despite their acknowledged expertise as leading financiers.[40] Fortunately new letters of credit reached Vaughan in Antwerp on 25 June but as he tried to explain a week later to the Privy Council in London, the 'howesos' of the Vivaldi bank were still unprepared to lend more than 50,000 crowns. He was dealing with 'foxes and wolves which are shrewd beasts whose natures are well known to your Honors'. Another practical issue was the need to count all the money received (which was in a mixture of currencies) before paying it out; the overworked Vaughan could not do this without help, particularly if his usual assistants were absent on missions to the English forces and the ever-troublesome mercenary bands.[41] More or less simultaneously the Duke of Norfolk, the English commander in the field, was complaining to the council that no money had come from Vaughan to his encampment and he did not have sufficient funds for more than eight days' pay for the mercenaries.[42] The wrangling over the letters of credit and the precise source and amount of each tranche of the loan continued through early July, although small sums of money were delivered to the captains concerned. Gaspare Ducci might indeed be 'a fox', in Vaughan's opinion but 'they must use him or he would work to their hindrance'.[43]

As well as these negotiations Vaughan was also continually distracted by the question of the king's lead. The possibility of using the sale of the considerable stockpile of lead stripped from the roofs of dissolved religious buildings had been one of the first suggestions made by the council in London to increase the royal 'cash flow'. Unfortunately royal advisers had little idea of how the market in this commodity worked and how it must be managed to the king's advantage.

Vaughan had at first been receptive to the idea: he felt that a stockpile of royal lead in Antwerp could be useful security for the repayment of loans: 'some great quantity of lead to remain here, the sight whereof only would get us credit for where we now seek credence by that means credence would seek us.' The council, however, wished to sell the whole quantity available at once which led to a crash in the market for the commodity and extreme difficulty for Vaughan in selling any of it at all even at prices which gave the Crown little if any advantage. The constant exchange of nagging letters on this topic with the council over the summer of 1544 only made more difficult the raising of the essential loans in cash needed to pay the mercenaries.[44]

It was not until 21 July that Norfolk could report to the council that he had received substantial funds from Vaughan and that the king himself had landed at Calais ready to proceed against the French with the intention to lay siege to Boulogne.[45] Vaughan remained at Antwerp and now had sufficient time to write to Paget, on the same date, that his diets (payments for daily expenses) were in arrears and in consequence he was in personal financial difficulties. He also begged Paget to allow him more assistance, 'some other sober sad and witty folks.' He continued, 'it is too much for me alone in th'absence of Dymok and Lock, (his assistants) both to receive money keep account of money run and go to and fro the merchants without ceasing and when the money is received see it well and safely kept whiles I, being out of my lodging, shall be driven to run so many ways.'[46] This pressing business was not the only claim on his time and energy. He was also expected to do personal errands for people like Paget. In the same letter he reported that Paget's order of linen cloth was now in Vaughan's wife's hands in London.[47] Twelve days later on 26 July a certificate regarding the repayment of the last tranche of the loan was issued.[48] He had also successfully set up a new line of credit with the Affitadi and the Bonvisi at a reasonable rate of interest.[49] The king's business finally seemed to be on a much more even keel. Vaughan himself was, however, still without any news of his diets and this time sweetened his request by sending Paget 'a little barrel of sturgeon'.[50]

By this time the king had arrived at the siege of Boulogne which had begun with the rapid capture of the lower part of the town. The attack on the Haute Ville began with a furious barrage on 3 August and there was every expectation of success. From Vaughan's point of view the immediate pressure on him lessened; he even had time to quibble with Damsell, acting as the royal agent buying supplies for the English army, over the cost of fifty lasts of gunpowder for the royal army.[51] His major preoccupation now shifted to the arrangements for the repayment of the loans already made to the king. It was necessary to remind

Paget and the king that the creditor merchants would expect two-thirds of their money in gold and the rest in silver. In his view there was no way around this requirement even though obtaining sufficient 'valued gold' would add from ¼ to 2 per cent to the costs of the loans. Vaughan felt strongly that the Bonvisi bank in Antwerp was profiting at the expense of the king but this condition could not be avoided.[52] Finally at the beginning of September all seemed to be going well. The only real problem seemed to be a shortage of gunpowder on the market, which as Vaughan pointed out could be more cheaply and quickly delivered to the king's army by water than by land. Much relieved, Vaughan could write cheerily to Paget: 'God send you health and good luck with Bulleyn.'[53]

Ten days later, Vaughan was faced with disastrous news from London. His wife was 'sore sick and in jeopardy of her life'. He needed urgently to return home; as he put it to Paget in a letter written on 20 September, 'I have many young children which, wanting a mother and lacking the presence of a father may soon tumble into many displeasures. I have also young daughters and many other folks whose youth is no trusty guardian to itself.'[54] Four days later Vaughan in great distress (his usual neat handwriting becomes a hasty scrawl) wrote to Paget, 'In the reverence of God get me home or else all my poor things shall stand in great hazard.'[55] This seemed impossible. Antwerp and the Bourse were awash with rumours that the emperor was about to make peace with France without any participation from Henry VIII in the wording of the proposed treaty or consideration of his interests. This disastrous news from the English point of view was in fact true; the accord between Francis I and Charles V had been signed at Crépy on 18 September. Another rumour claimed that as a consequence the Dauphin was marching towards the English forces at Montreuil with 36,000 cavalry and foot soldiers. Vaughan did not know what to believe; could the emperor really be so devious? He was afraid there was some 'trumpery or guile in the matter'.[56] The confirmation of his wife's death within days of reporting all this to Paget was the final blow. Both his personal affairs and those of the king whose representative he was, seemed to be in crisis. Yet even in this situation not only his devotion to his family but also his care for the efficient conduct of business shines through; amid all the bad news he sent to Paget was the confirmation that two hogsheads of wine and a camp bed he had ordered was on its way to Boulogne where Paget was presently with the royal army.

Fortunately public affairs apparently became less threatening within days, although full confirmation of the treaty made at Crépy had still not reached Vaughan in Antwerp. He believed the peace rumours and the Dauphin's march 'were but a dream'; he should have taken more notice of the fact that merchants on the Bourse were betting in favour of peace with France.[57] Nevertheless, perhaps as a result of this unfortunately false report, Vaughan was given permission to go home. Arrangements for the repayment of the king's loans had been made successfully. His aides, Dymok and Lock, would be responsible for this with the help of Ducci even though 'John Dymok can skill of no reckonings making but Lock can'. Either by the end of September or in early October Stephen was in London, travelling by way of Calais able for once to look after his own affairs. This was only a brief respite. By 15 November he was on his way to Antwerp again once more facing urgent competing calls on his time and expertise.[58] On the one hand Paget gave him time-consuming personal commissions like finding and despatching to London twenty-five ells of the best crimson damask velvet and a particular set of fireirons while on the other he had to deal with sending good intelligence to the council and the continuing problems of renewing the king's loans. The arrangements for the loans were inextricably mixed up with the personal commercial dealings of Ducci, Vaughan's wily but indispensable broker. Stephen's personal affairs in London were also by no means on an even keel; his household was now headed by his brother-in-law and his deputy at the Augmentation Office neither of whom had much idea of how to look after his children or his household in Stephen's eyes

The king's loans, whether negotiating new ones or repaying those outstanding, had precedence. Here the problem was that Ducci clearly would do little for the king till his own demands were met. These included the question of compensation for a cargo of herrings and a consignment of woad taken in the course of commerce raiding by English ships in the Channel which had to be dealt with by the authorities in England. Vaughan suspected Ducci of 'colouring other men's goods' that is falsely claiming that the goods of Frenchmen, which were lawful prizes as the king's enemies, were in fact his. Ducci also had his fingers in other pies such as trying to induce the king to take part of his loans in alum, for which Ducci held a monopoly on the market in the Netherlands. Another idea was to involve the most prominent and 'fattest' members of the Company of Merchant Adventurers like the Greshams and Ralph Warren in a ploy to use their credit on the market in Antwerp to buy goods in demand like pepper and fustians. These goods would then be sold for cash and the money used for the king. There was also the need to negotiate the sale of the remaining stock of lead in his charge; as always the king and council had little understanding of commercial realities and expected an unrealistic and unrealizable level of profit.[59]

Moving from one banking house to another or talking to merchants on the Bourse in furtherance of these schemes, Vaughan also picked up information quickly relayed to London from his various contacts. Much was mere gossip and rumours but he could pass on useful titbits like the fact that the new imperial ambassador in London, Francis van Delft, was both 'honest and learned and has ever been friendly to the king's merchants here'.[60] As far as his own affairs were concerned he still had worries about the situation at home in London. Vaughan's plea to Paget for help in finding a wife is a sign of his desperation; his children in London were 'young and without discretion to order themselves'. In these circumstances he needed a 'sad trusty and womanly matron' to look after them. Not surprisingly he did not want anyone 'sharp, foolish, drunken or sluttish' but one above all with an 'honest mind'. To find such a paragon he would 'be much trained and ruled by your (Paget's) advice and counsel'. The real issue here was perhaps that it was only his link with Paget which held out some hope that he might be allowed to return to London for long enough to sort out his personal problems. He also needed to sort out the question of the money (a considerable sum of over £300) owed by the Crown for the work done for the queen's household by his late wife. Paget might possibly be flattered into helping Vaughan. Stephen much needed not only a wife but also to have his accounts as the king's agent in Antwerp audited something not done for some time. If this was concluded he could hope to have his discharge from his increasingly onerous obligations.[61]

He probably knew there was little hope of this happening in the near future. Ten days later a further letter to Paget dealt exclusively with royal business; he reported on such matters as the money that might be forthcoming from English merchants as surety for the repayment of the king's debts, the continuing problem of selling his stock of English lead at a good price in Antwerp and visits from unemployed Spanish mercenaries who were hoping to serve with the English as peace between the empire and France had led to a collapse in the demand for professional fighting men. Last but not least were his further efforts to curry favour with Paget by obtaining for him the damask cloths, towels and napkins that were his latest commissions to Stephen.[62] The most important development, however, was a meeting with Ducci at the beginning of December at which the wily merchant put forward a scheme which would occupy Vaughan's attention for much of the following year. Ducci would come to England if he was given a licence to bring into the country gold plate and jewels, the property of the Fuggers for sale to the king, together with a commitment for these items to be taken out of the country paying no customs if not in fact sold. Vaughan was very cautious about this; if Ducci's request was granted it would probably become much easier to raise money in Antwerp since he had so much influence with other merchants and bankers. Ducci, however, was 'witty and subtle' and also 'glorieth in being master of the emperor's finances' and 'had lustily risen into great wealth' after twice 'falling into decay'. This deal potentially involved a great deal of money and Vaughan was well aware that Ducci's main concern was always his own profit. As Vaughan wrote to Paget 'so fickle and wayward I find him and so lothe to hop over our seas'.[63]

Vaughan's sense of unhappiness, disillusionment and frustration at the effects of the events of the last months of 1544 clear in this letter and others written in December 1544 was not surprising. Both his professional duties for the king and his personal life seemed beset by difficulties. Despite the death of his wife, the mainstay of his affairs in London as well as the mother of his children, more and more work had been loaded onto him in Antwerp. Some of it required his skill and experience in the ways of the Bourse and the crafty bankers in the city and depended for its success on the way he had embedded himself in the merchant community there. Other tasks, however, were time-consuming, trivial and brought little in the way of reward or thanks. One can easily imagine his exasperation when in the midst of all his problems with satisfying the king's needs, he was also expected to find a new cook for Sir Richard Southwell, a privy counsellor. He was meanwhile stuck in Antwerp where there was no good French wine to drink only inferior Rhenish and moreover was short of money for his own needs because of the bad exchange rate for English pounds. On 5 January he wrote to his colleague John Dymok who was at that time in London, 'we may chance so to be sarpled abroad as we shall not meet togethers a good whiles.'[64] He was not mistaken in this; the need for his services became ever more evident in 1545.

From the English point of view the situation in both the Netherlands and regarding relations with France was fraught with problems. The emperor had concluded a peace treaty with France but Henry VIII had not done so and his forces were still in the field. Any mercenary who was by origin a subject of the empire was legally unable to remain in service against the French since they were no longer enemies of the empire. The winter of 1544–5 was disastrous as far as the remaining English forces were concerned; lacking food and other supplies, most had fallen back on Calais. The only good news was that a sustained attack by the French on Boulogne in early October had failed. After this one success further military efforts were suspended until the spring.[65] This did not mean, however, that Henry had reluctantly abandoned the war against France; as Vale has stated 'his determination to revive old claims and renew the Hundred Years War never died'.[66] Even though Paget believed that continuing the war was so impractical 'as my heart bleedeth in my body when I think of it'.[67] In early 1545 Henry was still determined on this course and it was Vaughan's duty to endeavour to find the funds to allow him to fight on.

7

The final years in Antwerp

In the first days of January 1545 the political situation in Western Europe especially in the Netherlands and the imperial lands was extremely volatile (Figures 9 and 10). Charles V was bed-bound with a severe case of gout or perhaps only of 'melancholy' induced by the realization that his treaty with France signed the previous summer was not the triumph it had initially seemed.[1] In Antwerp, merchants, gossiping as usual at the Bourse, were aware that there was little certainty about the emperor's intentions regarding peace and war. One worrying rumour for any Englishman was that exports of gunpowder from the Netherlands to England might soon be prohibited.[2] Equally in England, the king seemed intent on continuing the war with France despite his financial difficulties. It was not at all clear how this desire related to Henry's presumed wish to maintain his alliance with the emperor. Despite the usual winter lull in war-like activities the way forward for both Henry and Charles was unclear.

Personally Vaughan's attention was at first focussed on the scheme put forward by Ducci just before Christmas to provide new funds for the king. The scheme involved the king buying a selection of jewels owned by the Fuggers instead of asking them for a straight loan. Vaughan felt that Ducci's apparent eagerness to come to England to complete this deal could possibly be to the king's advantage but he also knew from experience how difficult it was to get Ducci to commit to anything like this. In the midst of these worries, on 6 January Vaughan was faced with a sudden and dramatic change in his situation. As he was sitting at dinner with Damsell one of his aides, the 'scowte' (constable) of Antwerp arrested them both; it was done, said Vaughan, 'very gently' but nevertheless all their goods were impounded and all their chests and papers were sealed up.[3] The same actions were taken against all English merchants in Antwerp or Barrow (Bergen op Zoom). The governor of the Merchant Adventurers in Antwerp was informed that this action was taken as a reprisal for the seizure and pillaging of vessels from Zealand by English men of war.[4] These ships were

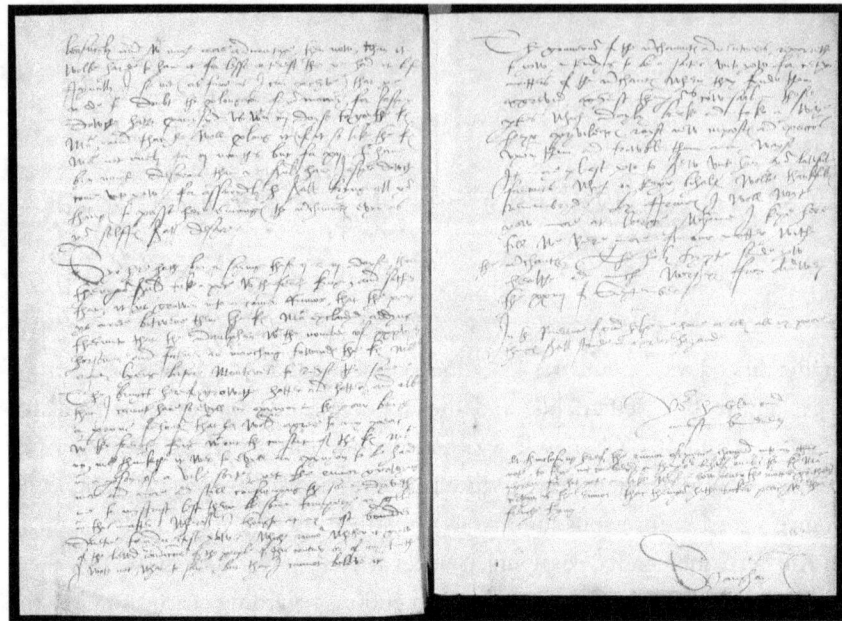

Figure 9 A holograph letter by Vaughan to Paget written at the time of the death of his first wife. Permission granted by the National Archives at Kew, UK.

Figure 10 A decoration in the dining room of the house built by Gaspar Ducci on the outskirts of Antwerp (undergoing restoration). Permission granted by Mechelen Museum, Belgium.

carrying the goods of French merchants (and thus legitimate prize goods) but the cargoes according to the English were 'coloured' (being passed off) as those of Flemings, that is subjects of the emperor. If genuinely in Flemish ownership the seizure was piracy. The arrest was by order of Mary of Hungary acting on the instigation of the emperor. Vaughan had had some prior warning from Nicholas Wotton the English ambassador at Mary's Court having received this somewhat enigmatic message; 'The Emperor taketh pepper in the nose with the taking of his subjects with which yet I was warned as a damsel overnight to be married in the morning',[5] but the arrest was still a surprise With this on top of his personal money worries and the continuing problems at home in London, Vaughan must have felt beleaguered on all sides.

Equally suddenly around a week later the gloom lifted a little. Vaughan received notice from the Privy Council that Ducci's licence to come to England in relation to the jewellery project had been granted on generous terms.[6] Ever optimistic Stephen happily began to plan to leave for England in a fortnight's time in company with Ducci sure that the arrangements regarding outstanding royal loans in Antwerp could be handled by his aides, and that the arrest would not be an impediment to his departure. Even so, he knew it would be hard 'to bring forth so wily a fox but I think to drive him thither'. The situation in Antwerp itself, however, was becoming worse and worse because of the stop on trade with England. Merchants in particular were in a bad way, 'their hearts damped and made cold with great fear that they had never to recover again such things as were taken upon the seas.' Unemployment had soared in the textile trades and many now believed, 'it were better for this country to have xx years wars with France than one with England'. Many traders agreed that the goods taken by the English were a lawful prize; even Ducci had accepted that when the incident actually occurred. There was little support in the city for the emperor's precipitate action in putting a stop on trade with the English.[7] Vaughan's clear expectation was that the arrest would be very short-lived and might even eventually be to the advantage of the English since the trade in cloth and other goods was so important to the prosperity of the Netherlands. All this optimism evaporated, however, after a meeting in Brussels between Ambassador Wotton and the emperor's principal advisers including Granvelle. Wotton's long and detailed report makes clear that, as so often in the past, the arrest of merchants and the stop on trade was a cover for the need to re-set the relationship between England and the empire which had worsened ever since the emperor's conclusion of peace with France. This had left England still in a state of war with its ancient enemy with the king and Privy Council feeling that the emperor had betrayed his ally and broken the treaty between them. The treaty in question between England and the empire signed in 1543 had terms which conflicted with that between Francis I and Charles V signed at Crépy in September 1544. It had had no input from English negotiators. The meeting between Wotton and Granvelle ended in a somewhat fractious stalemate. Neither side showed any desire to modify its position. There would be no relaxation of the arrest until all ships of the emperor's subjects and the goods they carried, which had been held in England, had been released. The arrest of Vaughan himself was agreed to be a mistake, as Imperial officials had thought he was the governor of the Merchant Adventurers rather than the king's agent in Antwerp, but this did not lead to his release from the restrictions on his activities and movements. Otherwise a great deal of old ground was trodden over, including the matter of compensation for Ducci's herrings and the bad behaviour of Landenberg and his mercenaries when discharged from service with England the previous summer. As Wotton finally concluded, however, 'neyther for the teatye nor amitye nor necessite, I coude have enye other answer but as they had declaryd the Emperours mynde unto me before, requyring ever that Your Majeste wolde take it yn good parte.' It was the case that they 'speake stille of thamitye and nothing of the treatye and when I alledge enye article of the treatye they saye not, that they will stand by the treatye but by summe evasion or cavillacion elude the true meaning of it'. Wotton may have been well received and made merry with the emperor's advisers but as he told Paget, 'words and countenances do not move me half so much as sometimes they have done'.[8]

The consequences for Vaughan were that not only was there no speedy lifting of his arrest and that of other merchants but also that the deal with Ducci was stymied. Ducci himself put forward endless reasons for the delay since one of his prime aims was always to maintain good relations with the emperor. Vaughan had already suspected that his early optimism was misplaced when Ducci began to show reluctance to make the journey to England before Wotton's meeting with Granvelle and spoke only of his confiscated cargo of herrings and his need for compensation.[9] Wotton also faced problems with any new negotiations over the arrest and the whole issue of relations with the empire because of Charles V's ill health. The emperor was still laid up with an attack of gout in his shoulder hands and knees, although there were suspicions that this was employed as a delaying tactic by Granvelle and his colleagues.[10] Stephen, meanwhile, was faced with the problem of finding the cash to repay the loans made by the Bonvisi in the summer. The stop of trade meant that there was no cash available to him in Antwerp even by way of forced loans from the Staplers and Merchant Adventurers. None could sell any cloth or receive money from their creditors with these restrictions in operation.[11] Although not without danger for him personally, Vaughan meant to get what money he could secretly to cover the king's debts since, 'if the creditors are not now served the credit will not hereafter be recovered'.[12] All his work in establishing the king's good name on the Bourse would go for nothing. By the middle of February his frustration at the stalling of any negotiations and worries about the king's affairs and his own family problems could hardly be contained. It was clear to him that Ducci was a wicked fellow whose word could not be trusted.[13] Vaughan believed he was a double-dealer simultaneously arranging loans for the French king and in fact working to 'prevent Henry getting more money here', rather than promoting English interests.[14]

At home things were no better. Vaughan could only repeat his pleas to Paget that, 'for the friendship and love that hath between us be good to my poor children which be babes and cannot help themselves'.[15] Even in Antwerp there was little respite because in general 'things are very suspiciously handled'. On 21 February he seemed almost in despair. He begged for a licence to go home. He knew Wotton would not approach the Regent for this licence unless ordered to do so by the king.[16] Vaughan was depressed and felt useless; he had nothing to do and no money and the merchants were 'unable to pay what they are appointed'. He was sure his aide Damsell could take over his duties. He was, however, aware that there was considerable apprehension in England about the intentions of the French, the renewal of hostilities and even the possibility of an invasion.

Despite his complaint of having nothing to do, he continued sending reports to the Privy Council of suspicious persons encountered in Antwerp seeking to make their way to England. Were they in fact French spies? Some of them as described by Vaughan sound like characters in a modern thriller. One suspect came to the English house asking for help but he was poorly dressed in a shabby yellow cloak with a black beard growing the 'breadth of iii fingers beneath his chin'. This fellow had an elaborate tale of fleeing from Venice because of a fight; but despite good English he was suspected of being a French man in disguise.[17] Vaughan arranged for him to be followed until he reached English territory at Calais where he could be arrested. He then warned Lord Cobham in Calais that this was a weighty matter and after being searched for papers the suspect should be watched so that 'he kill not himself'.[18] On another occasion a broker came to Vaughan in Antwerp with an elaborate story of two men who were going to London ostensibly to sell a pack of canvas but really intending to 'view the Isle of Sheppey, Margate and the ground between that and London' for a possible invasion route. The invading force, it was claimed, would have victuals and small ordnance and would make for a hill 'from whence their ordnance may beat the town. This hill as I guess should be about Fynsbury or More Fields'. Their knowledge of the geography of London was, perhaps, faulty and the hill in question at Blackheath. One of these men had a bad squint, or had lost an eye, a black beard and a 'coleric complexion'.[19] These reports were again taken seriously and letters were found when suspects were searched at Calais. There is, however, no way of knowing if the so-called invasion plans had any substance. They were also nevertheless reported to Wriothesley in London and Cobham in Calais.

At the end of February negotiations with the emperor about the treaty and the arrest were re-started. Wotton now had the aid of Paget, something of a personal friend, whose high status as a privy counsellor and secretary of state, it was thought, might help advance matters. Paget travelled to Brussels with orders to engage directly with the emperor's advisers together with Wotton. Initially no progress seemed to be made and extra complaints were aired including a rumoured arrest by the English of Spanish ships and merchants from Burgos. By the beginning of April, however, a way of settling the trade dispute emerged. The most important points of this agreement were that men, goods and ships arrested by either party should be freely released. Commissioners from both sides would be appointed to meet at Calais, Mark or Gravelines on 1 May to resolve disputes and 'griefs' about seized goods, compensation and other complaints by both English and Flemish merchants. Article six of the agreement also stated hopefully that 'subjects of both Princes shall at sea treat each other as friends'.[20] This was not always the case and incidents at sea continued to be reported but even so the English Commissioners for the meeting had been appointed by the end of April. These were Edward Carne, Thomas Thirlby, bishop of Westminster, William Petre, Stephen Vaughan and Thomas Chamberlain; all of whom had extensive experience in diplomatic negotiations or commercial matters. Thirlby was a distinguished civil lawyer as well as a member of the Privy Council and Petre was also of the council and a secretary of state; this was a high-powered delegation a clear sign of the importance to the king of sorting out the problems in relations with the empire.[21] This had become a matter of some urgency as the general situation had worsened. There was a fresh outbreak of fighting with France while the threat of an invasion was growing and seemed imminent. Further English raids into Scotland were being prepared and no firm allies for Henry could be found among the Protestant princes of Germany.

Vaughan, Carne, Thirlby and Petre were all in Calais in early May, ready to go to Gravelines for the scheduled meeting. Before this could happen both sides agreed to exchange lists of the alleged 'griefs'. The imperial delegation was not happy to travel to Calais rather than to stay at Gravelines or even move to St Omer because of an outbreak of plague in the town and also the poor health of Chapuys their prime negotiator.[22] Petre and Thirlby were, however, much encouraged by a private conversation with Chapuys which seemed to promise renewed friendship and true 'amity' between Henry and Charles.[23] By the end of May negotiations had proceeded reasonably well. The vague 'doleances' and 'griefs' had been specified and identified so that remedies might be found. The main obstacle to the commissioners' work seemed to be the plague outbreak in Calais which had caused justifiable alarm. Petre wrote, 'I was not more afraid of the like in all my life.' He had a reason for this as one of Carne's servants had caught the infection and later died.[24] The Privy Council's reaction at this point was to urge the delegation not to concede more than the other side did and 'if they by theyr wont understandinges will interpret the words at theyr pleasure you must do the semblalble'. At this point in the negotiations, at the end of May, however, a sudden order came from the king himself that Vaughan was to leave immediately for Antwerp as there were more important things for him to do there.[25]

This abrupt change of direction for Vaughan was undoubtedly caused by the deep financial difficulties of the king at a moment when every effort was needed to counter the apparent threat to his realm posed by France.[26] There was little if any ready money available to pay the wages of mercenaries or to buy war supplies especially gunpowder. New loans were urgently needed, possibly including a large one from the Fuggers. This in consequence brought about a reconsideration of the importance of the earlier Ducci deal involving the purchase of jewels which were the property of the bank. It had been in limbo since January. Vaughan's expertise and experience were urgently needed to deal with both matters. When he returned to Antwerp, Vaughan immediately set about reopening his talks with Ducci trying to do this in such a way that Ducci did not realize the urgency of the situation. He tried to appear very casual, asking about the jewels as a side issue in a discussion about a large loan of 200,000 crowns at 10 per cent for a year.[27] A meeting to view the jewels at the Fugger house was agreed but Vaughan was careful to insist that he would only take part in this after his chosen valuer had had an opportunity to establish their worth. He also suggested that he would only get authority from the king to proceed with a loan if a much larger sum was in prospect. By 20 June Ducci himself wrote to Paget with details of the deal which seemed to be on the verge of completion. He informed Paget that the valuables had cost the Fuggers 50,000 ducats and they were in no hurry to sell, being quite prepared to wait for a better price. However, if the king paid the asking price now he would also get a loan of 250,000 ducats on good terms, 'a good bargain compared with what other princes pay'. Once it was known that the Fuggers had allowed him credit for such a large sum 'every merchant will wish to employ money in his service'. The jewels and one-third of the money would be delivered at the 'Pentecost fair' with repayment a year later. On the side as it were, he also suggested that if given a suitable present by the king, he would be happy to drop the matter of compensation for his cargo of herrings.[28] We don't know how Paget reacted to this missive but Vaughan pointed out that the deal over the sale of jewels by the Fuggers had the effect of raising the interest rate paid by the king on the whole bargain above 18 per cent, an extortionate amount. It was never to be forgotten that Ducci was a man 'so greedily hunting after gain', that his own advantage was always his prime aim. The only benefit for the king was that the Fuggers would accept a personal royal bond for repayment rather than the Privy Council being compelled to find sureties for the loan among London merchants or the representatives of Italian banking houses in London.[29] It was also the case that Vaughan himself, perhaps unaware that Ducci's letter mentioned the still unsold royal lead to Paget, was running the risk of going behind Ducci's back with a separate bargain with another group of traders. He had found two Spanish merchants and made a preliminary agreement with them. They were apparently prepared to supply the king with alum (an easy commodity for the king to sell profitably) to be paid for by their accepting in return some of the royal lead which had up to this time proved to be such a drag on the market.[30]

All this bargaining was taking place against the background of increased tension over conditions of trade between the Merchant Adventurers and the Staplers, and the authorities in the Netherlands. Rumours of conspiracies got up by the French against the English forces in Boulogne and Calais were also spreading rapidly. According to Vaughan, English merchants were attempting to reduce their stocks of goods in Antwerp and elsewhere as stories spread about the state of the negotiations with the emperor's commissioners in Gravelines again thought to be heading to a stalemate. Likewise, agents of the emperor were attempting to discover the value of goods belonging to Spanish and Flemish merchants in England. Both groups feared another arrest and tit-for-tat reprisals if the talks were finally to break down.[31] The war talk was all about French plots to suborn the garrisons of English forts, for example at Hammes in the Pale of Calais or in Boulogne, so that the fortifications could be handed over to the French without any fighting.[32] Vaughan himself fully expected to be rearrested on 4 July but nothing happened.³³ It seemed confusion reigned on all sides. He wearily concluded on 8 July that 'all things are here very suspicious and I exceeding sorry to see that the malice of the time will not suffer me to do the King's Majesty any better service. Please let me know what to do.'³⁴

One of the problems for both Vaughan and his associates in Antwerp and for the king's officers and councillors in London, and undoubtedly a source of some frustration was the uncertainty and irregularity of communications. Although letters would occasionally be intrusted to apparently trustworthy individuals who were known to be about to make the crossing to England, most letters addressed to the king in London were carried by regular couriers very familiar with the routes concerned. Even so letters, queries and replies crossed each other causing confusion or the situation (usually in Antwerp) changed abruptly so that instructions from London were no longer appropriate.³⁵ All this added considerably to Vaughan's difficulties in the summer of 1545. Another issue was that it was correct that Ducci was playing, as usual, a double game. He was simultaneously leading Vaughan on into the intricacies of the Fugger jewellery and the linked loan arrangement while covertly preventing any such deal from becoming a reality at the behest of Charles V. The emperor did not want Henry to take up any loans in the market at a time when he too was in need of funds for a possible war with the Turks or actions against restive German princes.³⁶ Ducci brought up the subject of the confiscated cargo of herrings whenever things looked favourable from Vaughan's point of view, a sure route to delay. Charles V also complicated the relationship with England by taking up the case of merchants in Burgos who had suffered losses to English commerce raiders in the waters of Biscay or in the Channel. One incident of a fleet of Spanish ships intercepted when leaving Bordeaux with woad also included cargo shipped by Ducci giving him a further cause to seek compensation in England. By 19 July Vaughan was on the verge of finally losing patience with Ducci and to his relief a German banker, Christoffel Haller, willingly came forward to offer a loan to the king. Haller would provide a total of 200,000 crowns on good surety and 'shows good affection to the King'.³⁷ Things at last seemed to be on a more even keel, a feeling increased by signing the contract for the alum/lead deal some five days later.³⁸ News that the French fleet was off the Isle of Wight and of the inconclusive engagement of in the Solent did not reach him till 28 July when it was all over. His focus was by necessity on the matter of the king's need for money but he hoped the failure of the French attack would be seen as good news that would go down well in Antwerp and on the Bourse.

It was, of course, impossible in the close-knit and gossipy world of the merchants of Antwerp and the brokers on the Bourse to keep the new loan for the king to be provided by Haller from the ears of Ducci. The result should perhaps have been anticipated by Vaughan. August and much of September passed in prolonged, detailed and somewhat ill-tempered negotiations between Ducci and Vaughan with interventions from Paget and other members of the Privy Council in London over new loans and repayments. Wriothesley, the Treasurer had warned Paget that there was virtually no money available from the usual sources; he had 'swept the house bare'. The large repayments due in Antwerp could be met only with great difficulty and yet Paget was continually demanding 'pay pay pay prepare for this and for that'.[39] At the beginning of August at first things were quiet; the Ducci deal had been approved by London. Stephen had been ill with a fever which had left him weak 'with a pair of lean cheeks', but he was delighted that the king had rewarded his efforts by granting him the fee simple of a parcel of properties in Spitalfields of which he had earlier been granted the rents. Fortunately, Thomas Chamberlain had been able to take charge of the king's affairs while he was ill. A letter to the king dated 12 August followed up by one to Paget set out the deals underway and their progress. Even the vexed question of the Ducci herrings seemed to be included in the arrangements with him and the Fuggers. The total loan due from them was 300,000 ducats, with the jewels accounting for 40,000 of that. The alum deal was underway while the Haller loan was for 60,000 crowns. Payments had also been made as directed to mercenaries engaged for the defence of Boulogne.[40] Warning of trouble to come perhaps lay in the news reported a few days later that Ducci was 'in a great rage' because of the Spanish alum bargain.[41] Stephen, however, was still hopeful that as 'these finances are made' and Chamberlain could deal with the receipt of money, he could at last get home. The man he had left in charge there had gone back to Wales and things were in a bad way.[42] The problems centred on a maid called Anne Kydney. She had, 'by evil enticement fallen into great lightness drawing to her a great rout of lewd fellows who use his house as their own and threaten his servants'. As Vaughan wrote to Paget it drove him out of his mind, 'to be so shamefully abused while serving his Prince in a strange country' and this was 'worse than twenty fevers'. He begged Paget to send one or two 'honest and sad men' to his house to talk to his servants and to get the maid out of the house as quietly as possible. They should speak to her, 'in such a way as rather to win her from evil than to drive her to it by despair'. His main concern was the influence she might have on his children. He would send a letter for his brother-in-law to read to his maid making everything clear. Finally in this situation he felt there was no solution to his domestic difficulties but to re-marry. Paget was once more asked to help him achieve this.[43]

Probably before this letter reached Paget, Vaughan was again thrown off course by an outburst of cold fury from Ducci. The latter now had the details of the loan made by Haller to the king. Vaughan should have realized that the emperor had given Ducci oversight of all loans to foreign rulers and all such bargains had to be approved by him. The emperor, he pointed out, 'often needed money and it was not meet that the money of the Bourse should serve other princes besides his knowledge'. There would clearly be a need for more intricate bargaining before the money reached the king, money which was needed urgently to pay mercenaries. Vaughan and Haller were at first relatively sanguine about the outcome of this row. (Haller said he cared not a fig for Ducci.)[44] Ducci's influence on the authorities, however, did have an effect in a way which while not entirely unexpected threatened to prevent any loans from reaching Henry. Vaughan was summoned to the Margrave's residence in Antwerp. He was told that he 'went about to undo the country' (Flanders). The basis of this accusation was that Vaughan intended to send large amounts of both gold and silver bullion to England there to be taken to the Mint and recoined into English coins of lesser value with a lower bullion content. It was, of course true and well known to all bankers and traders, that Henry was in the process of carrying through a debasement of the English coinage, a manoeuvre which had greatly helped the king's finances while bankrupting some traders. Vaughan was able to refute the idea that any recoinage was directly involved in the loans from the Fuggers or others. Nevertheless the Regent, at the behest of the emperor, imposed an absolute embargo on any transport of valued gold or silver. Vaughan had in fact already received much of the money in question and some of the jewels, the most notable being 'a dagger of gold garnished with stones and pearls'. The problem was that nothing could be moved from his premises in Antwerp not even the small amount, 'not in the Emperor's coins' needed to pay 'the King's Almains'.[45]

Stephen was given no clear explanation of the reasons for this arrest beyond the wild charge of wanting to destroy the Low Countries. He wondered if the fact that he held a position in the Mint in England (performed by a deputy while he was abroad) had something to do with it. He was sure that Ducci's plotting was involved in some way, complaining bitterly that 'in all the days of my life was I never so craftily handled'. The only action he could take was to go to Brussels with his colleagues Thirlby and Carne to speak directly to the Regent and her advisers. A somewhat tense interview between the two sides did result in an agreement that while valued gold was still embargoed, other coins like French crowns or angels could leave the country.[46] In Vaughan's mind Ducci's machinations were behind the affair. Ducci was a 'crafty and lewd man' obsessed by the business of compensation for his cargo of herrings. Back in Antwerp, Vaughan spent the next week arranging as far as possible the exchange of the cash value of the Fugger's loan from imperial currency (largely 'gilderns') to 'florins'; a further visit to Brussels would hopefully result in a licence to carry out 'valued gold'. This time the embassy to Brussels met with greater success; the emperor even told Thirlby and Carne that I (the emperor) 'am and always will be his (Henry's) good brother and friend'.[47] It was agreed that Vaughan could export cash other than in the emperor's coins, that he would be helped with the necessary exchanges and that a licence would be granted for the export of 10,000 or 12,000 gilderns in valued gold. For Vaughan the news of this agreement could hardly have been more welcome. While he was dealing with this urgent business regarding loans or the king, he was also distracted by another complex and acrimonious matter regarding the hiring of mercenaries in the German lands. His worries about the situation at his house in London had also not abated. The one individual whom he fully trusted to look after his children, a schoolmaster called Cobbe, 'of sober honest and virtuous life' had got into trouble over his religious beliefs and had been summoned before the bishop of London's chancellor.[48] Vaughan needed more than anything to go home to set up adequate care for his family. He still had hopes of re-marrying but finding a suitable partner was not easy based, as he was, out of the country. His pleas to both Wriothesley and Paget for help to get home come from an urgent postscript to letters mostly concerned with the details of the loans and the transport of the money. He ended one letter in this way on 1 October repeating the plea already made on 20 and 26 September:

> I beseech you help me home. The Emperor will not license me to carry away any gold of his own coin so that I must change his crowns for French. All the money I will send to Calles shall be French crowns 12,000 in valued gold and the rest in English gold and silver.[49]

Stephen's plan was that he should escort the king's money to Calais and then continue with it across the Channel and so home at last.

He was finally able to implement this scheme by the beginning of November but not without some further problems rearing their heads. One concerned securing the necessary sureties for the Haller loan but this matter was in the end aborted. Ducci's influence had won out. Another concerned getting the necessary passports to transport the cash to Calais from the emperor. Three different ones would be involved all with precise terms as to the amount and nature of cash they covered. Vaughan was also desperate to ensure that Ducci was kept ignorant of the details of the alum deal with the Spaniards as knowledge of this might prompt Ducci to put more stumbling blocks in the way of getting the loan money and jewels to England. Ducci was as always, 'wondrous troublesome'.[50] By 10 October, twenty-five bags of money were in the hands of Thomas Gresham (Vaughan's courier for this task) for delivery to Wotton in Calais.[51] The final problem he had to be dealt with, however, concerned mercenaries and their endless demands. In the summer it had become clear that more troops were needed to defend Boulogne, a cause very dear to the king's heart. The French, equally strongly wished to retake the town and erase the humiliation of its loss. Negotiations had been opened by the king's Commissioners in June with one Friedrich von Reiffenberg from Coblenz in the territory of Philip of Hesse to supply a large force of both horse and foot to the English. All at first seemed to go well but the deal began to fall apart when the force was mustered in early September. Not all the men contracted for were present and many were not properly armed. When Reiffenberg finally set out against the French, supposedly aiming for Mezières on the Meuse, things rapidly went from bad to worse. It was suspected by the commissioners that they had been greatly deceived and that Reiffenberg and his men had never intended to leave German territory. They had been marching about in the territory of the bishop of Liége, a vassal of the emperor, to little purpose and with no plan to go against the enemy. They were in fact demanding an extra month's pay to go home. Vaughan was expected to supply this money just as he was deeply involved in getting the cash for the king's loans to Calais. The king initially refused the mercenaries' demands but Vaughan's hands were forced. The commissioners, including Vaughan's friend and colleague Thomas Chamberlain, were seized by the mutinous mercenaries, placed in irons and threatened with death unless the money demanded was immediately forthcoming.[52] It was clear that Chamberlain and Fane were 'now in the hands of no reasonable men but in the cruel handling of a most cruel and wicked sort; God which holpe Daniel in the midst of the lions deliver them out of the hands of so wicked a people.'[53] It was not until 4 November that Vaughan was able to write to Paget that he had managed to lay his hands on enough money to pay off the Almains. He had eventually been able to get hold of £72209 14s 1d to pay them off (some of it supplied by Ducci who did have his uses!).[54] A report went to the Council on 8 November that the matter was settled. Vaughan, however, could not leave Antwerp immediately and only on 8 December was Stephen finally able to tell the king that he had arrived at Calais with the king's jewels but would not be able to leave until an escort could be found for his ship.

The transport of so large an amount of money and valuables had been no light matter; he had had to find at least three cases for the jewels and five firkins for the money as well as 'mats ropes canvas and trussing and binding of the same'.[55] Happily any delay this time was brief; he reached Dover only a day later after 'the fairest passage that ever man had'. His pleasure at being once more on home territory made the whole journey a delight.[56]

In one respect his brief return to London in December 1545 was more successful than he could have reasonably expected. Although at home for only about three weeks he was at last able to resolve his personal difficulties in a way that brought him a chance of some happiness and the likelihood of the security and the good governance of a well-managed home that he had always wanted for his children. In this brief interval away from his responsibilities in Antwerp, he was able to meet and propose marriage to the widow of Henry Brinklow. Under the pseudonym of Roderyck Mors, Brinklow had written at least two pamphlets, *The Complaynt of Roderyck Mors* and *The Lamentacion of a Christian*.[57] These polemical works embodied much of the thinking of the group of reformers known as the Commonwealth Men, blaming much of the current unrest they saw in society on economic matters like the spread of enclosures and the way the debasement of the currency had worsened the plight of the poor. In religion Brinklow, a mercer by trade, was an ardent reformer but with no clear adherence to any organized group. He had died probably shortly after the making of a will dated 20 June 1545, leaving a young wife, Margery, and one child.[58] As a young man just starting out on a career initially as a Merchant Adventurer, Vaughan had been a member of a group known as the Brethren, many of whom had similar views on both social and religious reform to Brinklow's. Vaughan's views had not changed greatly since his youth as is clear from his attitude to Tyndale and his work in the 1530s, and the way he had carefully chosen as tutor to his children, Stephen Cobbe, a scholar also known as a supporter of religious reform. It is possible that Henry and Vaughan had been at least acquaintances, if not close friends. Vaughan's desperate need for a wife was no secret. He had even written to both Wriothesley and Paget in September asking for their help in making an offer of marriage to the widow of the recently deceased provost of the Mint who had been 'left substantial'.[59] He and Margery may well have been drawn quickly together to make a match which, while it had an element of calculation about it, also had a sound basis in similar outlooks and even, perhaps, some prior attraction. Vaughan told both Paget and Wriothesley of his intention to marry Brinklow's widow in letters dated 22 January when he had already returned to Antwerp once more. He explained to Paget that she was not wealthy but of 'a person and honesty I like well enough' and 'remembering my declining now towards age and that riches is the gift of God but an honest woman that feareth God is above all riches'; a clear indication of his cast of mind. A later letter in March when he was trying to make arrangements for his wedding made clear that he had in fact 'long known the woman'.[60] This was not something hastily got up on the spur of the moment, notwithstanding his worries about the state of affairs for his children in London. At the same time he was not entirely indifferent to an opportunity to better his finances. He had spent some time in London lobbying for an opportunity to buy a small property if chantries were dissolved as seemed likely.

While in London Vaughan also could not be entirely free of worries stemming from his work in Antwerp for the king. Even though the king was pleased with the jewels and spoke pleasantly with Vaughan for about two hours when they were presented to him, there was still a problem with Ducci. It appeared that when the package of jewels was examined by Paget two rings were missing and Vaughan was blamed for this discrepancy.[61] Later, writing from Antwerp, Ducci furiously denied that there was any chicanery involved in this; these rings had never been part of the deal. He was an honourable and honest man still not fully recompensed for the jewels, and he yet again brought up the matter of his cargo of herrings, and his need for some favour from the king.[62] His explanation seems to have been accepted and the matter was allowed to rest.

Vaughan, back in Antwerp by the middle of January with new instructions from the king, found the situation in the city was still difficult. There were food shortages after a poor harvest. In addition to his many other responsibilities, he was now also expected to find and arrange supplies of victuals and munitions for the English forces in Calais, Boulogne and elsewhere. The king had been tentatively engaged in peace negotiations with France in the autumn but was now once more preparing to reactivate the campaigns in the Low Countries and on the Borders. This increased the pressure to negotiate on him to negotiate new loans for the Crown. Wriothesley had bluntly declared at the end of 1545, 'I am at my wits' end how we shall possibly shift for three months following and especially for the next two.' Vaughan, however, discovered to his evident horror that the strategy of including the purchase of jewels in any bargains with the English king seemed to have become popular among the 'foxes and wily pies' (magpies) he had to deal with on the Antwerp Bourse. One John Carolo of the Affitadi bank had shown him 'a tabled diamond set in an owch (jewel) of gold'; a 'jewel of wondrous price' with 'a great fair round pearl hanging thereat'. Vaughan wanted only money without jewels and if the 'Welsars' would not help in these circumstances 'will leave no bourse or bank untried'. What money he could raise would be packed hidden in a chest with velvets and sent to Calais where the exchange rate for crowns was in the king's favour. This was to avoid the danger of money being confiscated if sent out of the emperor's territory without proper authorization.[63]

Despite this unsatisfactory initial approach to the Antwerp bankers, the next two months in early 1546 were largely occupied with the complex and tangled negotiations necessary to fulfil the king's urgent need for money as the war threatened to reignite. Apart from the large sums of money needed, Vaughan had to deal with the problems of finding sureties for repayment that were acceptable to the lenders. This involved squabbles about interest rates and the currencies to be used in repayments for the original loan and fears about the actions of either the emperor or the Regent. Hovering in the background all the time was the possibility that another embargo might be placed by the rulers of the Netherlands on the transport of large sums of money in cash through their territory to Calais, and the difficulties which they might place in the way of any licence to allow such transit. The funds available on the Bourse were also drying up as it became more evident that the emperor was preparing for war against the Lutheran princes and was himself in need of large loans. Despite the discussion of bargains with other merchant bankers like John Carolo, it was the case that only a deal fixed by the agency of Ducci with the Fuggers was likely to come to any conclusion. It was also the case that any deal would probably involve a trade-off of some kind, if not with jewels then with some other commodity like fustians or alum. A further problem was that Vaughan could only conclude a deal with the written authorization of the king and the Privy Council in London. Although Vaughan had normally good relations with Wriothesley and Paget, both were so worried about the king's overall financial situation that neither at times seemed to understand fully the way in which the Antwerp loan market operated. In Vaughan's view, they blandly assumed that he had merely to follow their instructions to conclude an advantageous deal for the king. Ducci, as had always been the case in the past, was a slippery customer but also indispensable. He was inclined at first to promise that loans were easily available for the asking. The whole flimsy edifice of the proposed deal would then collapse in days in some acrimony but, or so it seemed to Vaughan, in such a way that it always ensured higher fees or commissions for Ducci himself.[64]

Vaughan was adamant about some things; he would not in the future agree to any deal involving jewellery, however beautiful or valuable. The king should not be pestered with jewels; he 'already has more than most of the princes of

Christendom'.⁶⁵ If Vaughan gave way on this it would be impossible to borrow any money without taking jewels as well. At the end of January, Ducci, who was in high good humour because of a personal grant from Henry, attempted to curry favour with Vaughan by bringing him intelligence about yet more French plots involving the corruption of captains at Boulogne.⁶⁶ At the same time he came up with a bargain involving buying fustians for a proportion of the loan, with additional complicated arrangement involving the alum bought from the Spanish the previous summer. There were also vague hints of a larger deal but with the unacceptable inclusion of a jewel (this time a pointed diamond set round with others like a rose). The negotiations on this proceeded slowly because Ducci had misjudged the emperor's reaction to his personal grant from Henry. To his chagrin Ducci was forced to give up the grant.⁶⁷ Vaughan, in his turn, was blamed by the Privy Council for the problems posed by the disputes and quibbles over the deal proposed. He reacted strongly to the injustice of this accusation. by pointing out to Paget it was no easy matter to borrow large sums in Antwerp. Such sums were not to be found in every man's house. No one 'will disburse so huge sums of money before they be honestly assured to be repaid again'. The sureties offered had to be acceptable to the lenders and the merchants in Antwerp would not accept the 'bonds of noblemen in England'. Too hasty acceptance of a deal was not 'meet for the King's majesty's advantage'. It could both 'hinder the bargain and raise the interest'.⁶⁸ Despite this outburst of fury born out of his frustration at what Vaughan saw as a lack of support and appreciation in London of all his hard work in Antwerp, an agreement was made a matter of days later with bonds backed by the king and the city of London; the final accord was for 3,000 florins in money and 10,000 florins in fustian from the Fuggers at 6 per cent for six months. The immediate crisis seemed to have passed.⁶⁹

Vaughan's deputies had also had some success in the hunt for victuals for the troops both in Calais and Boulogne and on the Borders. They had found cheese, bacon and butter available in Antwerp but grain was more of a problem. For this they had to travel to the Baltic lands especially the big Hanseatic trading ports of Bremen and Danzig. The agent here for the English was the house of Erasmus Schetz of Antwerp which was able to obtain rye and wheat in Danzig for shipment to Newcastle as soon as the seaway was free of ice. Vaughan was also happy to be able to renew his contacts with Christopher Haller. Despite the deal that Vaughan had made with him the previous summer collapsing, this German banker was again willing to offer 60,000 crowns to the king for nine months to a year.⁷⁰ These deals, others with the Bonvisi and that with Ducci relieved the immediate pressure on Vaughan. At the end of February he had time to fulfil some personal commissions for his friends Lord and Lady Cobham in Calais. He was able to send Lady Cobham the cinnamon she had requested but not the black satin from Venice she also wanted. Also tucked into a letter to her husband about possible attacks on English merchant ships by a squadron of French warships from Dieppe was 'a little clout with needles' for their daughter. The markets in Antwerp were far better provided with both necessities and luxuries than those in Calais.[71]

Vaughan had a particular need at this time to consolidate his friendship with the Cobhams. The matter of his second marriage was much on his mind. He was anxious for the wedding to take place as soon as possible. He had two plans to achieve this aim; the first was to approach his friend and supporter in the Privy Council, William Paget. At the end of February he wrote to Paget in the final sentences of a letter dealing with the Fugger loan and other business matters begging him to meet his future wife. He asked if Paget would invite her to his home to meet Lady Paget. His bride needed 'some cheer' because 'she is like to have none of me awhile'. Above all he prayed for the end of the war with France so 'that I might in mine old days live in rest'.[72] Ten days later he made a more specific request; he asked for a licence for his wife to travel to Calais and for the marriage to take place at the deputy governor's (Lord Cobham's) house. This could happen within a matter of weeks with her journey secured by a protecting escort of armed ships for he 'was loth the Frenchmen should have her by the way'.[73] The day before this he had also written to Cobham saying frankly that he needed to get married as quickly as possible because of the state of affairs at his home and there was little chance he would be able to get to England before the autumn. His plan was for his intended bride to come to Calais. If this could be arranged he begged Cobham 'to give her lodging and marry her in his chapel without any foolish wondering as he could only stay two or three days but must return and so shall she'.[74] Despite this request Vaughan did not give up on the hope that he could after all come to London for this purpose. He asked both Paget and the king directly for this favour in a letter dated only a few days later. He was worried about 'the peril upon the seas and the peril also in Calles upon the coming thither of soldiers and of the pestilence'.[75] It is not entirely clear when or where the marriage did in fact take place. Margery Brinklow was entertained by Paget at his house in London probably in early March; Stephen was very pleased by this because the letters she had sent to him in Antwerp had been lost on the way by the courier.[76] It also seems that Paget was in favour of Vaughan coming to England. A journey to escort the king's treasure could easily include a wedding. This journey was arranged with him expecting to leave from Calais around 5 April. The king's treasure securely packed was expected to leave Antwerp for Calais on 2 April.[77] After some delay caused by the need for passports and an uproar in Antwerp caused by attacks on shipping in the Channel Vaughan with the treasure eventually reached Calais on 14 April, intending to depart 'when wind and weather' allowed.[78] There is no doubt that he was in England for at the very least a few days at this time. He was directed to return to Flanders by the Privy Council on 6 May.[79] The evidence that he delayed in Calais till almost the end of the month for the marriage to take place rather than arranging the ceremony in London relies on a licence dated 26 April from the archbishop of Canterbury for him to marry in Cobham's chapel. Wherever the wedding was finally celebrated, the future of his personal life now looked both happier and more settled.

Once back in Antwerp Vaughan found that he could expect no similar respite in his business life. The king's acute 'cash flow' problems had led to the creation of the situation where most short-term loans were destined in part for the repayment of earlier borrowing. The political situation was, however, more encouraging. At the same time as he was concerned with his wedding the arrangements for peace talks between envoys of the French and the English were getting underway. Henry had changed his mind from his show of belligerence in January and February and was now prepared to come to terms with Francis I. This meant that the focus in the coming summer would be on complex arrangements to repay loans falling due and efforts to maintain Henry's credit on the Antwerp Bourse without the pressure caused by continuing hostilities with France. Even though he and the council well knew that Ducci was 'of extreme greediness', he also clearly had the power to put obstacles in the way of Vaughan raising money on the money market both now and in the future. It was necessary to pay attention to his claims even that concerning the cargo of herrings. Vaughan also reminded the council that it was essential to repay loans in valued rather than current money; only this was acceptable to the bankers in Antwerp an opinion backed up by the leading London financiers, Ralph Warren and the Gresham brothers, John and Richard. In conjunction with receiving this advice, there was an unforeseen added complication for Vaughan. At the end of May, the factor in charge of the Fugger Bank in Antwerp suddenly fell dangerously ill of the palsy; he could not speak and his life was despaired of.[80] At a time when Vaughan was trying to get the big Fugger loan extended this made things very difficult. To cap it all at the end of May, Stephen also became embroiled in an unexpected fracas in Amsterdam where his colleagues were buying supplies for the English army. As reported to him by John Dymok, one of those involved, one Sunday he (Dymok) had been invited to a meal at the house of the 'ballowe' of Amsterdam; other officials were there and soon all were very drunk. These men started asking him half jocular questions saying this was all for their ears only (under the rose was the phrase used). These included questions about a rumour current in the Low Countries at this time that Anne of Cleves had been taken back by Henry and had two children. They then turned to religious matters and began claiming that the English were all heretics and despised the pope. Dymok did his best to answer truthfully but finally claimed that in his view the emperor would like to follow Henry's example over the dissolution of monasteries and control of the church. The next day his questioners now sober realized that this was a dangerous conversation if reported back to England or to the emperor. Dymok was summarily arrested and imprisoned in Dordrecht.[81] The matter could not be ignored because if the local law was upheld by the authorities Dymok faced the death penalty for his unwise words about Charles V.

Trying to sort out this affair was exactly the kind of task Vaughan did not need when faced with the fact that since the Fuggers had refused to extend Henry's loan 'no one will emprunt any convenient sum towards so great a payment as is due to the Fugger'.[82] Fortunately the Regent ordered Dymok's release and substituted banishment from the emperor's territory for execution but the whole incident was an unwelcome distraction in his negotiations over the loans.[83] Vaughan had devised what he hoped might be a solution to the imminent problem of repaying the Fugger loan due at the end of August. He would repay part of the loan early if the terms of the large remainder could be extended for six months. He informed the Fuggers of this through Ducci since their Antwerp factor was 'sick and raving'. The plan was not acceptable to the Fuggers something for which Vaughan was blamed. He claimed in turn that he had only been doing his best for the king. At this point the council in London unusually took matters into its own hands and communicated directly with the bank in Augsburg via the Fugger factor in London. This direct appeal had some success although Ducci was as ever annoyed at being cut out of a deal and claimed that Henry's approach to the Fuggers had had the effect of raising interest rates for all borrowers on the Antwerp Bourse, including of course the emperor. A well thought-out memorandum, probably the work of Wriothesley, confirmed in a letter from Vaughan to the king, brought the matter to a close. The king understood Ducci's concern but the arrangement with the Fuggers was necessary to preserve the king's honour; the whole Fugger loan would be discharged save for a sum of 200,000 crowns which will be held over to be covered from a loan from Ducci at the next mart of 150,000 crowns in money and 50,000 the value of a consignment of copper 'at such price and upon such interest for the whole as mentioned in your letter'. This was in the region of 12 per cent though likely to be increased by the payment of various charges and fees.[84]

Negotiating this matter with Ducci and the Fuggers with the frequent intervention of the Privy Council had worn Stephen out. He was desperate that his own accounts should be properly audited as otherwise with the need to both value and account for all the money passing through his hands he was likely to be out of pocket. He was also unwell, suffering particularly with 'the stone' more than I 'am able to endure'.[85] Somewhat theatrically he concluded that 'if I die whilst they [my accounts] hang over my head all I have should be lost and my wife and children go a-begging'. He spoke the truth about the burden of the work involved in receiving coined money. More than a hundred different types of coins could be involved and each individual gold coin had to be weighed and valued.[86] Moreover since the debasement of the English coinage in progress since 1544 the new angel, the new 'crown of the rose' was now worth considerably less than before on the exchange market. There was in fact great reluctance in Antwerp to accept English crowns and other coins, most merchants preferring French coins or those of the emperor. The only bright spot for Vaughan was that since peace had been agreed with the French at the Treaty of Camp signed on 6 June, the crisis atmosphere of the earlier part of the year had considerably abated. As far as rumours of war were concerned all the news was of Charles V's preparations for war against the Protestants. Vaughan reported to Henry VIII that at the end of July it was widely believed that if these armies meet, there will be a bloody fray.[87] Trade in consequence was at a standstill which was creating great difficulties for English merchants contracted to contribute to the loan repayment. He had nevertheless by tapping every other possible source of funds managed to accumulate almost enough money to repay the Fuggers in full on the appointed day 15 August. Haller and Erasmus Schetz, he reported, had even approached him to let them borrow some of the funds destined for the Fuggers for very short-term loans to others, so tight was the money market and so anxious were they to make even the smallest profit.[88] What he really needed was precise direction regarding the loan repayment. This was received on 5 August; 60,000 florins should be paid on 15 August and another 25,000 in September. Vaughan set out the particulars as known to him at that date in a memo to the council. Most of the debts were covered though there might be a small deficit of £1,000 for interest to certain Italian creditors in lieu of their payment in valued money.[89] This memo did clarify the situation, which was in danger of becoming utterly marooned in a sea of confusing details.

There were of course minor changes in these particulars in the following weeks; some related to difficulties with the 'side deal' in copper that was part of the Fuggers' agreement; others to the kind of unexpected addition to the account of an individual creditor he had come to expect. For example John Carolo of the Affitadi demanded an extra ½ per cent as provision 'for acceptation and payment' of a bill of exchange, something no other merchant had ever asked for. Vaughan, however, needed to clear the king debts as quickly as possible. He was in no position to refuse to pay charges like this. The difficulties which arose repeatedly over the details of any repayment are well illustrated by problems over repaying a loan from the Bonvisi bank in early September. The head of the Bonvisi bank was owed 9,000 florins which Vaughan could only pay in angels; this was unacceptable to the Italian. He would 'take no more angels or English coin and, for his credit as a merchant, must bring a notary and protest against me for non-payment'.[90] Vaughan was now in a quandary; such a suit would 'touch the King's honour'. He asked for more time and then with the help of Chamberlain and Damsell frantically began to scrape together and count enough valued money to clear the debt. Some came from the loan that was due from the king's merchants, some from other sources in dribs and drabs. In the end the team in Antwerp was successful but articulated their usual suspicion that somehow Ducci was again responsible for Bonvisi's refusal to accept payment in angels. At one point Vaughan summarized the arguments over the currency in which repayment should be received as 'no less hard to please both than to please a shrew wife'.[91] He did not get much sympathy from the council for his problems. The councillors were inclined to take the view that the general refusal to take angels was not because of the debasement of the coinage but somehow because Vaughan made too much of this. He should keep quiet in their view: 'the great speaking thereof might give occasion to mistrust lest we devised by some new angels made for the nones to deceive them and so indeed put them in fear without cause.'[92] Happily the council were also prepared now at last to grant him permission to return home once he had handed over his responsibilities to Chamberlain and Damsell and the repayment process was complete. On 1 October Vaughan could at last write to Paget that he 'today pays all the merchants strangers for their valued gold and provision and then returns homewards'.[93] His journey would not in fact to be undertaken quite so speedily but the end of his sojourn in Antwerp was in sight. It was not in fact until the very end of the month that he reached Calais on his way home. He had been delayed not through any more business with the loans but because he had been commissioned to escort the money in payment of the king's French pension (reinstated by the Treaty of Camp), from Calais to London. All the money had as usual to be counted and its bullion content certified by a goldsmith. It was in the region of 50,000 crowns.[94] Packed in marked bags, the whole consignment had reached London in Vaughan's care by 29 November. On that date he inquired of Paget what he should do with all this money. Not surprisingly its final destination was the Mint.[95] Vaughan's formal discharge from this duty came in the following January. The Treasurer of the Mints then certified the precise sum of the pension for half a year as 52058cr. 16s *Tournois*.[96]

Vaughan's only remaining duty for the Crown was to attend the final audit of his accounts for the period of his time in Antwerp. His diets and expenses were recorded in January 1547 as paid in the Augmentations Book of that date. In the meantime for the first time in many years, he had no other duties for the Crown beyond those belonging to his long-standing appointment as a Chancery clerk in the Augmentation Office. There is no record of any plans he might have had for his retirement from the post of the king's agent in Antwerp. Anything he might have intended was also thrown up in the air by the king's death on 28 January. Vaughan himself was in poor health; he had suffered from a recurrent fever in 1545 and bad attacks of the stone in 1546. His letters make clear how overburdened he had felt in his final months in post as king's agent. He had also had little time to order his own affairs and those of his family. Since his hurried re-marriage in April he had only spent a matter of days with his new wife. To modern eyes a period of rest and relaxation was long overdue. His financial affairs in respect of his work for the Crown were sorted out reasonably promptly. What he was owed in respect of diets and expenses was dealt with by the Court of Augmentations in the last month of Henry's reign. His overall accounts for his involvement in Henry VIII's affairs in Flanders and 'High Almayn' were settled in early June 1547 before a commission made up of his friends and colleagues William Paget, William Petre and Ralph Sadler.[97] There was every chance that they would deal with this business with sympathy and understanding. It was also necessary to complete the sale of the fustians, which were an element in the last loan for the late king arranged with the Fugger Bank. In April of the same year this matter was dealt with by Sir John Gresham, who sold them to a group of London merchants.[98]

In what would be his last involvement with official affairs, Stephen was elected as a Member of Parliament for the borough of Lancaster in the first Parliament of the new reign. His nomination was probably the work of Paget who was chancellor of the Duchy of Lancaster.[99] It has been suggested that he had little personal reward for all his labours in Antwerp and that he was deliberately overlooked by those in power under the young king Edward VI. This may well have been a consequence of his poor health rather than any official disapproval. His outlook on religion as a committed supporter of reform but not a Lutheran or member of any other sect would have been in tune with that of the new court and Edward's advisers. We can speculate that after the frantic activity and considerable stress of his years in Antwerp he had no overwhelming wish for more responsibilities of a like nature. He had, it is true, been acutely disappointed to be passed over for the office of treasurer of the Chamber in early 1546 and had also been unsuccessful in getting the grant of a house he and his new wife coveted in Wood Street. Now back in London and with his expenses at last paid and his accounts closed, perhaps what he wished to do was hasten the conversion of the property he did have in the former St Mary Spital into a suitable mansion house for himself and his family. He had earned the right to spend more time with both his new wife and his children.

Tables 1–4 The financial situation in 1545

Loans and repayments negotiated by Stephen Vaughan

Based on the data in Oscar de Smedt, 'Stephen Vaughan, Agent van de Engelsche Kroon en de Antwrpsche geldmarkt in de Jaren 1544–1546', *Antwerpen Archievenblatt* III 1928, 244–5.

1 Old Crown Debts

Expiration day	Creditors	Amount in £ Fl	Origin of the debt
March 1546	J.C. Della Affitadi, Bart. Fortuni in London the factor in London	6,000	Unknown
	Ger. Deodati and Vincent Baltasar Guinigi for Ant. Bonvisi in London	6,000	Presumably the previously mentioned 5,500 £ Fl and ten months' worth of interest at 10%
April	Ant. Bonvisi and Ant. Salvago in London	18,000	Nominal amount of loan, previously arranged; net revenue was £ FL 16,896.2.10

15 August	Anton Fugger and Nephews		108,733. 6. 8	(=362.200 ducats)	
15 August	Same		1,646. 13. 4	(contingencies)	
			Total 140,380.		

2 New Crown Debts

Date	Expiration date	Interest p. a.	Lenders	Amount in £ Fl	Origin
February 1546	15.VIII.46	12%	A. Fugger & Nephews	31,800	In specie 3 30,000 Interest £1,800
Same	Same	Nihil	Same	10,000	Value of fustians to be sold by the Crown
March	September	11 ½%	Affitadi (factor Fortuni)	6,000	Extension of loan made in March
15.VII	15.X.46	?	Bart.Campagna	6,000	Extension of loan which expired on 15.VII

3 New Crown Debts, Agreed by the Privy Council in London

Date	Expiration date	Interest p.a.	Lender	Amount	
15.I.46	15.VII.46	10%	B. Campagna	6,000	
6.III	6.IX	?	Ant. Bonvisi (with Deodati of Lucca)	9,000	Remitted to Vaughan per exchange
15.III	15.IX	?	Ant. Vivaldi, Salvago &Co	6,000	Same

Money due to be repaid in 1546

Old debts	. . .	140.380.- £ Fl	
New debts	53,800.-		
	21,000.-	74,800.- £ Fl	
		215,180.- £ Fl	

4 Loans to Be Repaid in 1547

Date	Expiration date	Interest p. a.	Lenders	Amount in £ Fl	Origin
July 1546	15.VIII.47	Nihil	A. Fugger and Nephews	20,000	Secured on the value of a consignment of copper
Same	15.II.47	13%	Same	60,000	Partial extension of earlier loan of £Fl 152,180

August	Same	Not known	Erasmus Schetz and Sons	20,000	
				Together 100,000.- £ Fl	

Repayment of Above Loans

Expiration 1546	Lenders	Amount owed £ Fl	Paid off £ Fl	Long extension £ Fl	Short extension £ Fl
March	Affitadi	6,000			6,000
Same	Deodati/Guinigi Bonvisi/Salvago	6,000	6,000		
April		18,000	18,000		
15.VII	Campagna	6,000			6,000
15.VIII	Fuggers 108,733. 6. 8 1,646.13. 4 41,800. -. -	152,180	92,180	60,000	
September	Affitadi	6,000	6,000		
6.IX	Deodati	9,000	9,000		
15.IX	Guinigi/Balbani	6,000	6,000		
15.X	Campagna	6,000	6,000 143,180 + 12,000		
			155,180 + 60,000	60,000	12,000
		215,180 £ Fl	215,180 £ Fl	Transferred on 1547	

At the end of 1546 the Crown owes Antwerp

For 15.II to Erasmus Schetz & Sons . . . 20,000 £ and 6 months' interest.
For 15.II to Anton Fugger & Nephews . . . 63,900 £ = 60,000 + 6 months'. interest at 13% p.a.
For 15.VIII.47 to the same . . . 20,000 £

8

Stephen's legacy

By the end of 1549 Vaughan's health was clearly giving real cause for concern (Figure 11). It was the custom at the time to delay making a will until recovery from illness seemed unlikely. Vaughan's will is dated 16 December 1549. He died a week later on Christmas Day. The will stated that he wished to be buried in St Mary le Bowe, his parish church, not far from his old family home in Three Legges alley. Following the usual custom, as a livery man of the Merchant Taylors Company, his coffin would have been borne to the church covered with the company's beautifully embroidered hearse cloth, followed by a procession of his fellow liverymen in their robes.[1] In the opening words of the will he declares. 'I bequeath my most wretched and sinful soul to the most blessed and Holy Trinity the Father the Son and the Holy Ghost in person one God.' This wording is not unusual for the time but is in tune with Reformed views of justification by faith and a hint of his favouring of the new ways of the Church of England. There are also no charitable bequests or payments for candles or any of the accompaniments of an old-style ceremony. There are only a few personal bequests; a gold ring to left to Ralph Sadler his colleague from the early days in Thomas Cromwell's office but now in high favour at court and similar gifts to colleagues from the assay office at the Mint and at the Augmentations office. Otherwise apart from the wages to his servant all Vaughan's property went to his wife and the children. His wife would have control of his landed property, that at St Mary Spital, Three Legges and in Baynards Castle, Westchepe and Watling Street until Stephen junior was of age. His daughters (both unmarried at his death) were also provided for. They would get the rent of Three Legges for at least nine years while their brother was a minor. John Gwyneth, his brother-in-law from the time of his first marriage and always close to Stephen, was charged with supervising the children's welfare and would continue to live at the Three Legges, even keeping a room there after the children were all of age.[2] The total value of his landed estate was around £67 per annum which doesn't seem much

Figure 11 The Hearse Cloth of the Company of Merchant Taylors. Permission granted by the Company of Merchant Taylors and the V&A.

after a lifetime of service to the Crown but it is probable that his ready money, plate and valuables, goods and chattels were worth a great deal more, certainly his wife remarried shortly after his death perhaps because she was considered a wealthy widow.[3] The major landholdings were held of the Crown as fractions of a knight's fee as was made plain at the inquisition post-mortem on 17 June 1550.[4] Looking back over Stephen's career would he have felt content that he had both lived as an upright citizen of London and father of a family and also had served his monarch well?

His personality, as revealed in his letters and other sources, was that of a somewhat emotional man of great integrity, open to and aware of the new currents of thought and opinion to which he was exposed. He was not originally of high social status though granted a coat of arms as befitted a gentleman in 1539. He did not acquire a large landed estate or great wealth either from his private business or his work for the Crown. He was in modern terms, 'comfortable' being assessed as owing £16 13s 4d for the subsidy of 1541 as a resident in the parish of St Mary le Bowe in Chepe ward in the city with a further £15 due from property in Middlesex.[5] This was a considerable amount for a merchant but dwarfed by the wealth of a family like the Greshams. Most of those contributing to the subsidy in his parish paid less than 20s but his assessment was equalled or surpassed by several others in his parish and the rest of the ward. Significantly his largest property holding was in London, the grounds and buildings of St Mary Spital outside Bishopsgate granted to him by the Crown in fee simple in 1544. He was born and remained a Londoner all his life and seems to have been immune to the desire for a country estate that most successful Londoners succumbed to. Much of the wealth of Sir Richard Gresham, for example, derived not from his activities on the Bourse at Antwerp but from his dealings in monastic property. It has been calculated that between 1538 and 1545 he poured a fortune of thousands of pounds into properties extending from Kent to Yorkshire and Cheshire.[6]

Moreover Vaughan as an individual confounds many of the stereotypes of a man of the middling sort in early Tudor England. As a family man he proved himself to be caring and thoughtful for the future of his children in a way not often seen as typical of the age in which he lived and the level of society from which he came. Although a practical man who had to rely on his own efforts to support himself, well aware of the advantages of a 'good' marriage, there is no doubt that he and his first wife, Margery Awpart née Guinet or Gwyneth had a strong relationship. She was a widow with some property from her first husband, Edward Awpart, a member of the Girdler's Company. Any economic benefit, however, was probably not the sole motive for the match.[7] Vaughan seems to have been prepared to take on the care of her children from her first marriage. There is also no mistaking the anguish he felt when news came to Antwerp of his wife's illness and it proved impossible for him to return home before her death. As well as running a large household Margery was his partner in business matters. Letters, other directions and parcels of goods came from Antwerp to her at their family home on the clear understanding that she could deal with them. As well as this she had her own career as a silk-woman to the queen (Anne Boleyn), a career that at one point Stephen claimed was the sole support of his family. This was clearly no sinecure since there are records of her obtaining supplies needed for her work for the queen. Equally Vaughan's care for his children was deep-seated and concerned not only with the practical matters of their upbringing but also with their education and nurture in what he felt to be the right way. This was particularly the case after the death of their mother. He clearly spent some thought on finding a tutor for them and chose for this task one Stephen Cobbe, a colleague and friend of many of the printers and booksellers caught up in the anti-Reformist drive led by Bishop Gardiner in 1543. In October 1544 Cobbe was himself arraigned before the court of aldermen in the city for having reformed views but escaped punishment through the intervention of one of Queen Katherine Parr's servants. A year later he was summoned before the chancellor of the bishop of London again for having suspect views.[8] Vaughan called this young man 'a jewel' as an educator of his children but was forced to send him away from his home after this arrest. Because Lord Cobham's son was lodging at Vaughan's house in London and thus was also taught by Cobbe, Stephen wrote sadly to his father in Calais

> Mr Cob goes from me I dare no longer keep him.... I think there is no honester man and I leave his opinions to be judged by others. It is a great displeasure to me to lack so sad a man as he is in my house to teach my children specially seeing I am driven so often from home.[9]

Vaughan even tried to find Cobbe another position providing, in a letter to Paget, what amounted to a reference for his children's former tutor. He was 'of right good learning and wit'. Moreover 'he is a very good Latin man – I think none like him within the King's realm – a good Grecian and speketh well the French tongue' a true humanist educator.[10]

The choice of this man as a tutor for his children like his remarriage to Robert Brinklow's widow allows us to understand a little better Vaughan's religious opinions and probable views on social questions of the day. As a young man there is evidence that he was a member of the group known as the Brethren, early supporters of the reform of the church. His involvement in the efforts to get Tyndale back to England reveals his sympathy for him and his own absolute conviction that the Bible should be made available to all in English. At the same time Vaughan was clearly no Lutheran and one suspects that, as someone working for the Crown, he was not overly keen to be identified as a reformer or activist in religious matters. In his own household it was a different matter. There is an intriguing hint that his first wife may have shared he husband's views to some extent. An analysis of the biography of Anne Boleyn included in Foxe's Book of Martyrs has suggested that Anne may have received controversial books on religious matters published in Antwerp through the help of one of her silk-women, Joan Wilkinson. Mrs Vaughan, a fellow royal silk-woman, is not mentioned by name but would have been well placed to arrange this for Mrs Wilkinson through Stephen who often bought books wanted by Cromwell in Antwerp.[11] Stephen certainly took trouble to ensure that his children were brought up to favour reformed views, something which may have become more obvious after his second marriage. His second wife, also Margery, during her marriage to Robert Brinklow, had been part of a close-knit circle of friends holding advanced views not only on religion but on society in general. Brinklow, in his pamphlet the *Lamentacyon*, had attacked the rich citizens of London writing that 'the great part of these inordinate rich stiff-necked citizens will not have in their houses that lively Word of our souls nor suffer their servants to have it'.[12] Cobbe was part of the same group. Moreover he taught all Vaughan's children not just his son, also Stephen, but equally his daughters Anne and Jane. It was not only women in the highest levels of society, like Lady Elizabeth and Lady Jane Grey who might be educated according to humanist principles but also those who were part of the middle ranks of London mercantile society. Also probably present in Cobbe's school room were Vaughan's stepchildren from his wife's first marriage. His letters speak at the time of his wife's death of having 'many young children' and of 'many other folks whose youth is no trusty guardian to itself'.[13] His stepchildren were probably between eighteen and eleven years old at the time of their mother's death, the right age to be described as potentially unruly 'youth'.

Stephen himself seems to have lacked the fervent and sometimes intolerant adherence to a particular doctrine or a particular sect which characterized so many reformers among his own contemporaries. Despite the fact that he had supported the need for church reform since his youth, Vaughan happily shared his home, for most of his life after his first marriage, with his brother-in-law, the priest John Guinet or Gwyneth. At the end of his life, in his will Stephen made Gwyneth the guardian of his children Anne, Jane and Stephen, a task the priest had earlier undertaken for his sister's first family, Stephen's stepchildren. It may be that Gwyneth's support for the old ways of the Catholic Church became more obvious and more vocal after Stephen's death. In July 1553 after the accession of Mary as queen and the restoration of the Catholic Church in England, Gwyneth preached a sermon in the parish church at Luton finding parallels between the new queen and the Virgin Mary which created enough of a stir to be printed and widely distributed.[14] His zeal for the restoration of the Catholic Church may also have had a great influence on Stephen's daughter Jane. She was probably around fourteen years old when her father died. She married a known supporter of the old religion, Thomas Wiseman of Braddocks, a property in Wimbush in Essex between Thaxted and Saffron Walden.[15] It seems likely that by the time of her marriage she had also become a devout supporter of the papacy. Of her eight children, her oldest son inherited the property, another died fighting for the Spanish in the Low Countries and two further boys became Jesuits. All four of her daughters entered religious orders on the continent.[16] Jane herself suffered under the penal laws in the reign of Elizabeth. She was one of the many who fell under the spell of the young John Gerrard, the Jesuit priest; around 1591 he was said to be acting as a chaplain in her household. She was eventually arrested as 'a great harbourer of priests and other bad persons' c. 1594 at much the same time that Gerard was also captured by the authorities. She was only released on the accession of James I, having at one time faced the appalling prospect of suffering *peine forte et dure* (crushing to death for failure to plead).[17] Her prominence among stories of Elizabethan recusants indicates her strength of character, determination and devotion to the old ways. A nineteenth-century biography of John Gerard attributes both her devotion to the Catholic Church and her marriage to Wiseman to the influence of her uncle John Gwyneth. The writer John Morris extols her as a holy widow who would have welcomed the opportunity of martyrdom for her faith.[18] John Gerrard's own *Autobiography* written in the early seventeenth century (Gerrard had become something of a celebrity among the missionary priests because of his successful escape from imprisonment in the Tower of London *c.* 1594) also praises her character and her efforts to assist several Jesuit missionary priests including Gerard himself. Gerard described her answering her accusers in court after her arrest for harbouring priests 'very boldly more like a free woman than a wronged and persecuted lady'.[19]

Closer to Stephen, in her religious outlook was her older sister Anne. She was as fervent a supporter of reformed religion as her sister was of the old ways. Not only her father's views and the teaching of her tutor Cobbe, but also the example of her stepmother seems to have had a great influence on her own opinions. Her life also reveals how much could be achieved by a determined and clever woman at this time who also had the support of family members and a close group of friends of like minds. Anne was probably around sixteen or seventeen years old at her father's death.[20] Two years later in 1551 she married Henry Locke, the well-to-do youngest son of the prominent London mercer Sir William Locke.[21] This marriage embedded Anne even more securely among the leading supporters of the reformed religion in London. Her father-in-law Sir William Locke who had died just before her marriage had publicly demonstrated his support for reform as early as 1534 when he tore down a copy of the pope's anathema of the king. Her sister-in-law Rose Hickman in her memoir wrote of the way her mother brought all her family up in the new ways reading to them in private from heretical books smuggled into London by her father's factors.[22] Her brothers-in-law were all similarly supporters of reform including the younger William, who was sent by his father to Flanders and France to 'learn their languages and to know the world'. He very probably met Stephen Vaughan at the English House in Antwerp. The Locke family lived in Bow Lane with a shop in Cheapside not far from the Vaughans. Sir William's wife like Anne's mother and stepmother was a silk-woman so the ties between the two families were probably cordial and long-standing.

Not long after their wedding John Knox lived for a period with the young couple. During this time Anne and John became close friends. After the death of Edward VI in 1553 and the restoration of the Catholic Church by Mary, Knox became convinced that she was both in actual danger after the execution of Latimer and Ridley and also faced spiritual jeopardy now that the religious opinions she held were outlawed. Writing to both 'Mistress Locke and Mistress Hickman merchandis wyffes in Londoun' he urged them to 'leif your native countrie', suggesting that they should only inform their husbands of their desire to leave the country after the decision had been made. A second letter written in November only to his 'loving sister Mistress Anne Locke wife to Mr Harie Locke Merchand nygh to Bow Kirk in Chaip syd in Londoun' was more insistent stating his eagerness to see her again in Geneva where an English congregation under his leadership following Calvin's teaching had been established. His last plea to come to Geneva was written in December 1556, pointing out that Geneva 'was the most perfyt schoole of Chryst that ever was in the era since the days of the apotollis'.[23] Though she was only about twenty-two years old at the time, Anne finally left London with her two young children and only her maid Katherine for company. She reached Geneva on 8 May 1557. Four days later the Livre des Angloys recorded that her baby daughter, Anne, had died. Despite this tragedy Anne stayed in Geneva until the summer of 1559, when she felt it was safe to return to London and her husband. She did not waste her time in Geneva but spent some time translating four of Calvin's sermons from French to English and certainly began to compose her major work, a sonnet sequence based on Psalm 51 entitled *A Meditation of a Penitent Sinner*. The poems make up a sequence, probably the first known example of this form of poetic work in English, something which became much used in the later sixteenth century. Her skill as a poet compares not unfavourably with that of her compères and in the eyes of Michael Spiller betrays evidence of familiarity with the works of both Wyatt and Surrey.[24]

The sonnets which appear at the end of the volume of sermons, *Sermons of John Calvin upon the songe that Exechias made after he had bene sicke* were published in 1560. The original publication now survives in only two copies. One is in the Folger Library and the other in the British Library. This copy has on the cover the handwritten inscription, *Liber Henrici Locke ex dono Annae uxoris suae 1559*, hardly that of a husband who actively opposed his wife's endeavours. The publication of this book and the journey to Geneva epitomize Anne's life and her significance. She was, as Patrick Collinson wrote, representative of 'a generation of women who were highly educated in classical and modern languages and other intellectual skills thought proper to their sex by Vives, Erasmus and other Renaissance educators'.[25] She was also more than this, demonstrating both personal courage coupled with determination and a degree of intellectual daring. In her life she combined the roles of wife and mother along with those of a writer and poet and of one thoroughly involved in the politics and networking of the later sixteenth-century community of committed Protestant reformers. Her work as a writer has most recently come to the fore with support from feminists and other critics. Her personal life demonstrates well the way in which women of the middling sort at the time apparently found little difficulty in combining these roles. On her return to London via Frankfort from her adventures in Geneva she and Henry Lock had a further two children in quick succession; a second Anne who was baptized in October 1561 and Michael in the same month a year later. None of this prevented her from resuming her correspondence with Knox. She was in many ways acting as the official contact of the Scottish reformers in London. Knox sent her a series of letters offering personal spiritual advice but also giving detailed news of events in Scotland which she was expected to make sure reached the right ears. There was also a hope that she might be able to organize financial aid for the Scottish reformers from among London merchants. In a letter of November 1559 he wrote, 'I cannot; becaus I trust yee suspect me not of avarice I am bold to say to you that if we perishe in this our enterprise the limits of Londoun will be straiter than they are now within few yeeres.' Events in Scotland might well influence how events developed in England.

The last letter between Anne and Knox was written in 1562. Wider political events, the dislike of Knox among many in England and his own personal circumstances may have been responsible for the end of this contact. What is clear, however, is that the end of this connection did not signify the end of Anne's support for what she would have considered the true way for religious reform in England. When Henry Locke died in 1571 leaving her all his worldly goods, she married Edward Dering, a London Puritan preacher much in the mould of Knox. His proposal to her manifested both Puritan scruples, 'I atempte nothing but that which is veryse laufull ans becometh any Christian', and also a charming bashfulness, 'I am afearde to write unto you', and was 'careful to shunne your good companye' . . . 'yf your affection shalbe enclyned as I doo wyshe it to be bent, God's name be praised'. His health was, however, poor and he was also soon in trouble with the authorities for his views. Facing possible imprisonment he was able to write, 'My wife hathe beene I thank God in no trouble . . . ; if any fall God hath made her rich in grace and knowledge to give account of her doing.' His death in 1576 brought this short and somewhat troubled union to an end.[26]

Anne's final marriage in 1579 to Richard Prowse heralded a more peaceful and productive period in her life. Richard was a wealthy and respected burgess of Exeter who had made his fortune as a draper or cloth merchant. He was wealthy enough to have a tennis court and bowling alleys on his property in the town. He was also mayor in 1579, the year of his marriage and again in 1589 as well as MP in the Parliament of 1584–5. In Parliament he concerned himself with local matters like the salmon in the haven but also was put on a committee for a bill regarding better observation of the Sabbath day. Prowse contributed generously, perhaps at his wife's urging, to the appeal for help made in 1582–3 by the city of Geneva faced with an attack by the Duke of Savoy. The city was described as the nursery of God's church in the appeal words which would have recalled to Anne the phrase used by Knox in the letter which had led to her expedition to the city in 1557. Prowse also signed the Bond of Association to defend Elizabeth from her Catholic enemies and was one of the first to do so in Exeter. He and his family were securely embedded in a network of wealthy and educated families with strongly held reformed views on religion based in the West Country where Anne would have enjoyed the company of a group of educated women with views which chimed with her own.

Her move to the West Country clearly also did not lead to the end of her connection with London Puritan propagandists and activists. The clearest sign that this marriage did not herald any slackening of Anne's support for reformed religion nor of her desire to write is the publication of her last work. This appeared in 1590 and was a translation from French of Jean Taffin's book *Of the Markes of the Children of God*. This was an account of the tribulations suffered by reformers in the Low Countries by a pastor and scholar who was close to William the Silent leader of the Dutch revolt. This book became a classic of Protestant literature and (in a modern translation) is still in print. It is not surprising that Anne's version was also widely read and reprinted with the last edition appearing in 1634. Anne's choice of subject may well reflect her father's long connection with the Low Countries and his support and sympathy there for early reformers. The book was dedicated to the countess of Warwick and includes a short poem by Anne entitled: 'on the necessitie and benefit of affliction'.

> Then we with David shall confesse
> That God from Heaven above
> By humbling us) doth well expresse
> His mercie and his love.
>
> For ere we felt the scourging rod,
> We er'de and went astray

But now we keepe the law of God
And waite thereon always.

Anne undoubtedly shared these feelings with her daughter, also Anne who had married Robert Moyle, a gentleman from Bake just across the Tamar near St Germans. She had clearly been as carefully educated as her mother. She was praised by Charles Fitz Geoffrey in a collection of Latin poems published in 1601 as 'Doctissimum, Pietissimum', with a 'manly heart', 'learned in both Greek and Latin'.[27]

Stephen would have rejoiced to see the way his careful choice of a tutor for his children and his care for them after they had lost their mother had borne fruit. His elder daughter Anne's literary work is now well studied by literary scholars and has revealed how the Renaissance enthusiasm for education did not only benefit the uppermost ranks of society and was not confined to men.[28] Among well-to-do merchants and country gentlemen networks of women with lively minds and good education created a vibrant level of society in which new ideas of all kinds could be discussed. The lives of Anne and Jane also demonstrate how deeply felt was the schism in society caused by the reformation. Stephen himself supported reform but cautiously and with a degree of ambiguity. His only clear statements of his own views reveal his strong support for the provision of the scriptures in English as widely as possible, but also his acceptance of the royal supremacy and all that this entailed for religious doctrine as well as the organization of the church in England. His daughters were less inclined to hide their views no matter what repercussions this might bring upon them. It is sobering to remember that at much the same time that Anne in Exeter was publishing her book *Of the Markes of the Children of God*, a key text to this day for Calvinists, her sister was facing the horrors of the *peine forte et dure* for her support of Popish priests, including the charismatic John Gerard in Essex. Similarly most of Jane's children entered religious orders while Anne's included not only Anne junior whose views echoed those of her mother but also her son Henry. Henry wrote a large amount of religious poetry, including a verse rendering of Ecclesiastes. He entered the service of the Crown as an agent for both Robert and William Cecil in Scotland and elsewhere. He finally fell into debt and ended his days in the Clink. He has been characterized as 'an indifferent religious poet' with an equally unfruitful career as a courtier.

Vaughan's only son, also Stephen, was the youngest of his children born in October 1537. Less is known about the details of his life than those of his sisters. His education continued after he lost Cobbe as his tutor following a much more conventional route for a young gentleman in London in the mid-sixteenth century. He was matriculated at Gonville Hall in Cambridge in 1554 and ten years later joined the Inner Temple. The family was based at the property his father had been granted at St Mary Spital, now including a mansion house, outside Bishopsgate in London. There is no record of him practising law although he might have been drawn to such a career by the fact that his stepmother married, about two years after his father's death, George Rolle, a successful lawyer. His guardian and uncle John Gwyneth was also involved in litigation in Chancery, principally with his stepmother's third husband Sir Leonard Chamberlain, over the terms of his father's will.[29] Stephen junior's main occupation was probably concerned with managing his property which consisted of the former family home in Three Legges, an alley off Cheapside as well as the site of St Mary Spital. After he was of age the Cheapside property was let as a mixture of shops and warehouses largely to clothworkers and drapers. His much larger property formerly the precinct of St Mary Spital was also divided among various lessees some of whom had been in occupation before Stephen Vaughan senior acquired the full title to the land. In one case, just before his death, this had led to violence. One of Vaughan's servants had attacked the occupier of a property over the gatehouse and his servant, 'would have been sore hurted and wounded to the greate Jeopperdye of his lyffe yf presenr Recue had not thenben'. The occupier also claimed to have been daily threatened with 'opprobrious words and perpetual imprisonement' and to face difficulties because Vaughan was a 'man of great Substaunce possessions and estimacion and greatly fynded alyed and supported'. Stephen junior came into occupation of the whole property on his majority now described as a 'mansion house at St Mary Spittell with the gardeyn and orchard thereunto belonging'. It remained in the family until the late seventeenth century. No traces of the original hospital or the 'mansion house' remain, although the site has been extensively excavated. After being left to his second son Rowland, all this property eventually came into the ownership of the Earl of Bolingbroke in 1685.[30]

Stephen junior perhaps lacked the enterprise of his sisters. He was, however, not lacking in religious conviction even if not with the fervour they both showed. In 1591 in the Middlesex Sessions he was found guilty of not attending his parish church while in the following years he was brought before the ecclesiastical commissioners for the same reason. He was bound over in the sum of £100 to ensure that he would receive instruction twice a week on his religious beliefs. This was to continue throughout the summer of 1592 with a variety of divines but there was evidently little sign that he would modify his belief that he was justified by Christ only without works of his own.[31] He may, however, have finally consented to attend his parish church since there is no record of any other action against him. He had been caught up in the growth of anti-Puritan feelings in Elizabeth's government which culminated in the Act of 1593. This set out severe penalties against failure to attend the parish church and attendance instead at 'unlawful assemblies conventicles or meetings'.[32] He was perhaps minded in these circumstances to conform and publicly acknowledge his fault. He seems to have maintained some connection with the Merchant Taylors' Company since he witnessed the deed regarding a sale of land and a bond on behalf of two fellow members of the company in 1576.[33] The only other record of his activities is a possible connection with his family's original home in Radnorshire in the Marches of Wales. In 1564 a survey was made of the 'Great Forest of Radnorshire'. The jury declared that it extended to 3,000 acres much of it 'waste heath' or 'wild fogge Moorish ground', in fact scrubland largely overgrazed by goats and 'wild beasts'. Only two hundred acres could be described as good pasture for cattle and sheep. The profit of the 'said Forest' was only £19 per annum due to Stephen Vaughan who currently held the position of under forester. This grant according to the jury went back to a grant by letters patent in the reign of Henry VIII of which, however, there is no sign on the Patent Rolls.[34]

The lives of Stephen Vaughan and his immediate family, therefore, cast a somewhat different light on the sixteenth century than that focussed on the court and the nobility. Stephen himself seems in some ways a typical merchant intimately concerned with the nuts and bolts of doing business in a world which was becoming increasingly complicated and interconnected. He also, however, confounds in another way much of the stereotypical view of men of his level in society at this time. The eruption of prolonged and deeply felt discussions over the precise nature of Christian belief did not pass him by but affected his personal and family life. At the same time this family life was of great importance to him even though his many absences abroad made its enjoyment something of an occasional pleasure. The careers of his children also reveal the way in which the controversies and divisions in many areas of life at this time could divide families. The climate of debate and study behind these controversies also allowed the emergence of a culture where there were many more opportunities for an individual to carve out their own path. His children were able to make their own way in the world not tied to a family tradition.

When we turn to Vaughan's service to the Crown, it is clear that his work in Antwerp for Henry VIII is the most important aspect. The operations of the Bourse at Antwerp in its relatively brief heyday saw the beginnings of a truly international financial system with all that the meant for rulers and ruled. The glittering figures of the very wealthy Gresham clan and their confreres have perhaps obscured the work done by Vaughan and his friends and colleagues in establishing England as fully engaged in this system. During his last two years in Antwerp as the king's agent, Stephen raised a total of £272,821 15s in loans from foreign banks, principally that of the Fuggers of Augsburg. This total includes the value of jewels sold to the king (40,000 crowns), and also that of fustians (£30,000 Flemish) sold to the king which was part of a deal in which the king expected to sell them on at a profit. A further £27,000 came by letters of credit from Italian banking houses like that of the Bonvisi of Lucca which had branches in both London and Antwerp. At the time a crown was worth about 4s 4d and one pound Flemish was valued at about 15s sterling but these values varied considerably according to the political situation and the demand for funds on the Bourse. Repayments were covered by credits from the English Treasury with sureties provided by prominent London merchants such as the Gresham brothers and the Companies of the Staplers and the Merchant Adventurers.[35] In the circumstances of 1544–6 this was the result of much hard work and considerable achievement. Even more striking is the fact that when Vaughan left the Low Countries at the end of 1546 all the loans had been repaid except for those falling due in the following year; this included £20,000 Flemish from Erasmus Schetz and £80,000 Flemish from the Fuggers secured on a cargo of copper. These debts were paid in 1547 by Edward VI after the death of Henry VIII on 28 January of that year.[36] No other representative of the English Crown had ever successfully brought to a conclusion such a series of financial deals on the European money market.

The total sum borrowed was not enormous taking into account the overall cost of Henry's French war of 1543–6 being a little over 10 per cent of the final amount. This money, however, provided essential 'cash flow' in ready money. Wriothesley was not mistaken when he claimed in late 1545 that there was no cash available in all the various organs of the Henrician government to pay immediate expenses. Nor was Henry in denial when he also believed that England and its people had ample resources to support a war. The problem was that the royal government at that time had no effective way of quickly raising a large sum of money and was therefore forced to rely on various expedients, some more successful than others, to get around the problem of a lack of cash. Henry VII's treasure had been spent early in his son's reign largely on the king's first French war. The riches which came to the Crown from the dissolution of religious houses which had flowed into the Court of Augmentations had also been largely exhausted, being treated as income rather than hoarded as a possible royal 'endowment'. Every effort had also been made to increase the revenue from the sale of land, and to squeeze every last penny from royal rights like wardships and from fines of all kinds. Even the profits to the Crown from the debasement of the coinage had proved to be insufficient. Peter Cunich has estimated that the total cost of war and defence from 1534 to 1547 was £ 2,267,117, or 55 per cent of royal expenditure. Vaughan's activities on the Antwerp Bourse produced a mere 0.8 per cent of all expenditure by the Crown in the same period. Nevertheless the loans were essential in providing ready cash to cover the costs of keeping Henry's forces in the field. Most of this money was needed in 1544–5. Never before had there been such an expensive war. Between 1542 and 1545, among Henry's advisers, 'confidence quickly turned to desperation . . . as the crown registered disastrous deficits'. Vaughan's activities and his successful establishment of Henry's credit on the money market prevented the bankruptcy of the English Crown and enabled the war to continue.[37]

Under the young king Edward, attempts were made to continue to use the Bourse in Antwerp in the same way. Using loans from the Fuggers to alleviate immediate financial problems continued. The young king recorded in his journal in an entry for May 1551 that his council was having to make special arrangements to prolong a loan from the Fuggers including paying 100,000 crowns for 'a very faire jewel of his [the Fugger's] fower rubies marvellous big one orient and great diamount and one great pearl'. When editing the journal in the nineteenth century Nichols also added a note pointing out that in August 1552 Thomas Gresham had reminded the Duke of Northumberland in a letter how when 'the king's majesty's father dyd first beggyne to take up money upon interest Mr Stephen Vaugan being his agent a took the fee penny in merchandise eyther in jewels copper gunnepowder or fustians. And soe the matter hayth passid ever since taking of wares when the king's majesty made any prolongacyone'.[38]

William Damsell, Stephen's assistant and after his retirement his successor, was not, however, able to repeat Vaughan's successful management of this policy. One problem was that he received only minimal support from the Privy Council in London. There is some evidence that he was fatally undermined by a web of machinations and deceit spun by Thomas Gresham who coveted the post of royal agent on the Antwerp Bourse for himself. The good standing of the English king on the Antwerp Bourse so carefully nurtured by Vaughan, was then squandered by the results of the policies of the Duke of Somerset. The wars with both Scotland and France were renewed despite the worsening economic situation in England. The forced further debasement of the coinage, in particular the much-used testoon or shilling and a collapse in the cloth trade with the Low Countries, made it exceedingly difficult to raise any new loans for the Crown or to re-schedule old ones except at what were considered in London to be exorbitant interest rates. After Northumberland had taken over control of the council from Somerset in 1549, Gresham succeeded in his aim to discredit Damsell. Damsell had finally managed to roll over debts due to the Fuggers in March 1551 but only, as the king noted, on the condition of also buying a quantity of fustians and jewellery, the very type of transaction which Vaughan had earlier found should be avoided at all costs. This time Damsell had little alternative but to agree because of the hopeless state of royal finances. Gresham successfully managed to convince Northumberland that the poor deal was due to Damsell's 'slackness' rather than the activities of the royal government itself.[39] On 6 April Damsell was recalled from Antwerp and Gresham installed in his place. He was confident that he better than any other merchant could manage things differently devising, 'what way with least charge his majesty might grow out of debt'.[40]

It was certainly true that one of the achievements of Thomas Gresham, when he became Elizabeth's banker, was to ensure the end of the need for foreign loans. Guy suggests that Gresham's financial manoeuvring was successful not by the use of his expertise in the markets but by using the surpluses accumulated by William Cecil.[41] In his career as a whole, Gresham's manipulations of the market seem to mirror in some respects the activities of Gaspar Ducci, albeit on a larger scale. He acted of course on behalf of the English monarch rather than as an unreliable ally of that monarch's agent but was following the example set by his predecessor. Both Vaughan and Gresham served the Crown well at a time of financial difficulty but can it be argued that all their efforts on the Antwerp money market had little long-term significance? It was the case that Antwerp itself ceased to be the centre of European finance as a result of the changes in the political situation in the 1560s, including the stop of trade with England in 1569 culminating in the sack of Antwerp by the forces of the Duke of Alva in 1576. By the last years of Elizabeth's reign, Gresham had established his reputation as one of Elizabeth's most successful advisers and was revered for his financial acumen. He also became personally very wealthy in the process. Did Vaughan on the other hand, rise from obscurity only to die inconspicuously and to be soon forgotten as Richardson suggests?[42] This judgement gravely underestimates both the value of his personal service to his king and his country and the significance of his career. Personally he has often been treated somewhat dismissively by earlier writers. He has been accused of 'a lack of proportion and of a propensity for self-righteous ranting', at least as a young man by Diarmaid MacCulloch.[43] Richardson further characterized him as little more than a royal messenger, a 'practical business man unversed for the most part in the subtleties of the new Renaissance statecraft', loyal and hardworking but engaged only in 'tedious and unromantic' financial work. In his view, Vaughan's real importance, such as it was, was that 'he had advanced the interest of a nation of busy traders whose future position in world commerce was now assured'.

There is, however, more to be said of him as a royal servant than this assessment of his days as a diplomat and royal agent in Antwerp. It is clear from his career and that of many contemporaries just how important the mercantile element in English society was to the continued progress of the kingdom. Looking at English society in the reign of Henry VIII it appears that much of its dynamism came from those who were loosely classified as merchants. New ideas in secular, religious and also economic and commercial matters could be found at court but it is arguable to a much greater extent among the merchants. By his long residence in the Low Countries, principally in Antwerp, Vaughan was involved in the life of one of the most vibrant and intellectually active cities in Europe. He lived among wealthy men prepared to patronize some of the most skilled artists and craftsmen of the period. As well as the Bourse he knew and visited Antwerp's bookshops and printing houses whether seeking out books for Thomas Cromwell, or looking for them on his own account. He was involved with jewellers and artisans in many different trades in the most sophisticated market in Western Europe for luxuries of all kinds. The ferment of religious ideas in the city was something he was actively engaged in. His openness to the life of a city at the peak of its prosperity and cultural primacy is clear from casual asides in his business letters, from his reports on the Tyndale affair and even the personal commissions to find special luxuries in the markets in the city, with which he was so often entrusted by courtiers and others. He had many personal connections among the merchant elite of Antwerp and also in the court of the Regent and the emperor himself. Through negotiating as a diplomat he became familiar with court life and its elaborate etiquette but was not afraid to speak his mind to those like Granvelle the emperor's adviser or even the Regent herself. His business relationships in general seem to have been cordial with men like the bankers Haller and Schetz. That with Gaspar Ducci was at times somewhat fractious but survived its ups and downs until Vaughan left the city. As his client, Vaughan was close to someone who had one of the most splendid mansions in Antwerp decorated in the very latest Renaissance style in a way hardly to be found in London at this date. Ducci's house outside Antwerp reflected the latest developments in the layout and interior design of buildings of this type. Notably it contained two parlours, one small and one large, designed for the dinner parties which had become 'a central component of social and business life for Antwerp's prosperous business men'.[44] Vaughan certainly visited this mansion and was entertained there. Vaughan's letters also often mention that he has been visited or has received official guests while at dinner. This had become a common way of conducting important business. Many other Merchant Adventurers and Staplers who attended the marts in the Low Countries and who stayed in the English house in Antwerp or the Adventurers' base in Middelburg were equally open to the stimulating effects of the cultural life of the Low Countries as a whole and Antwerp in particular. We can see this effect, particularly in the considerable traffic in controversial religious texts between England and Antwerp's printing houses. Tyndale's works were not the only ones of great importance to English intellectual and religious culture which were first printed in the city. The striking portrait of Thomas Gresham dating from 1544 to 1545 by an unknown Netherlandish artist, probably painted in Antwerp, also testifies to the way English merchants enjoyed and were exposed to a sophisticated cultural environment in the city.

Apart from these cultural contacts, in the increasingly important world of interstate relations, English envoys at this date were also frequently engaged in negotiations which had a commercial aspect. Success depended on employing envoys, ambassadors or commissioners with mercantile experience in discussions of this nature. Because the focus of English trade as a whole was on both exports and imports to or from the Low Countries, there were frequent negotiations of this kind as we have seen, either with the court of the Regent of the Netherlands or with the emperor himself. A particular bone of contention was incidents related to attacks on seaborne trade in the Channel by either English ships or those from other coastal states. They led to a great deal of argument and litigation about the rights and wrongs of each case and the compensation which might or might not be due. The case of Ducci and his cargo of herrings taken by English mariners off a French ship in time of war is only one example. Was this cargo the property of a subject of the emperor or were the goods 'coloured' by some French merchant using Ducci's name? Ducci was prepared to spend a great deal of time and effort demanding his 'rights' even when involved in issues of national importance for both Henry VIII and the emperor. Such cases could not be progressed without men from a mercantile background involved as advisers. Similarly negotiations regarding the commercial clauses of treaties were also common, leading to disputes about the conditions of trade-like liability to tolls, for example. Vaughan often acted for the Crown in matters of this nature. In these circumstances his commercial experience was essential. This was something that Vaughan shared with colleagues like John Hutton, John Hackett and Thomas Chamberlain, all Merchant Adventurers who also worked for the Crown. A considerable part of the work of the governors of the Company of Merchant Adventurers based in the Low Countries was concerned with acting in disputes of this kind for individuals as well as on behalf of the Crown. Only the collapse of the wool and cloth trade in the later sixteenth century reduced the importance of the employment of merchant ambassadors.

For himself Vaughan's devoted service to the Crown was not perhaps rewarded as lavishly as that of some others but his record and that of many of his colleagues exemplify the extent to which Henry VIII relied on men like him to carry out his policies and ensure the good governance of the realm. His career as a whole also makes clear that until the collapse of the cloth trade to the Low Countries and the end of the glory days of the Antwerp Bourse the continuing importance of these trade routes is often overlooked. It is very easy to discount the importance of the 'old' trade routes in favour of the opportunities which opened up in the reign of Elizabeth I and later. Vaughan was involved in the development of new ways in the money market but dealt in goods in the ways common to his predecessors from at least the fourteenth century. In some ways his career formed a bridge between the old ways and new developments in European commercial society. Far from being a mere functionary Stephen and his colleagues, both as individuals and in their service to the Crown, helped to lay the foundations of the mercantile world of the late sixteenth century and the rise of England as a trading power.

Notes

Introduction

1. The only previous discussion of his life is in W. C. Richardson, (1953), *Stephen Vaughan, Financial Agent of Henry VIII: A Study of Financial Relations with the Low Counties*, Baton Rouge: Louisiana State University Press. He is mentioned briefly in, for example, Diarmaid MacCulloch 2018 *Thomas Cromwell: A Life*, London: Allen Lane and John Guy's (2019), *Gresham's Law: The Life and World of Queen Elizabeth's Banker*, London: Profile Books.
2. These letters are to be found in TNA State Papers vols. They are calendared in *Letters and Papers of the Reign of Henry VIII*.
3. Quoted from C. G. A. Clay, (1984), *Economic Expansion and Social Change; England 1500–1700, II Industry Trade and Commerce* in Thomas Leng, (2020), *The Merchant Adventurers and the Restructuring of English Commerce 1582–1700*, Oxford: Oxford University Press, 2.
4. Heather Dalton, (2016), *Merchants and Explorers: Roger Barlow, Sebastian Cabot and Networks of Atlantic Exchange 1500–1560*, Oxford: Oxford University Press.
5. Felicity Stout, (2015), *Exploring Russia in the Elizabethan Commonwealth: The Muscovy Company and Giles Fletcher the Elder, (1546–1611)*, Manchester: Manchester University Press.

Chapter 1

1. D. J. Keene and Vanessa Harding, (1987), *Historical Gazetteer of London Before the Great Fire Cheapside; Parishes of All Hallows Honey Lane, St Martin Pomary, St Mary Le Bow, St Mary Colechurch and St Pancras Soper Lane*, London, The family had interests in a property called The Three Legs near the site of 33 Cheapside, off the main thoroughfare.
2. In his will he was said to be forty-nine at the very end of 1549.
3. ODNB entry for Stephen Vaughan.
4. There are no entries for the name of Vaughan in the city of London records for the fifteenth century.
5. https://archives.library.wales/index.php/lewis-family-of-harpton-court. The Welsh archives have estate papers for the property beginning in 1541.

6 Evan T. Jones and Margaret M. Condon, (2016), *Cabot and Bristol's Age of Discovery; The Bristol Voyages 1480–1508*, Bristol: University of Bristol.
7 S. McShaffrey and N. Turner, (2003), *Lollards of Coventry 1486–1515*, Cambridge: Cambridge University Press.
8 Eamon Duffy, (1992), *The Stripping of the Altars Traditional Religion in England 1400–1580*, New Haven: Yale University Press, 77.
9 Stephen Alford, (2017), *London' Triumph: Merchant Adventurers and the Tudor City*, London: Allen Lane, 4–11.
10 Caroline Barron, (2000), 'London 1300–1540', in D. Palliser ed., *The Cambridge Urban History, Vol. I*, Cambridge: Cambridge University Press, 435.
11 http://www.panoramaofthethames.com/pott/wyngaerde-pan/wyngaerde-1543
12 Alford, *London' Triumph*, 13.
13 Barron, 'London 1300–1540', 398.
14 William Dunbar, (1900), 'In Honour of the City of London', in Sir A. Quiller-Couch ed., *The Oxford Book of English Verse*, Oxford: Clarendon Press, 26–30.
15 This was the route most often used by one of the Cely brothers, merchants of the Staple, when en route to Calais.
16 Alison Hanham, (1985), *The Celys and their World: An English merchant Family of the Fifteenth Century*, Cambridge: Cambridge University Press, 187–980.
17 Ian Blanchard, (2009), *The International Economy in the Age of the Discoveries: Antwerp and the English Merchants' World*, Stuttgart: Franz Steiner Verlag, 79–84.
18 Richard Ehrenberg, (1963), *Capital and Finance in the Age of the Renaissance: A Study of the Fuggers and Their Connections*, New York: Kelley, 196–201.
19 Caroline M. Barron, (2005), *London in the Later Middle Ages: Government and People 1200–1500*, Oxford: Oxford University Press. Appendix 1, The Mayors and Sheriffs of London, 342–51.
20 Anne F. Sutton, (2005), *The Mercery of London: Trade, Goods and People 1130–1578*, Aldershot: Ashgate, 182.
21 Quoted from BL Cotton MSS Otho E X, f.45 in John Guy, (2019), *Gresham's Law: The Life and World of Queen Elizabeth I's Banker*, London: Profile Books, 142.
22 Barron, *London in the Later Middle Ages*, 150.
23 Sutton, *The Mercery of London: Trade, Goods and People 1130–1578*, 476.
24 Barron, *London in the Later Middle Ages: Government and People 1200–1500*, 10, 13, 18–22.
25 The medieval wool trade is discussed in some detail in Susan Rose, (2018), *The Wealth of England: The Medieval Wool Trade and Its Political Importance 1100–1600*, Oxford: Oxbow Discussion of the Company of the Staple in the fifteenth century will be found in Chapter 9, 145–56.
26 Rose, *The Wealth of England*, 123. By 1536 there were only forty Staplers.

27 E. M. Carus-Wilson and O. Coleman, (1963), *England's Export Trade 1275–1547*, Oxford: Clarendon Press, 196.
28 Anne F. Sutton, (2002), 'The Merchant Adventurers of England: Their Origins and the Mercer's Company of London', *Historical Research* 75.3, 27.
29 Sutton, 'The Merchant Adventurers of England', 46. A full discussion of the history of the Mercers' Company and their links with the Adventurers will also be found in Sutton, *The Mercery of London,* The earliest grants of privileges to the Merchant Adventurers can be found in Anne E Sutton and Livia Visser-Fuchs, (2009), *The Book of Privileges of the Merchant Adventurers of England 1296–1483*, Oxford: Oxford University press for the British Academy.
30 Sutton, *The Mercery of London.*

Chapter 2

1 Quoted in Blanchard, *The International Economy in the Age of Discoveries, 1470–1570*, 99.
2 Dr Giles ed., (1865), *The Whole Works of Roger Ascham*, vol. I part II, London, 212. 'Dii Boni! Non Brabantiae, sed totius mundi ditissimum emporium. Splendida magnificaque structura sic emeinet ut eo modo superet reliquae omnes urbes quas ego vidi'.
3 Michel Limberger, (2001), 'No Town in the World Provides More Advantages; Economies of Agglomeration and the Golden Age of Antwerp', in Patrick O'Brien et al. eds, *Urban Achievement in Early Modern Europe: Golden Ages in Antwerp, Amsterdam and London*, Cambridge: Cambridge University Press, 42–3.
4 Figures recorded in the Introduction of the catalogue of the exhibition held in 1973–5 *Antwerp's Golden Age; the Metropolis of the West in the Sixteenth and Seventeenth Centuries*, 17.
5 S. T. Bindoff, (1945), *The Scheldt Question,* London: Allen and Unwin, 34, 64, map 96.
6 Peter Spufford, (2002), *Power and Profit; the Merchant in Medieval Europe*, London: Thames and Hudson, 389–95. A map on 352 shows these routes.
7 Spufford, *Power and Profit; The Merchant in Medieval Europe*, 208.
8 Herman vander Linden, (1914), 'Le voyage de P. Tafur en Brabant, en Flandre et en Artois, (1438)', in *Revue du Nord*, 5 1914.19, 216–31.
9 Piet Lombarde, (2001), Antwerp in its Golden Age, 'one of the largest cities in the Low Countries' and 'one of the best fortified in Europe', in *Urban Achievement in early Modern Europe: Golden Ages in Antwerp, Amsterdam and London*, 107–8, 120–1.
10 A quotation from an article by J. H. A. Munro cited in J. L. Bolton and F. G. Bruscoli, (2008), 'When Did Antwerp Replace Bruges as the Commercial and

Financial Centre of North-Western Europe? The Evidence of the Borromei Ledge for 1438', in *Ec. H. R.* 61.2, 360–79.

11 Ehrenberg, *Capital and Finance in the Age of the Renaissance*, 236.

12 Bolton and Bruscoli, 'When did Antwerp Replace Bruges as the Commercial and Financial Centre of North-Western Europe? The Evidence of the Borromei Ledge for 1438', 360–79.

13 J.-A. van Houtte, (1940), 'La Genèse du grand marché international d'Anvers à la fin du Moyen-Age', in *Revue belge de philosophie et d' histoire*, 19, 115.

14 Ian Blanchard, (1996), 'Credit and Commerce: From the Mediterranean to the Atlantic in the Sixteenth Century', in H. Diederiks and D. Reeder, eds., *Cities of Finance*, Oxford, 21–34.

15 Letter 241, 242–4 in Hanham, *The Cely Letters 1472-88*.

16 Bolton and Bruscoli, 'When did Antwerp Replace Bruges as the Commercial and Financial Centre of North-Western Europe? The Evidence of the Borromei Ledge for 1438', 372.

17 Linden, 'Le voyage de P. Tafur en Brabant, en Flandre et en Artois, (1438)', 216–31.

18 Kathedraalarchief, Antwerp. Archives of the fabric of the cathedral of Our Lady, Antwerp; Originele Rekeningen de annis 1431–1560; registers 7–15. Dan Ewing, (1990), 'Marketing Art in Antwerp. 1460–1560: Our Lady's *Pand*', in *The Art Bulletin*, 72.4, 558–84.

19 Lorne Campbell, (1976), 'The Art Market in the Southern Netherlands in the Fifteenth Century', in *The Burlington Magazine*, 118, 188–98.

20 Ewing, 'Marketing Art in Antwerp. 1460–1560: Our Lady's *Pand*', 563.

21 Ewing, 'Marketing Art in Antwerp. 1460–1560: Our Lady's *Pand*', 567.

22 The picture is now in the ownership of the Mercers' Company.

23 Werner Waterschoot, (2001), 'Antwerp: Book, Publishing and Cultural Production before 1585', in P. O' Brien et al. eds, *Urban Achievement in Early Modern Europe: Golden Ages in Antwerp, Amsterdam and London* Cambridge: CUP, 233–40.

24 Thomas More, (1972), *Utopia,* trans. Paul Turner, London: Folio Society, 37–8.

25 L. Guicciardini, (1521–1589, 1593), *The Description of the Low countreys and of the prouinces thereof, gathered into an epitome out of the historie of Lodouico Guicchardini*, London: By Peter Short for Thomas Chard (no page numbers).

26 Raymond de Roover, (1967), *San Bernardino of Siena and Sant' Antonino of Florence: Two Great Economic Thinkers of the Middle Ages*, Boston: Harvard Business School, 33–8.

27 Blanchard, *The International Economy in the 'Age of Discoveries' 1470–1570*, 19.

28 Raymond de Roover (1953), 'Anvers comme Marché Monétaire au xvi siècle', in *Revue Belge de Philologie et d' Histoire*, 31-4, 1010.

29 Quoted in Limberger, 'No Town in the World Provides More Advantages', 59.

Chapter 3

1. Blanchard, *The International Economy in the 'Age of Discoveries' 1470–1570*, 11–15.
2. Blanchard, *The International Economy in the 'Age of Discoveries' 1470–1570*, 19.
3. Florence Edler, (1938), 'The van der Molen, Commission Merchants of Antwerp: Trade with Italy 1538 44', in *Medieval and Historiographical Essay in Honor of James Westfall Thompson*, 84, 86–9, 100, 103, 107, 117. The originals of the letters can be found in Antwerp Municipal Archives. Insolvente Boedelskamer 2030, Pieter van der Molen Brievenkopij 1538–44.
4. Ehrenberg, *Capital and Finance in the Age of the Renaissance*, 240–1.
5. The question of the influence of bribes on the election of Charles V is fully discussed in Henry J. Cohn, (2001), 'Did Bribes Induce the German Electors to Choose Charles V as Emperor in 1519?' in *German History* 19.1, 1–27.
6. Herman van der Wee and Ian Blanchard, (1992), 'The Hapsburgs and the Antwerp Money Market: The Exchange Crises of 1521 and 122–3', in Ian Blanchard et al. eds, *Industry and Finance in Early Modern History*, Stuttgart: Franz Steiner, 27–57 at 31, 40–1 (tables of interest rates).
7. A full discussion of the operation of the money market in Antwerp including details of the changes in interest rates can be found in Herman van der Wee and Ian Blanchard, (1992), 'The Hapsburgs and the Antwerp Money Market: The Exchange Crises of 1521 and 1522–3', 27–57 and in Blanchard, *The International Economy in the Age of Discoveries' 1470–1570*, 19–44.
8. de Roover, 'Anvers comme Marché Monétaire au XVI Siècle', 1003–47, at 1027, 1035.
9. G. L. Harriss, (1988), *Cardinal Beaufort: A Study of Lancastrian Ascendancy and Decline*, Oxford: Clarendon Press, 406, 411–13.
10. The most elaborate arrangement was the deal between the Crown and the company of the Staple made in 1466 whereby the Company took financial responsibility for the defence of Calais in return for the reimbursement of outstanding loans from the Customs revenue to the tune of £3,000 per annum. Rose, *The Wealth of England*, 152.
11. G. L. Harriss, (1963), 'Aids, Loans and Benevolences', in *The Historical Journal*, VI.1, 17.
12. Mark R. Horowitz, (2009), 'Henry Tudor's Treasure', in *Historical Research*, 82, 577.
13. Horowitz, 'Henry Tudor's Treasure', 560.
14. Mark R. Horowitz, (2009), 'Policy and Prosecution on the Reign of Henry VII', in *Historical Research*, 82, 457.
15. A. H. Thomas and I. D. Thornley eds, 1938), *The Great Chronicle of London*, London: George W. Jones, 274–5.
16. TNA E36/14, 232; E34/2, 87.
17. Hannes Kleineke, (2003), 'Morton's Fork?- Henry VII's "Forced Loan" of 1496', in L. Visser-Fuchs ed., *Tant d'emprises; the Ricardian XIII; Essays in Honour of Anne F. Sutton*, Richard III Society, 315–27.
18. Thomas and Thornley, eds., *The Great Chronicle of London*, 348.

19 Horowitz, 'Henry Tudor's Treasure', 560–579 at 578.
20 *Letters and Papers, Foreign and Domestic, Henry VIII, Volume 2, 1515–1518*, ed. J. S. Brewer, London, 1864 Item 1475. Hereinafter cited as L & P. followed by the volume number and the item number.
21 L & P 2, 1816.
22 L & P 3 1021.
23 L & P 4, 1721 and 1722.
24 J. W. Burgon, (1839), *The Life and Times of Sir Thomas Gresham*, London: Robert Jennings, I, 31–3. And Richard Gresham ODNB. His son Sir Thomas Gresham was finally able to set up the Royal Exchange to provide this much desired facility for merchants in the late 1560s with building being completed in 1567.
25 Elizabeth Frances Rogers, (1971), *The Letters of Sir John Hackett 1526–1534*, Morgantown: West Virginia University Library, 7 letter 6.
26 Elizabeth Frances Rogers, (1971), *The Letters of Sir John Hackett 1526–1534*, 9, letter 7 Robert Wingfield to Wolsey.
27 Sutton, *The Mercery of London*, 419.
28 Elizabeth Frances Rogers, (1971), *The Letters of Sir John Hackett 1526–1534*, 28, letter 12 John Hackett to Wolsey.
29 Elizabeth Frances Rogers, (1971), *The Letters of Sir John Hackett 1526–1534*, 27, letter 14, Hackett to Brian Tuke.
30 Elizabeth Frances Rogers, (1971), *The Letters of Sir John Hackett 1526–1534*, 43, letter 23, Hackett to Wolsey.
31 Elizabeth Frances Rogers, (1971), *The Letters of Sir John Hackett 1526–1534*, 80, letter 36, Hackett to Wolsey.
32 Elizabeth Frances Rogers, (1971), *The Letters of Sir John Hackett 1526–1534*, 351, letter 168, Hackett to Cromwell.

Chapter 4

1 Vanessa Harding, (2012), 'Houses and Households in Cheapside c. 1500–1550', in M. Davies and J. A. Galloway eds, *London and Beyond: Essays in Honour of Derek Keene*, London: Institute of Historical Research, 134–54.
2 Harding, 'Houses and Households in Cheapside c.1500–1550', 135–54.
3 He is recorded in Michael McDonnell, (1977), *The Registers of St Paul's School 1509–1748* but the entry states only 'may possibly have been educated at St Paul's School'.
4 Michael McDonell, (1909), *History of St Paul's School,* London: Chapman and Hall, 40.
5 The tutor he found for his children, a Mr Cobbe taught them both Latin and Greek.
6 TNA SP1/53 f.176. L & P 4. Item.
7 L & P 3 5429.

8 The cases concerned are TNA C1/ 587/41 and 587/15; C1/553/35 Richard's insolvency; C1/689/39 breach of covenant. Unfortunately some of the details of the deal are obscure because the documents are illegible.
9 Thomas Leng, (2020), *Fellowship and Freedom: The Merchant Adventurers and the Restructuring of English Commerce 1582-1700*, Oxford: Oxford University Press, 118.
10 John Johnson a wool merchant never recovered his previous prosperity after being declared bankrupt. Barbara Winchester, (1955), *Tudor Family Portrait*, London: Jonathan Cape, 294-318.
11 Matthew Davies and Ann Saunders, (2004), *The History of the Merchant Taylors' Company*, London: Maney, 270.
12 Edward Salisbury, (1897-8), 'List of Liverymen and Freemen of the City Companies A.D. 1538', in *Middlesex and Hertfordshire Notes and Queries*, 3-4, 81-2.
13 Kent History and Library Centre U1384/E10.
14 'Memorial XIII: Inventory of Effects 1512', in C. M. Clode, ed., *Memorials of the Guild of Merchant Taylors of the Fraternity of St John the Baptist in the City of London*, London, 1875, 84-92. The kind of embroidery used was that done by silk-women like Vaughan's first wife.
15 *Memorials of the Guild of Merchant Taylors of the Fraternity of St. John the Baptist in the City of London*, C. M. Clode, ed., London, 1875, memorial XXVIII the burial of a deceased brother.
16 Davies and Saunders, *The History of the Merchant Taylors' Company*, 270.
17 TNA CP 40/1038, MacCulloch, *Thomas Cromwell*, 27.
18 LP4/ii 5034, MacCulloch, *Thomas Cromwell*, 35.
19 Diarmaid MacCulloch, (2018), *Thomas Cromwell, a Life*, London: Allen Lane, 65.
20 MacCulloch, *Thomas Cromwell, a Life*, 121.
21 MacCulloch, *Thomas Cromwell, a Life*, 72.
22 SP1/141,ff 126-7, L & P v 221. When Miles Coverdale returned from exile in Germany on the accession of Edward VI, one of the first sermons he preached was at a festival for the Merchant Taylors at St Martin Outwich, perhaps with Stephen Vaughan present. ODNB Miles Coverdale.
23 Susan Brigden, (1989), *London and the Reformation*, Oxford: Clarendon Press, 106-19 and 'Thomas Cromwell and the Brethren', in M. Claire Cross et al. eds (1988), *Law and Government under the Tudors,* Cambridge: Cambridge University Press, 31-49.
24 ODNB Ralph Sadler.
25 L & P iv 5772.
26 Merriman I. letter 1.
27 TNA PROB 11/21/398.
28 Heather Dalton, (2009), 'Negotiating Fortune: English Merchants in Early Sixteenth Century Spain', in Caroline Williams et al. eds, *Bridging the Early Modern Atlantic World: People, Products and Practices on the Move*, Aldershot: Ashgate, 57-74.

29 TNA C1/484/37.
30 Philip John Ward, (1999), 'The Origins of Thomas Cromwell's Public Career: Service under Cardinal Wolsey and Henry VIII 1524–30', PhD London, 36–42.
31 *A History of the County of Kent*, ii, VCH Kent 1926, 165–7.
32 Item 5115. 'Henry VIII: December 1528, 26–31', in J. S. Brewer, ed. *Letters and Papers, Foreign and Domestic, Henry VIII, Volume 4, 1524–1530*, London, 1875, 2208–54. *British History Online* http://www.british-history.ac.uk/letters-papers-hen8/vol4/pp2208-2254 [accessed 19 October 2020]. Misdated 1528; in fact from 1526.
33 TNA SP1/52/40. Quoted in Ward, 'The Origins of Thomas Cromwell's Public Career: Service under Cardinal Wolsey and Henry VIII 1524–30', 90.
34 TNA E36/165. L & P iv 2217/1.
35 Ward, 'The Origins of Thomas Cromwell's Public Career: Service under Cardinal Wolsey and Henry VIII 1524–30', 132.
36 TNA SP1/235/67. L & P ADD. i 488.
37 L & P iv 5398 dated 23 March 1529.
38 L & P iv 4107 dated 28 March 1528.
39 For example in L & P iv 5787.
40 L & P iv 3674 dated 19 December 1527.
41 L & P iv 4613; Also printed in Ellis ser.2 vol. 2 141.
42 L & P iv 5034.
43 L & P iv 4884 dated 29 October 1528.
44 The position of Cromwell in relation to the fall of Wolsey and the king's Great Matter from late 1528 to the early months of 1530 are discussed in MacCulloch, *Thomas Cromwell*, 87–103.
45 L & P iv 5772.
46 L & P iv 5823.
47 Sutton, *The Mercery of London*, 347–8.
48 L & P iv 1529.
49 L & P iv 6036; also Ellis series 2 vol. 3, 171.
50 L & P iv 6196.
51 L & P iv 6429.
52 L & P iv 6744.
53 L & P iv 6487.
54 E. F. Rogers, (1971), *The Letters of John Hackett 1526–1534*, Morgantown: West Virginia University Press, letter 23, 41–3.
55 ODNB William Tyndale; http;//DOI.ORG/10.1093/REF:ODNB/27947. Diarmaid McCulloch, *Thomas Cromwell, a Life*, 110.
56 McCulloch, *Thomas Cromwell, a Life*, 135–7.
57 L & P iv 6754.
58 L & P v 65; Cotton Galba B/X f.46.
59 L & P v 201.

60 L & P v 153.
61 L & P v 248.
62 MacCulloch, *Thomas Cromwell, a Life*, 151–3.
63 L & P v 247.
64 L & P v 246.
65 L & P v 303.
66 L & P v 1260 item 20.
67 Richardson, *Stephen Vaughan, Financial Agent of Henry VIII*, 14.
68 L & P v 533,542.
69 ODNB George Constantine.
70 L & P v 574.
71 L & P v 618.
72 Keene and Harding, 'St Mary le Bow 104/32', in *Historical gazeteer of London before the Great Fire Cheapside: Parishes of All Hallows Honey lane, St Mary Pomary, St Mary le Bow St Mary Colechurch and St Pancras Soper Lane*, 356.
73 L & P vi 559 30 May 1533.
74 L & P vi 917 30 July 1533.
75 L & P x 914 1537.
76 L & P x 914 1537.
77 Will of Stephen Vaughan, TNA PROB 11/33/117.
78 Gwynneth [Gwynedd] also Guinet, John, ODNB.
79 A. à Wood ed. P. Bliss, *Fasti Oxoniensis or Annals of the University of Oxford part 1 1500–1640*, London 1815, 86.
80 Gwynneth [Gwynedd] also Guinet, John, ODNB.
81 L & P xx pt I 250 February 1545.
82 Thomas Lodge, ODNB.

Chapter 5

1 Chapuys's career and his informative reports to the emperor are examined in detail in Lauren Mackay, (2015), *Inside The Tudor Court; Henry VIII and His Six Wives through the Eyes of the Spanish Ambassador*, Stroud: Amberley.
2 Luke MacMahon, (1999), 'The Personnel of English Diplomacy c.1500–c.1550', PhD U. of Kent Canterbury, 63–5.
3 L & P XIV I 209 Wriothesley to Cromwell 2 February 1538.
4 MacMahon, 'The Personnel of English Diplomacy c.1500–c.1550', 151.
5 Betty Behrens, (1933), 'The Office of the English Resident Ambassador: Its Evolution as Illustrated by the Career of Sir Thomas Spinelly 1509–1522' in *TRHS* 16, 161–95.

6 BL Cotton MSS Galba B VII 263 L & P III 2833 Sir Robert Wingfield to Wolsey February 1522. All the surviving letters either by or to Hackett are printed in E. F. Rogers ed., (1971), *The Letters of Sir John Hackett 1526–1534*, Morgantown: West Virginia University Library.
7 BL Cotton MSS Galba B VII I69. L & P III 3366. Dr William Knight to Wolsey 28 September 1523.
8 BL Cotton MSS Galba B IX 39. L & P IV 2569 Hackett to Wolsey.
9 BL Cotton MSS Galba B X 46 L & P V 65.
10 L & P VI 313, Sir Thomas Elyot to Hackett.
11 I have had news which doesn't seem good to me.
12 L & P VI 371 To the Duke of Norfolk.
13 L & P VI 372 To Cromwell.
14 L & P IV 2628.
15 Letter to Wolsey 15th November 1526 L & P IV 2628.
16 L & P IV 141.
17 BL Cotton MS Galba B X 26 Vaughan to Cromwell.
18 BL Cotton MSS Galba B X 3 Vaughan to Cromwell; Hackett Letters 304–5.
19 Hackett Letters 305.
20 BL Cottom MSS Galba B X 37v.Hackett Letters 306.
21 L & P V 946 Hackett Letters 307–12.
22 Blanchard, *The International Economy in the Age of Discoveries, 1470–1570*, 214–15. Blanchard attributes the difficulties in the cloth trade at this date to enhanced transaction costs in the Netherlands and the competitive advantage of English 'light' draperies that is, mainly kerseys.
23 L & P V 870. This phrase was used at the time to mean something on the lines of cutting off your nose to spite your face. It was used by Cranmer in his *Answer to Fifteen Articles of the Rebels Devon Anno 1549*.
24 M. L. Robertson, (1975), 'Thomas Cromwell's Servants: The Ministerial Household in early Tudor Government and Society', PhD, University of California Los Angeles, 325.
25 L & P V 129 She was created a Marquis in her own right and thus did not use the consort's title of Marchioness.
26 L & P V 1602; wrongly stated to be from Wriothesley in L & P.
27 L & P V 1609.
28 MacCulloch, *Thomas Cromwell*, 209.
29 L & P V1609.
30 L & P v 1620.
31 Elizabeth I was born in early September 1533.
32 A letter to Cromwell dated 3 May 1533 details the tracking of individuals who seem to be involved in some sort of conspiracy, probably against the royal marriage, from Daventry to Coventry. L & P vi 434.

33 ODNB Christopher Mont.
34 L & P vi 917 and 934.
35 L & P vi 1082.
36 L & P vi 1150.
37 State Papers 1/79 f.64.
38 L & P vi 1324.
39 MacCulloch, *Thomas Cromwell*, 212–13.
40 L & P VI 1385.
41 L L & P Vi 1448.
42 Hackett, Letter 169, 27 January 1534.
43 Hackett, Letter 178, 31 March 1534.
44 Hackett will item 182 dated 26 October 1534.
45 Hackett Letters, 183, Jean Carondelet to Lord Lisle Valenciennes 27 October 1534.
46 Hackett Letters, 185 Thomas Leigh to Stephen Vaughan Antwerp 6 November 1534.
47 L & P vi 1534 7 December 1533.
48 R. Merriman Letters of Thomas Cromwell vol. ii letter 177; in L & P x 377.
49 L & P vi 302.
50 R. Merriman Letters of Thomas Cromwell vol. ii letter 178; in L & P x 378.
51 L & P vi 418.
52 L & P vi 300.
53 L & P vi 275.
54 Cal. S. P Spain 5 i 75.
55 Cal. S. P. Spain 5 ii 3. Dated 9 January.
56 L & P ix 309.
57 L & P ix 341.
58 L & P ix 663.
59 L & P ix 929.
60 L & P xii pt1 1092.
61 L & P xii pt1 310.
62 L & P xii pt1 745.
63 L & P xii pt1 133.
64 L & P xii pt1 332.
65 Gwynneth (Gwynedd) John ODNB.
66 L & P xii pt1 301.
67 MacCulloch, *Thomas Cromwell*, 446.
68 L & P xiii pt. 2 286.
69 L & P xii pt. 1 1061.
70 L & P xiii pt. 2 513, 286 (2), 512, 513.
71 L & P xiii pt. 2 506.
72 SP1/137 f.118.

73 Wriothesley and Vaughan had received letters from the English envoys at the French court informing them of this.
74 L & P xiii pt 2 581.
75 L & P xiii pt. 2 747.
76 L & P xiii pt. 1 690.
77 SP1/139 f.126.
78 L & P xiii pt.1 635 636.
79 *History of Parliament: The House of Commons 1509–1558*, (1982), S. T. Bindoff ed., Woodbridge: Boydell and Brewer Heading, Carne, Sir Edward (1495–1561) of Ewenyy, Glamorgan.
80 L & P xiii pt. 1 882.
81 L & P xiii pt 1 880.
82 L & P xiii pt 1 924.
83 L & P xiv pt1 6.
84 L & P xiv pt1 7.
85 L & P xiv pt 1 335.
86 L & P xiv pt 1 265.
87 L& P xiv pt 1 286.
88 L & P xiv pt 1 529 dated 16 March 1539.
89 Mackay, *Inside the Tudor Court*, 282–3.
90 Thomas Wriothesley, biography in S. T. Bindoff, (1982), *The History of Parliament: The House of Commons 1509–1558*.
91 Under entry 'Vaughan', the Visitation of London begun in 1678 parts 1–2, London Harleian Society new series vols. 16–17.
92 L & P xiv pt 1 1306.
93 L & P xiv pt 1 1216.
94 MacCulloch, *Thomas Cromwell*, 508, 512.
95 L & P xiv pt 2 541.
96 L & P xiv pt 2 356.
97 L & P xiv pt 2 553.
98 L & P xiv pt 2 591.
99 L & P xiv pt 2 634.
100 L & P xiv pt 2 634.
101 L & P xv 68.

Chapter 6

1 Statutes of the Realm vol. 3. 32 Hen viii *c*. 16, 765–6.
2 L & P xvi 906.

3   L & P xvi 910 dated 18 June.
4   Quoted in Mackay, *Inside the Tudor Court*, 304 from Hof und Staats archiv England Diplomatische Korrespndenz Karton 11.
5   L & P xvi 962 dated 3 July.
6   David Potter, (1995), 'Foreign Policy', in Diarmaid MacCulloch ed., *The Reign of Henry VIII: Politics, Policy and Piety,* Basingstoke: Macmillan, 120-4.
7   L & P xvi 962 dated 3 July.
8   L & P xvi 979, 1013.
9   L & P xvi 1064.
10 L & P xvi 1095; a council report to Henry VIII dated 14 August.
11 L & P xvi 1109; dated 22 August.
12 L & P xvi 1110.
13 L & P xvii 292.
14 L & P xvii 293.
15 L & P xviii pt 1 259.
16 L & P xvii Grants in November 1542 item 50.
17 Potter, 'Foreign Policy', 118-23.
18 Richard Hoyle, (1995), 'War and Public Finance', in Diarmaid MacCulloch ed., *The Reign of Henry VIII: Politics Policy and Piety,* Basingstoke: Macmillan, 90-7. Tables of total taxation and of the costs of warfare are on 90 and 93.
19 L & P xix pt1 271.
20 L & P xix pt1 188.
21 L & P xix pt 1 215.
22 L & P xix pt 1 208.
23 L & P xix pt 1 245, 246.
24 L & P xix pt 1 347.
25 L & P xix pt 1 279,280,282. 287.
26 L & P xix pt 1 347.
27 L & P xix pt.1 item 380 22 April.
28 L & P xix pt 1 item 83 in grants in May.
29 L & P xix pt 1 457.
30 L & P xix pt 1 667.
31 L & P xix pt1 752.
32 L & P xix pt1 695, 703.
33 David Potter, (2011), *Henry VIII and Francis I: The Final Conflict 1540-44*, Leiden: Brill, 313-15.
34 Ehrenberg, *Capital and Finance in the Age of the Renaissance*, 225-6.
35 Enrico Stumpo, (1992), *Biographical Dictionary of Italians,* 41, item Ducci, Gaspare.
36 Richardson, *Stephen Vaughan, Financial Agent of Henry VIII,* 52.
37 L & P xix pt1 578.
38 L & P xix pt1 630.

39 L & P xix pt1 725.
40 L & P xix pt1 759.
41 L & P xix pt1 822.
42 L & P xix pt1 836.
43 L & P xix pt1 887.
44 W. C. Richardson, (1954) 'Some Financial Expedients of Henry VIII', in *EHR* 7.1, 39–43. This article cover the matter in some detail.
45 L & P xix pt1 958.
46 L & P xix pt1 911.
47 L & P xix pt1 972.
48 L & P xix pt1 988.
49 L & P xix pt2 13.
50 L & P xix pt1 1018.
51 L & P xix pt2 31.
52 L & P xix pt2 66, 108, 169.
53 L & P xix pt2 171,178.
54 L & P xix pt2 178,220, 266.
55 L& P xix pt2 287.
56 L & P xix pt2 266.
57 L & P xix pt2 308.
58 L & P xix pt2 615.
59 L & P xix pt 2 733, 764. The whole issue regarding the sale of the king's lead is discussed in W. C. Richardson, (1954), 'Some Financial Expedients of Henry VIII', in *EHR New Series* 7.1, 21–34.
60 L & P xix pt2 723.
61 L & P xix pt2 724, 733.
62 L & P xix pt2 781.
63 L & P xix pt2 765.
64 L & P xx pt1 26.
65 G. J. Millar, (1980), *Tudor Mercenaries*, Charlottesvile: University of Virginia Press, 116–24.
66 Malcolm Vale, (2007), *The Ancient Enemy: England France and Europe from the Angevins to the Tudors,* London: Hambledon Continuum, 134.
67 Potter, 'Foreign Policy', 132.

Chapter 7

1 L & P xx pt 1 13.
2 L & P xx pt 1 27.

3   L & P xx pt1 30, 31.
4   L & P xx pt 1 32.
5   L & P xx pt 1 41.
6   L & P xx pt1 42.
7   L & P xx pt 1 65.
8   L & P xx pt 1 107. State Papers King Henry VIII v. 10 part V Foreign Correspondence MXCVII p 262, London: 1830–52.
9   L & P xx pt 1 96.
10 L & Pxx pt 1 144, 108.
11 L & P xx pt 1 164.
12 L & P xx pt 1 150.
13 L & P xx pt 1 171.
14 L & P xx pt 1 241.
15 L & P xx pt 1 xx4.
16 L & P xx pt 1 242.
17 L & P xx pt 1 196.
18 L & P xx pt 1 199.
19 L & P xx pt 1 240, 241.
20 L & P xx pt 1 282,494.
21 L & P xx pt 1 544. Chapuys to Mary of Hungary.
22 L & P xx pt 1 709.
23 L & P xx pt 1 710.
24 L & P xx pt 1 826.
25 L & P xx pt 1 829.
26 Henry VIII's financial difficulties in 1544–6 are discussed in W. C. Richardson, (1954), 'Some Financial Expedient of Henry VIII', in *E. H. R. New Series* 7.1, 33–48.
27 L & P xx pt 1 892.
28 L & P xx pt 1 996.
29 L & P xx pt 1 1008, 1010.
30 L & P xx pt 1 1009.
31 L & P xx pt 1 1099.
32 L & P xx pt 1 1067, 1125.
33 L & P xx pt 1 1115,1116.
34 L & P xx pt 1 1143.
35 An example of the kind of confusion which easily rose because of the uncertainty of communications occurred sometime before 17 July. Vaughan travelled to Calais expecting to go to England to arrange details of the Fugger loan only to discover once he reached the town two couriers on their way to Antwerp who had the documents he needed. Vaughan returned to Antwerp after a wasted journey.
36 L & P xx pt 1 1194.
37 L & P xx pt 1 1223.

38 L & P xx pt 1 1239, 1266.
39 Richardson, *Stephen Vaughan, Financial Agent of Henry VIII*, 62–3.
40 L & P xx pt 2 111, 113,114.
41 L & P xx pt 2. 153.
42 L & P xx pt 2 192.
43 L & P xx pt 2 217.
44 L & P xx pt 2 243.
45 L & P xx pt 2 362.
46 L & P xx pt2 393,407,411.
47 L & P xx pt 2 485 'que je suis et tous jours seray son bone frere et amye'.
48 L & P xx pt 2 416.
49 L & P xx pt 2 507.
50 L & P xx pt 2 550, 551.
51 L & P xx pt 2 559.
52 Millar, *Tudor Mercenaries and Auxiliaries, 1485–1547*, 139–43.
53 L & P xx pt 2 677, 756, 766.
54 L & P xx pt 2 726.
55 L & P xx pt 2 957.
56 L & P xx pt 2 956, 960.
57 Both published in one volume by the Early English Text Society ed. J. M. Cowper in 1874.
58 Brinklow's will was not proved until November 1545 but by this time Vaughan was actively arranging his marriage to Margery Brinklow's widow; for some reason the probate was delayed and did not follow shortly after the death as was usual practice.
59 L & P xx pt 2 363, 364.
60 L & P xxi pt 1 347.
61 L & P xx pt 2 1025 1055 1056.
62 L & P xxi pt1 39.
63 L & P xxi pt1 82, 95, 105, 106.
64 L & P xxi pt1 142.
65 L & P xxi pt1 127.
66 L & P xxi pt1 grants in January no.2, 164.
67 L & P xxi pt1 199.
68 L & P xxi pt1 197, 241, 264.
69 L & P xxi pt1 263,264 (2), 296.
70 L & P xxi pt1 211.
71 L & P xxi pt1 265, 270, 283.
72 L & P xxi pt 1 271 24 February.
73 L & P xxi pt 1 347 8 March.
74 L & P xxi pt1 349.
75 L & P xxi pt 1 367, 368 dated 10 March.

76 L & P xxi pt1 435.
77 L & P xxi pt1 523, 524.
78 L & P xxi pt1 605.
79 L & P xxi pt1 748.
80 L & P xxi pt1 933.
81 L & P xxi pt1 933, 935.
82 L & P xxi pt1 954.
83 L & P xxi pt1 983.
84 These negotiations took place over most of June 1546. They involved a brisk exchange of letter between the Privy Council and Paget and Vaughan which involved some misunderstandings and also some acrimony due to the complexity of the situation as much as anything. The despatches and reports concerned are L & P xxi pt1 962,1018,1042, 1044, 1045, 1049 1073 1113, 1187.
85 L & P xxi pt1 1044. 1188.
86 L & P xxi pt1 1210.
87 L & P xxi pt1 1261.
88 L & P xxi pt1 1283.
89 L & P xxi pt1 1421, 1434.
90 L & P xxi pt2 70.
91 L & P xxi pt2 42.
92 L & P xxi pt2 96.
93 L & P xxi pt2 xx5.
94 L & P xxi pt2 293.
95 L & P xxi pt2 465.
96 L & P xxi pt2 Documents by stamp January 30–31 no. 53.
97 CPR Edward VI, 136.
98 CPR Edward VI, 21, 140.
99 Bindoff, *History of Parliament*, Vaughan, Stephen.

Chapter 8

1 https://www.british-history.ac.uk/no-series/taylors-guild-london/pp131-138.
2 TNA PROB 11/33/117.
3 His widow remarried twice; both her second husband George Rolles and her third husband Sir Leonard Chamberlayne, of Woodstock were prepared to take legal action over the terms of Stephen's will which perhaps indicates that there was more at stake than appears at first glance. The suits are TNA C1/1319/9-11, C78/10/26, C1/1339/16-20.

4 Https://www-British-history-ac-uk.libezoproxy.open.ac.uk/inquis-post-morthem/abstract/no1/pp78-95#p44
5 '1541 London Subsidy Roll: Cheap Ward 'in *Two Tudor Subsidy Rolls for the City of London 1541 and* 1582 ed R. G. Lang (1993), 45–9.
6 ODNB Sir Richard Gresham.
7 Will of Edward Awpart. TNA PROB 11/24/211 and PROB 11/24/220.
8 Brigden, *London and the Reformation*, 344.
9 L & P vol. Xxi pt 1 494.
10 L & P vol. xxi pt2 52.
11 Thomas S. Freedman, (1995), 'Research Rumour and Propaganda: Anne Boleyn in Foxe's Book of Martyrs', *Economic History Review*, 4.3, 803.
12 Brigden, *London and the Reformation*, 408.
13 L & P vol. xx pt 2 266.
14 John N. King, (1987), 'The Account Book of a Marian Bookseller 1553-4', *British Library Journal*, 13.1, 39 and 42.
15 This house still exists complete with priest hole.
16 ODNB Wiseman [neé Vaughan] Jane.
17 The ODNB entry for Jane Wiseman names as her father one Cuthbert Vaughan a soldier of the Calais garrison who later also served on the Border with Scotland. This is incorrect; he was born c1519 and died in 1563; his will also makes plain that there was no issue of his marriage in 1550 to Elizabeth Roydon.
18 John Morris, (1881), *The Life of Father John Gerard of the Society of Jesus*, London: Burns and Oates, 89–94.
19 *The Auto Biography of John Gerard*, (2012), London: Ignatius Press.
20 Her parents probably married not earlier than 1533 since her mother's first husband did not die until 1532. Anne was probably the oldest child.
21 ODNB Locke [neé Vaughan; other married names Dering, Prowse] (1530–1607). Her life is set out in some detail in P. Collinson, (1983), 'The Role of Women in the English Reformation Illustrated by the Life and Friendships of Anne Locke', in *Godly People: Essays on English Protestantism and puritanism*, London: Hambledon Press, 272–85.
22 BL Add. Mss 43827 ff.1–180 printed in Maria Dowling and Joy Shakespeare, (1982), 'Religion and Politics in mid Tudor England through the eyes of an English Protestant woman: the recollections of Rose Hickman', *Historical Research*, 55.
23 Susan M. Felch (1995), 'Deir Sister: The Letters of John Knox to Anne Vaughan Lok', in *Renaissance and Reformation*, 19.4, 47–68.
24 Michael G. Spiller, (1997), 'A Literary First: The Sonnet Sequence of Anne Locke, 1560', in *Renaissance Studies: Journal of the Society for Renaissance Studies*, 11.1, 41–55.
25 Patrick Collinson, (2003), 'Not Sexual in the Ordinary Sense; Women Men and Religious Transaction', in *Elizabethans*, London: Hambledon, 123.

26 Collinson, 'The Role of Women in the English Reformation Illustrated by the Life and Friendship of Anne Locke', 282–3. The quotations from Dering's letter of proposal are from Kent Archives Maidstone, Dering MS U 350, C1/2 ff28v-29r.
27 Micheline White, (2005), 'Women Writers and Literary-Religious Circles in the Elizabethan West Country: Anne Dowriche, Anne Locke Prowse Anne Lock Moyle Ursula Fulford and Elizabeth Rous', in *Modern Philology*, 103, 187–214.
28 Susan M. Felch, (1999), *The Collected Works of Anne Vaughan Lock*, Tempe. Susan M. Felch, (2010), 'The Exemplary Anne Vaughan Lock', in Johanna Harris and Elizabeth-Scott-Baumann, ed., *Intellectual Culture of Puritan Women, 1558–1680*, New York: Palgrave Macmillan. Spiller, 'A Literary First: The Sonnet Sequence of Anne Locke, 1560', 41–55. Also see Jamie Quatro 'The hidden life of a forgotten sixteenth century female poet in *The New Yorker* for 5 August 2019.
29 These cases are TNA.
30 Survey of London 27, (1957) Spitalfields and Mile End New Town, London County Council, 39–51.
31 Middlesex Sessions Roll:1591 in *Middlesex County Records Vol. 1, 1550-1603*, ed. John Cordy Jeaffreson, London, 1886, 191–202. *British History Online*. http://www.british-history.ac.uk/middx-county-records/vol1/pp191-202. 'Queen Elizabeth-Vol. 242: July 1492', in Mary Anne Everett Green, ed., *Calendar of State Papers Domestic: Elizabeth, 1591–94*, London, 1867, 242–52, *British History Online* http://www.british-history-online.ac.uk/cal-state-papers/domestic/edw-elz/1591-4/pp242-252
32 35 Eliz cap 1 *An Act to Retain the Queen's Subjects in Obedience.*
33 Salters' Company Records H1/18/7 and 8 and H1/27/2
34 Rees, Thomas, (1815) *Beauties of England and Wales v. 25*, 880–3. A footnote states that the information regarding this inquisition comes from a 'curious instrument' given to the author 'by a Gentleman whom he has not the honour to know personal and whose name therefore he does not feel himself at liberty to mention'.
35 Details of these loan are in Chapter 7 and Table 1.
36 The loans taken out for the king by Vaughan in 1545 are summarized in the table.
37 Peter Cunich, 'Revolution and Crisis in English State Finance 1534–47'.
38 J. G. Nichols ed., (1857), *The Literary Remains of King Edward VI*, London: Roxburghe Club, vol.2, 315–6.
39 APC 1550–52, 252.
40 John Guy, (2019), *Gresham's Law: The Life and World of Queen Elizabeth I's Banker*, London: Profile Books, 44–52.
41 Guy, *Gresham's Law: The Life and World of Queen Elizabeth's Banker*, 242–8.
42 Richardson, *Stephen Vaughan, Financial Agent of Henry VIII*, 74.
43 MacCulloch, *Thomas Cromwell*, 212.
44 Claudia Goldstein, (2013), *Peter Bruegel and the Culture of the Early Modern Dinner Party*, Ashgate: Farnham, 126.

Bibliography

Manuscript sources

British Library

Add. MSS 5751
Harley MSS 283, 284
Cotton : Nero , Galba and Titus

The National Archives, Kew,

Enrolled Customs Accounts
Early Chancery Proceedings
State Papers
Probate Canterbury Wills

Antwerp Municipal Archives

Kathedraalarchief Antwerp

Kent History and Library Centre

Lambeth Palace Library

Fairhurst Papers

London Metropolitan Archives-City of London:

Merchant Taylors Company Records
Salter Company Records

Suffolk Record Office Bury St Edmunds

Primary sources online and in print

Acts of the Privy Council vol 1 1542–147 and vol. 2 1547–1550, HMSO 1890.
Calendar of Patent Rolls Edward VI vols. 1 and II.

Calendar of Sate Papers Domestic Edward VI, Mary, and Elizabeth 1547–80, HMSO 1856.
Calendar of State Papers Domestic , Elizabeth 1591–94 HMSO 1865.
Calendar of State Papers Spain HMSO 1888.
Cely Letters 1472–1488 ed. Alison. Hanham Early English Text Society 1975.
England's Export Trade 1275–1547 eds. E. M. Carus-Wilson and O. Coleman Oxford: Clarendon Press 1963.
Henry Brinklow's Complaynt of Roderyck Mors, somtyme a Gray fryre, vnto the parliament howse of Ingland his natural cuntry: for the redresse of certen wicked lawes, euel customs a<n>d cruel decreys, (about A.D. 1542) and The lamentacyon of a Christen agaynst the cytye of London, made by Roderigo Mors (1545)ed. Joseph M Cowper Meadows ed. Early English Text Society.
L. Guicciardini, 1521–1589. 1593, *The description of the Low countreys and of the prouinces thereof, gathered into an epitome out of the historie of Lodouico Guicchardini*, London, By Peter Short for Thomas Chard.
Letters and Papers, Foreign and Domestic, Henry VIII, HMSO 21 vols. ed. J S Brewer (London, 1920), *British History Online* http://www.british-history.ac.uk/letters-papers-hen8.
Life and Letters of Thomas Cromwell ed. R.B.Merriman vol.2 Oxford: OUP 1846.
Literary Remains of King Edward the Sixth: ed. From his autograph manuscripts, with historical notes, and a biographical memoir. Ed. J. G. Nicholls London: Roxburgh Club.
Memorials of the Guild of Merchant Taylors of the Fraternity of St John Baptist in the City of London. Ed. C. W. Clode, London 1875.
Middlesex County Records vol 1 1550–1603, Middlesex County Records Society 1886.
Original Letters illustrative of English History third series vols I and II ed. Sir Henry Ellis 1846.
State Papers online: 1509–1714: Early Modern Government in Britain and Europe. Gale, https://www.gale.com/intl/primary-sources/state-papers-online.
The Book of Privileges of the Merchant Adventurers of England 1296–1488 eds. A.F. Sutton and L Visser-Fuchs British Academy 2009.
The Ledger of Filippo Borromei and Co. of Bruges, 1438. J. L. Bolton , Francesco Guidi Bruscoli (online) http://www.queenmaryhistoricalresearch.org/roundhouse/default.html.
The Letters of Sir John Hackett ed. E. F. Rogers , Morgantown: West Virginia University 1971.
Two Tudor Subsidy Rolls for the City of London 1541 and 1580 ed. R. C. Lang London Record Society vol. 29 1992.

Secondary sources

Alford, Stephen (2017), *London's Triumph: Merchant Adventurers and the Tudor City*, London: Allen Lane.

Antwerp's Golden Age; The Metropolis of the West in the 16th and 17th Centuries Exhibition Catalogue 1973–5, Antwerp: Smithsonian Institute.

Archer, I. W. (2001), 'The Burden of Taxation on Sixteenth Century London', in *The Historical Journal* 14.3, 599–627.

The Auto Biography of John Gerard (2012), London: Ignatius Press.

Barron, C. (2004), *London in the Later Middle Ages: Government and People 1200–1500*, Oxford: Oxford University Press.

Barron, C. (2000), 'London 1300–1540', in D. Palliser ed., *Cambridge Urban History*, vol. 1. Cambridge: Cambridge University Press, 395–440.

Behrens, Betty (1933), 'The Office of the English Resident Ambassador: Its Evolution as Illustrated by the Career of Sir Thomas Spinelly 1509–1522', in *TRHS* 16, 161–95.

Bindoff, S. T. (1945), *The Scheldt Question*, London: Allen and Unwin.

Bishop, J. (2016), 'Currency Conversation and Control: Political Discourse and the Coinage in Mid-Tudor England', in *EHR* 131.551, 763–92.

Bisson, D. R. (1993), *The Merchant Adventurers of England: The Company and the Crown 1474–1564*, Newark: University of Delaware Press.

Blanchard, I. (2009), *The International Economy in the Age of the Discoveries: Antwerp and the English Merchants' World*, Stuttgart: Franz Steiner Verlag.

Bolton, J. L. (2017), 'How It Really Worked: Italian Banking in Northern Europe in the Fifteenth Century as Seen Through the Ledgers of the Borromei Bank', in N. J. Mayhew et al., eds, *Money and Its Use in Medieval Europe: Three Decades On*, London: Royal Numismatic Society, 85–100.

Bolton, J. L. and F. G. Bruscoli (2008), 'When did Antwerp Replace Bruges as the Commercial and Financial Centre of North-Western Europe? The Evidence of the Borromei Ledge for 1438', in *Ec. HR* 61.2, 360–79.

Brigden, S. (1989), *London and the Reformation*, Oxford: Oxford University Press.

Brigden, S. (1988), 'Thomas Cromwell and the "Brethren"', in M. C. Cross et al. eds, *Law and Government under the Tudors \; Essays Presented to Sir Geoffrey Elton*, Cambridge: Cambridge University Press, 31–49.

Brulez, W. (1968), 'Le commerce international des Pays-Bas 110-1|£7au XVIe Siécle : essai d'appréciation quantitative', in *Revue Belge de Philologie et d'Histoire*, 46.4, 1205–21.

Burgon, J. W. (1839), *The Life and Times of Sir Thomas Gresham*, London: Robert Jennings,

Campbell, Lorne (1976), 'The Art Market in the Southern Netherlands in the Fifteenth Century', in *The Burlington Magazine*, 188–98.

Challis, C. E. (1972), 'Currency and the Economy in Mid-Tudor England', in *Ec. HR* 25, 313–22.

Cohn, H. J. (2001), 'Did Bribes Induce the German Electors to Choose Charles V as Emperor in 1519?' in *German History* 19.1, 1–27.

Collinson, Patrick. (2003), 'Not Sexual in the Ordinary Sense; Women Men and Religious Transaction', in *Elizabethans*, London: Hambledon Press, 119–50.

Collinson, Patrick. (1983), 'The Role of Women in the English Reformation Illustrated by the Life and Friendships of Anne Locke', in *Godly People: Essays on English Protestantism and Puritanism*, London: Hambledon Press, 273-87.

Colson, Justin (2016), 'Commerce, Clusters and Community: A Re-evaluation of the Occupational Geography of London c.1400-c.1550', in *EcHR* 69.1, 104-30.

Cunich, P. (1999), 'Revolution and Crisis in English State Finance 1534-47', in W. Mark Ormrod, Margaret Bonney, Richard Bonney, eds., *Crises, Revolutions and Self-Sustained Growth: Essays in European Fiscal History, 1130-1830*, Stamford: Shaun Tyas, 110-37.

Dalton, Heather (2016), *Merchants and Explorers: Roger Barlow, Sebastian Cabot and Networks of Atlantic Exchange 1500-1560*, Oxford: Oxford University Press.

Davies, M. (2012), 'Crown, City and Guild in Late Medieval London', in M. Davies et al. eds, *London and Beyond: Essays in Honour of Derek Keene*, London: IHR, 247-68.

Davies, M. (2002), 'Governors and Governed: The Practice of Power in the Merchant Taylors' Company in the Fifteenth Century', in I. A. Gadd and P. Wallis eds, *Guilds Society and the Economy of London, 1450-1880*. London: IHR, 67-83.

Davies, M. (2000), *Merchant Taylors' Company of London Court Minutes 1486-1493*, Richard III and Yorkist History Trust, Stanford: Paul Watkins.

Davies, M. and Ann Saunders (2004), *The History of the Merchant Taylors*, Leeds: Maney.

Davis, E. J. (1924), 'The Transformation of London', in R. Seton-Watson ed., *Tudor Studies*. London: Longmans, 287-314.

Davis, Ralph (1976), ' The Rise of Antwerp and its English Connection, 1406-1510', in D. C. Coleman, ed., *Trade Government and Economy in Pre- Industrial England*, London: Weidenfeld and Nicolson, 3-20.

de Roover, Raymond (1967), *San Bernardino of Siena and Sant' Antonino of Florence: Two Great Economic Thinkers of the Middle Ages*, Boston: Harvard Business School.

de Roover, Raymond (1953), ' Anvers comme Marché Monétaire au xvi siècle', in *Revue Belge de Philologie et d' Histoire* 31, 1003-47.

de Smedt, O. (1950), *De Englese Natie de Antwerpen 1496-1582, vol. II*, Antwerp : no pub.

de Smedt, O. (1928), 'Stephen Vaughan, Agent van der Engelsche Kroon en de Antwerpsche Geldmarkt in de jaren 1455-1546', in *Antwerpsche Archieveinblatt* III, 229-56.

Dowling , M. and Joy Shakespeare (1982), 'Religion and Politics in Mid Tudor England through the Eyes of an English Protestant Woman :The Recollections of Rose Hickman', *Historical Research*, 55.3, 94-102.

Dr Giles ed. (1865), *The Whole Works of Roger Ascham*, vol.I part II, London.

Duffy, Eamon (1992), *The Stripping of the Altars Traditional Religion in England 1400-1580*, New Haven: Yale University Press.

Dunbar, William (1900), 'In Honour of the City of London', in Sir A. Quiller-Couch ed., *The Oxford Book of English Verse*, Oxford: Clarendon Press, 26.

Edler, F. (1938), 'The Van der Molen; Commission Merchants of Antwerp: Trade with Italy 1538-44', in J. L.Carte et al. eds., *Medieval and Historiographical Essays in Honor of James Westfall Thompson*. Chicago: University of Chicago Press, 78-145.

Edler, F. (1937), 'The Effects of the Financial Measures of Charles V on the Commerce of Antwerp 1539-42', in *Revue Belge de Philologie et d'Histoire* 16, 665-73.

Edler, F. (1936), 'Winchcombe Kerseys in Antwerp 1538-4', in *Ec. HR* 7.1, 57-62.

Ehrenberg, Richard (1963), *Capital and Finance in the Age of the Renaissance*, New York: Kelley.

Ewing, Dan (1990), 'Marketing Art in Antwerp. 1460-1560: Our Lady's Pand', in *The Art Bulletin*, 72.4, 558-84.

Felch, S. M. (2010), 'The Exemplary Anne Vaughan Lock', in Johanna Harris and Elizabeth-Scott-Baumann, eds, *Intellectual Culture of Puritan Women, 1558-1680*, New York: Palgrave Macmillan, 33-57.

Felch, S. M. (2009), 'The Public Life of Anne Vaughan Lock: Her Reception in England and Scotland', in J. D. Campbell et al. eds, *Early Modern Women and Transnational Communities of Letters* Farnham: Ashgate, 137-56.

Felch, S. M. (1999), *The Collected Works of Anne Vaughan Lock*, Arizona: Tempe.

Felch, S. M. (1995), 'Deir Sister: The Letters of John Knox to Anne Vaughan Lok', in *Renaissance and Reformation* 19.4, 47-68.

Freedman, T. S. (1995), 'Research Rumour and Propaganda: Anne Boleyn in Foxe's Book of Martyrs', *Ec HR* 4.3, 797-819.

Goldstein, C. (2013), *Peter Bruegel and the Culture of the Early Modern Dinner Party*, Farnham: Ashgate.

Gunn, Steven, David Grummitt and Hans Cools (2007), *War State and Society in England and the|Netherlands 1477-1559*, Oxford: Oxford University Press.

Guy, John (2019), *Gresham's Law: The Life and World of Queen Elizabeth I's Banker*, London: Profile Books.

Hanham, Alison (1985), *The Celys and their World: An English Merchant Family of the Fifteenth Century*, Cambridge: Cambridge University Press.

Harding, Vanessa (2012), 'Houses and Households in Cheapside c.1500-1550', in Matthew Davies and James A. Galloway eds, *London and Beyond:Essays in Honour of Derek Keene*, London: IHR, 135-54.

Harriss, G. L. (1988), *Cardinal Beaufort: A Study of Lancastrian Ascendancy and Decline*, Oxford: Clarendon Press.

Harriss, G. L. (1963), 'Aids, Loans and Benevolences', in *The Historical Journal* VI.1, 1-19.

Hildebrandt, E. (1984), 'Christopher Mont, Anglo;-German Diplomat', in *Sixteenth Century Journal* 15.3, 281-90.

Horowitz, M. R. (2009), 'Henry Tudor's Treasure', in *Historical Research* 82, 560-79.

A History of the County of Kent vol. 2 VCH 1926.

Hoyle, R. W. (1994), 'Crown Parliament and Taxation on Sixteenth century England', *EHR* 109, 1174-96.

Jones, Evan T. and Margaret M. Condon (2016), *Cabot and Bristol's Age of Discovery; The Bristol Voyages 1480–1508*, Bristol: University of Bristol.

Keene, D. J. and Vanessa Harding (1987), *Historical Gazetteer of London Before the Great Fire Cheapside; Parishes of All Hallows Honey Lane, St Martin Pomary, St Mary Le Bow, St Mary Colechurch and St Pancras Soper Lane*, https://resolver.ebscohost.com/Redirect/PRL?EPPackageLocationID=3597.526108.1982653&epcustomerid=s2947694.

King, John N. (1987), 'The Account Book of a Marian Bookseller 1553-4', *British Library Journal* 13, 33–57.

Kleineke, Hannes (2003), 'Morton's Fork?- Henry VII's "Forced Loan" of 1 496', in L. Visser-Fuchs ed., *Tant d'emprises; The Ricardian XIII ; Essays in Honour of Anne F. Sutton*, Richard III Society.

Limberger, Michel (2001), 'No Town in the World Provides More Advantages; Economies of Agglomeration and the Golden Age of Antwerp', in Patrick O'Brien et al. eds, *Urban Achievement in early Modern Europe: Golden Ages in Antwerp, Amsterdam and London*, Cambridge: Cambridge University Press, 39–62.

Lingelbach, W. E. (1901), 'The Internal Organisation of the Merchant Adventurers of England', in *TRHS* 16, 19–67.

Lombaerde, P. (2001), 'Antwerp in the "Golden Age" One of the Largest Cities in the Low Countries and One of the Best Fortified in Europe', in P. O'Brien, ed., *Urban Achievement in Early Modern Europe*, Cambridge: Cambridge University Press, 99–127.

Lyell, L. (1935), 'The Problem of the Records of the Merchant Adventurers', in *Ec. HR*, 5.2, 96–8.

Mackay, Lauren (2015), *Inside The Tudor Court; Henry VIII and His Six Wives Through the Eyes of the Spanish Ambassador*, Stroud: Amberley.

Manref, G. (1996), *Antwerp in the Age of Reformation :Underground Protestantism in a Commercial Metropolis*, Baltimore: Johns Hopkins Press.

McShaffrey, S. and N. Turner (2003), *Lollards of Coventry 1486–1515*, Cambridge: Cambridge University Press.

Millar, G. J. (1980), *Tudor Mercenaries and Auxiliaries, 1485–1500*, Charlottesville: University of Virginia Press.

Morris, John (1881), *The Life of Father John Gerard of the Society of Jesus*, London: Burns and Oates.

Oldland, M. J. (2008), 'The Wealth of the Trades in Early Tudor London', in *The London Journal* 31.2, 127–55.

Outhwaite, R. B. (1971), 'Royal Borrowing in the Reign of Elizabeth I: The Aftermath of Antwerp', in *EHR* 86, 251–63.

Outhwaite, R. B. (1966), 'The Trials of Foreign Borrowing: The English Crown and the Antwerp Money Market in the Mid Sixteenth Century', in *Ec. HR* 19.2, 289–305.

Potter, David (2011), *Henry VIII and Francis I: The Final Conflict 1540–44*, Leiden: Brill.

Potter, David (1995), 'Foreign Policy', in Diarmaid MacCulloch ed., *The Reign of Henry VIII: Politics, Policy and Piety*, Basingstoke: Macmillan.

Puttevils, Jeroen (2015a), 'Eating the Bread Out of Their Mouth: Antwerp's Export Trade and Generalized Institutions, 1544–5', in *Ec.HR* 68.4, 1339–64.

Puttevils, Jeroen (2015b), *Merchants and Trading in the Sixteenth Century: The Golden Age of Antwerp*, London: Routledge.

Quatro, James, 'The Hidden Life of a Forgotten Sixteenth Century Female Poet', in *The New Yorker*, 5 August 2019.

Ramsay, G. D. (1978), 'The Recruitment and Fortunes of Some London Freemen in the Mid-Sixteenth Century', in *Ec. HR* 31.4, 526–40.

Rees, Thomas (1815), *Beauties of England and Wales*, Vol. 18, London : no pub.

Richard, Hoyle (1995), 'War and Public Finance', in Diarmaid MacCulloch ed., *The Reign of Henry VIII: Politics Policy and Piety*, Basingstoke: Macmillan.

Richardson, G. (2008), 'The French Connection Francis I and England's Break with Rome', in G. Richardson ed., *The Contending Kingdoms France and England 1420–1700*, Aldershot: Ashgate, 94–115.

Richardson, W. C. (1953), *Stephen Vaughan, Financial Agent of Henry VIII: A Study of Financial Relations with the Low Countries*, Baton Rouge: Louisiana State University Press.

Richardson, W. C. (1954), 'Some Financial Expedients of Henry VIII', *EHR* 7.1, 33–48.

Rose, Susan (2018), *The Wealth of England: The Medieval Wool Trade and Its Political Importance 1100–1600*, Oxford: Oxbow.

Spiller, M. G. (1997), 'A Literary First: The Sonnet Sequence of Anne Locke, 1560', in *Renaissance Studies: Journal of the Society for Renaissance Studies* 11.1, 41–55.

Spufford, Peter (2002), *Power and Profit; the Merchant in Medieval Europe*, London: Thames and Hudson.

Stout, Felicity (2015), *Exploring Russia in the Elizabethan Commonwealth: The Muscovy Company and Giles Fletcher the Elder, (1546–1611)*, Manchester: Manchester University Press.

Survey of London 27, 19570 Spitalfields and Mile End New Town, London County Council.

Sutton, A. F. (2005), *The Mercery of London: Trade, Goods and People 1130–1578*, Aldershot: Ashgate, 182.

Sutton, A. F. (2002), 'The Merchant Adventurers of England: Their Origins and the Mercer's Company of London', in *Historical Research* 75.3, 27–46.

Thomas, H. and I. D. Thornley eds. (1938), *The Great Chronicle of London*, London: George W. Jones.

Vale, M. (2007), *The Ancient Enemy: England France and Europe from the Angevins to the Tudors*, London: Hambledon Continuum.

Van der Wee, Herman and Ian Blanchard (1992), 'The Hapsburgs and the Antwerp Money Market: The Exchange Crises of 1521 and 122–3', in Ian Blanchard et al. eds., *Industry and Finance in Early Modern History*, Stuttgart : Franz Steiner.

Van Houtte, J. A. (1961), 'Anvers aux xv et xvi siècles: expansion et apogèe', in *.Annales . Economies Sociétés* 16.2, 248–78.

Van Houtte, J. A. (1940), 'La Genèse du grand marché international á Anvers á la fin du Moyen Age', in *Revue Belge de Philologie et d' Histoire* 19, 87–126.

Van der Linden, Herman (1914), 'Le voyage de P. Tafur en Brabant, en Flandre et en Artois, (1438)', *Revue du Nord*, 216–31.

White (2005), 'Women Writers and Literary-Religious Circles in the Elizabethan West Country Anne Dowriche, Anne Locke Prowse Anne Lock Moyle Ursula Fulford and Elizabeth Rous', in *Modern Philology*, 187–214.xct

Unpublished theses

Ficaro, Barbara (1981), 'Nicolas Wotton: Dean and Diplomat', PhD Kent.

Harper, S. P. (2015), 'London and the Crown in the Reign of Henry VII', PhD SAS London.

MacMahon, Luke (1999), 'The Ambassadors of Henry VIII: The Personnel of English Diplomacy c.1500–c.1550', PhD Kent.

Ramsey, Peter H. (1958), 'Merchant Adventurers in the First Half of the Sixteenth Century', D.Phil. Oxford.

Richardson, Glenn John (1995), 'Anglo-French Political and Cultural Relations During the Reign of Henry VIII', PhD LSE.

Rider, C. M. (1992), 'Our City and Chamber of London: The Relationship Between the City and the Crown in the Reigns of Edward VI and Mary', PhD Swansea.

Robertson, M. L. (1975), 'Thomas Cromwell's Servants: The Ministerial Household in Early Tudor Government and Society', PhD, University of California Los Angeles.

Ward, Philip John (1999), 'Origin of Thomas Cromwell's Public Career: Service under Cardinal Wolsey and Henry VIII', PhD LSE.

Index

Alum 24, 107, 118–20, 123, 126, 127
Antwerp, *see also* Bourse; *pand* (art market)
    buildings 24
    communications 23–4
    money market 35–40
    population 21–2
Aragon, Catherine of 9, 42, 48, 55, 58, 72, 74, 81, 94

Barrow, *see* Bergen op Zoom
Bergen op Zoom 18, 24–5, 27, 44, 55–8, 61, 70, 111
Boleyn, Anne 55, 59, 64, 71, 74, 139, 140
bonds 41, 46, 50, 100, 127
Bonvisi (bank) 13, 33, 103, 105–6, 114, 127, 132, 134, 149
Borromei Bank 13, 27
Boulogne 105, 109, 118, 120, 123, 125, 127
Bourse 2–3, 14, 25, 31–40, 44–5, 55, 57, 64, 101–11, 115, 119–21, 125–6, 129–30, 148–52, 154
Brethren 51, 124, 140
Brinklow, Henry 124, 140
Brinklow, Margery, later Vaughan 108, 124, 128, 131–4, 137–8, 140
Bruges 3, 10, 13, 17, 21, 25–7, 30, 35, 99

Calais 9, 12, 15–16, 19, 26–7, 40, 74, 85, 89, 90, 95, 97, 105, 107, 109, 115–18, 122–3, 126 128–9, 132–3, 140
Canterbury, Archbishop of 68–9, 74, 84, 129
Captains of mercenaries 95, 99–101, 104, 127
Carne, Sir Edward 86–8, 91, 93–6, 116–17, 121–2
Cely family 12, 26, 43
Chamberlain, Leonard 147

Chamberlain, Thomas 98–9, 116, 120, 123, 132, 154
Chapuys, Eustace 48, 67, 81, 86–7, 93–7, 103, 115
Charles V, Emperor 1–2, 37–9, 44–5, 57, 61, 69, 71–2, 74, 81, 84, 87, 94, 96, 98–9, 101, 106, 111, 114, 119, 130
City of London, Corporation of 2, 11, 33
Cleves, Anne of 88, 94, 130
cloth trade 9, 16, 18–19, 63, 73, 151, 154
Cobbe, Stephen 122, 124, 139–42, 146
Cobham, Lord 115–16, 128–9, 140
Common Council 13–15, 17
Cranmer, Thomas 69, 74–5
Cromwell, Thomas 1, 3, 9, 14, 46–65, 71–80, 82–5, 87–90, 94, 103, 140, 152

Damsell, William 105, 111, 115, 132, 150–1
Denmark 71, 78–80, 89
diplomacy 67–8, 70
divorce 46, 62, 74, 86, 94
Ducci, Gaspar 103–5, 107–9, 111, 113–23, 125–7, 129–31, 151–3
Dymok, John 107, 109, 130

Edward VI 97, 134, 139, 143
Emperor, *see* Charles V
exchange dealings 3, 25–6, 30–2, 35–6, 40, 43, 46, 48, 55, 98–9, 104–5, 122, 126, 131–2

France, King of, *see* Francis I
Francis I King of France 3, 33–4, 37–8, 69, 74, 78, 84, 86, 94, 106, 114, 129
Frescobaldi (bank) 12, 43
Fuggers (bank) 102, 108, 111, 117–22, 126–32

Gerrard, John 141–2

Index

Granvelle, Nicolas Perrenol de   97, 100, 113, 114, 152
Gresham, family of   4, 7
Gresham, Sir John   114, 129, 133
Gresham, Sir Richard   18, 44, 114, 129, 139
Gresham, Thomas   29, 150–1, 153
Guinet (Gwyneth), John   65, 83, 137, 142, 147
gunpowder   45, 88, 105–6, 111, 117
Gwyneth, *see* Guinet, John

Hackett, John   70, 72, 77–80, 154
Haller, Christoffel   119–22, 127, 131, 152
Henry VII of England   9–10, 18, 41, 67, 70
Henry VIII of England, as a young king   33, 42, 44
  and Anne Boleyn   55, 59, 61
  and death of   149
  and foreign policy   74–6, 79, 84
  and Gaspar Ducci   126–7
  and need for loans   102
  and war with France   4, 92, 109, 134
  and William Tyndale and reformed religion   58–62, 65, 67, 80
Hochstetters (bank)   33, 43, 46

jewels   40, 108, 111, 117–18, 120–1, 123–7, 149, 150

Knox, John   5, 143–5

Leigh, Thomas   78–9
Lesnes Abbey   53
livery companies   13–14, 16, 19, 33
loans   2–3, 13–15, 19, 25–6, 30–40, 42–4, 97–8, 101–7, 113–26, 129–34, 149–51
Lodge, Thomas   66
London   2, *see also* City of London Corporation of; common council; livery companies; loans; Mercers' Company; Merchant Adventurers, Company of; Merchant Taylors' Company
  governance of   15
  merchant society   65–6
  port of   12
  religious life   10–11
  trade of   9, 15–16
Luther   29, 31
Lutheranism   59, 62, 75–7, 88–9, 94, 126, 134, 140
Lyon   2, 13, 36, 74, 102

Magnus Intercursus Treaty   9, 72
Margaret of Austria, *see* Regent of the Netherlands
Mary of Hungary, *see* Regent of the Netherlands
Maximilian   27, 37–8
Mechelen   28, 45, 57–8
mercenaries   58, 62–4, 79, 98, 100–1, 104–5, 108, 114, 117, 120–3
Mercers' Company   7, 14, 17–19, 44, 47, 49
Merchant Adventurers, Company of   3–4, 18–19, 25–7, 44–5, 48–9, 55–63, 70–3, 80, 83–4, 89, 91, 103, 107, 111, 114–15, 118, 149, 153–4
Merchant Taylors' Company   18, 49, 52, 65, 137, 148
Middelburg   19, 23, 25, 27, 45, 153
Milan, Duchess of   84, 86–7, 91
Mont, (Mond) Christopher   75–6, 77, 78, 100
More, Thomas   29, 58, 62

Paget, William   2, 47, 98, 100–1, 105–9, 114, 116–24, 126–8, 132–3, 140
pand (art market)   28–9
Parr, Katherine   139
Petre, William   98, 116–17, 133
Portuguese trade   9–10, 26, 35
printing, print industry   10, 29, 152–3
Privy Council   18, 82, 98, 102, 104, 113–20, 126–9, 143, 150

Regent of the Netherlands   27, 34, 44–6, 48, 57, 64, 70, 72, 75, 84–9, 91, 95–6, 115, 121, 126 130, 152–3

Sadler, Ralph   51, 88, 133, 137
St Mary Spital   96, 134, 137–8, 147
St Paul's Cathedral   12, 13, 142
Scheldt   23
Schetz, Erasmus   127, 131, 149, 152
silkwoman   65, 76, 139, 140, 142
Speyer   98–100
Spinelly, Sir Thomas   70–1

Spitalfields   4, 120
Staplers, Company of   15–16, 103, 115, 118, 149, 153

Tafur, Pero   24, 27
Three Legges (Vaughan family home)   82, 137, 147
trade fairs   2, 13, 18, 25–31, 35–6, 44, 118
Treaty of Camp   131, 133
Treaty of Crépy   106, 109, 111, 114
Tyndale, William   29, 51, 58–62, 65, 67, 80–3, 124, 140, 152–3

usury   31, 39

Vaughan, Anne Locke   5, 83, 141–6
Vaughan, Jane Wiseman   83, 141, 146
Vaughan, Margery, née Guinet   64–5, 76, 80, 83, 106–9, 139, 140–1
Vaughan, Stephen (junior)   2, 5, 83, 145–6
Vaughan, Stephen (senior)
  birth and family   7, 64, 82
  character   77
  as diplomat   67–90
  religious views   51–2, 63
  working as royal agent in Antwerp   91–109, 111–36
  working for Cromwell   52–7, 65
  working with John Hackett   46, 71, 91
  working with Merchant Adventurers   54, 56–7

Warbeck, Perkin   7, 9
Welsers (bank)   33, 102
Wingfield, Robert   44, 70
Wiseman, Thomas   141–2
Wolsey, Thomas   43–6, 52–4, 58, 60, 62, 68, 70–2, 90, 94, 103
wool trade   16, 40, 70
Wotton, Nicholas   89, 98–100, 113–15, 123
Wriothesley, Thomas   69, 84–8, 98, 103, 116, 120–6, 130, 149

www.ingramcontent.com/pod-product-compliance
Lightning Source LLC
Chambersburg PA
CBHW061833300426
44115CB00013B/2365